The Westerners

The Westerners
Dee Brown

HOLT, RINEHART AND WINSTON
NEW YORK · CHICAGO · SAN FRANCISCO

Published simultaneously in Canada by
Holt, Rinehart and Winston of Canada, Ltd

Library of Congress Cataloging in Publication Data

Brown, Dee Alexander
The Westerners

Bibliography: p.
1. The West–Biography. 2. The West–History.
3. Indians of North America–The West. I. Title
F591.B88   917.8′03′0922   73–15456
ISBN 0–03–088360–1

This book was designed and produced by George Rainbird Ltd,
Marble Arch House, 44 Edgware Road, London W2

House editor: Penelope Miller
Designer: Trevor Vincent
Maps: Tom Stalker Miller
Index: Irene Clephane

Text printed by Jarrold & Sons Ltd, Norwich, England
Color printed by Westerham Press Ltd, Westerham, Kent, England

Printed and bound in Great Britain

Contents

List of Color Illustrations

List of Maps

Introduction

The story of the American West has all the elements of the *Iliad* and *Odyssey*. It is a heroic world of quests and wars, of journeyings into remote lands, of daring hunts, last stands, and legendary exploits. It is an epic of mighty deeds, of triumphs and failures, of inconsistent heroes and heroines. The West is a tragedy relieved by interludes of comedy. It is a tale of good and evil, a morality play of personified abstractions. Only an epic poet, a Homer, could encompass the American West and sing its essence into one compact volume.

The narrative which follows is the story of the West told through the experiences of a few representative Westerners from the sixteenth to the twentieth century. Some of these men and women are well known in history, others not so well known, but all were typical of many thousands of Westerners like themselves who contributed something significant to the Western past.

In the beginning it was a search for the Western Sea and seven mythical cities of gold. Most of those who ventured there were driven by elemental greed. Its fabled riches rather than the grandeur and beauty of the land drew men and women from around the world. Instead of admiring the awesome splendor of the Grand Canyon, Coronado's men cursed its expanse because the chasm was a barrier to their search for gold. Some found wealth, others failed; to almost all of them the American West was a place where one journeyed to endure hardships, become rich, and then withdraw. They treated the West as a storehouse to be exploited for personal gain.

D. H. Lawrence who was a Westerner for a brief time in New Mexico, and was fascinated by the rootlessness of westward seeking Americans, said that men are free only when they belong to a living homeland, an organic community. 'Not when they are escaping to some wild west. The most unfree souls go west, and shout of freedom. Men are freest when they are most unconscious of freedom. The shout is a rattling of chains . . .'

Among the Westerners whose stories are told here, only three were truly seeking freedom, and one of these was a native, an American Indian who had lost his freedom. The others were seeking wealth along with freedom. At least a dozen wanted nothing but wealth, although some sought it while shouting the name of freedom. Only one wanted adventure exclusively; two hoped for wealth along with their adventures; others thirsted for knowledge of the unknown–adventure combined with understanding. Four went west in pursuit of glory, two of them demanding wealth with the glory. They were all, in one way or another, as the Texas Indians said of Cabeza de Vaca and his companions, Children of the Sun.

Of them all, perhaps Lewis and Clark had the purest motives; they were explorers who coveted intelligence of the country; they wanted wealth no more than any men want it; they wanted only to *know*. Yet even they were eager to inform the natives they met that American Indians were no longer subjects of European kings and emperors but were under the protection of a benevolent Great White Father in Washington. And where are the 'protected' tribes now? George Catlin's artistic endeavor was admirable, yet he was less interested in the survival of the harassed Indian tribes than in recording their doomed civilization with his paint brushes.

Some of the most famous Westerners were there for only short segments of their lives. Less than a dozen of those in this representative selection ended their days in the land their names are linked with, and some of them died violently before they could depart. The Mountain Men celebrated their unfettered life, the Big Sky, and the Shining Mountains, but after they had virtually exterminated the fur-bearing animals they went back to white man's civilization to die. They and the others won their wealth and glory, survived ordeals and adventures, or suffered bitter defeats. And then they went away.

The West was there to be exploited and in the accomplishment of this, in their march to the Western Sea, they and many of the thousands who followed them destroyed a native civilization and obliterated innumerable species of animals and birds. They ripped apart the delicate balance of Plains grassland, they gutted mountains for metals and poisoned the earth, they leveled forests and created wastelands. They raped, stripped, and plundered the land as if they hated the Garden of the West with a violent passion. They built large cities in waterless places where even the most primitive tribes knew that cities should never be built. Upon their city lawns the exterminators of wild animals placed iron effigies of deer and buffalo, and on the gables of killers of eagles rose gold-plated images of the great birds.

The untrod deserts and canyons, the forests and rivers, began to fill with debris, the litter and refuse of the conquerors–drift-heaps of glass and metal, avalanches of abandoned wagons, railroad cars and locomotives, the steel and rubber and plastics of castoff automobiles and airplanes. Whenever a national 'crisis' decreed that destructive forces be unleashed–deadly bacteria, lethal chemicals, or neutron bombardments in the

atoms of uranium–the Western land sustained the assaults.

The first Westerners were tough of fiber and filled with the vigorous juice of life. Some of those who stayed through the generations learned to love the land. Some came to be like Sitting Bull of the Teton Sioux who perceived what was happening and tried to avoid the menacing power by moving away from it, asking only to be let alone until at last he had to turn and fight. He could not escape the forces of destruction by fleeing to another country and he came back to his homeland to try to save what was left. 'Let us alone', he said. 'We want none of your gold or silver, none of your goods. We can live well if you will only let us alone.' But by then it was too late. The West he loved was doomed, and so was he.

The unspoiled Garden of the West was so magnificent that early descriptions were often dismissed as tall stories.

1. Children of the Sun

One May day of the year 1539, the Zunis who lived at Hawikuh pueblo in what is now New Mexico observed a strange assemblage approaching on the arid plain to the south. At the head of the procession was a half-naked black man with a pair of greyhounds running beside him. Following along were two or three hundred Indians from Mexico, among them a considerable number of handsome young women. All were on foot; there was not even a burro to share their burdens.

The black man wore a headdress with plumes so high that he appeared to be taller than any of his companions, and his muscular body was decorated with clusters of bright feathers and pieces of turquoise and coral attached to thongs around his neck. Fastened to his arms and legs were cascabels which jingled as he marched along in the manner of a king. He also carried a gourd rattle ornamented with red and white feathers and a string of tiny tinkling bells.

While still some distance from the terraced walls of Hawikuh, the black man whose name was Esteban halted the procession and sent runners forward to announce his coming to the Cibolans, the name given by the Spaniards to the Zunis of that time. One of these messengers was Bartolome, a young Indian from Petatlan much trusted by Esteban, and it was he who carried the gourd rattle to the walls of Hawikuh where the Zunis met with the strangers. When the head man of the Zunis took the offered rattle in his hands and saw the tiny bells attached to it, he hurled the gourd angrily to the ground. 'He told the messengers to leave immediately, for he knew what sort of people they represented, and that they should tell them not to enter the city or he would kill them all. The messengers went back and told Esteban what had happened. He told them that it was of no importance, that those who showed anger received him better.'

With his cascabels jingling musically, the fearless black man walked on to the walls of Hawikuh, accompanied by Bartolome, a few other Indians from Mexico, and his two greyhounds. Near sundown, the Zunis stopped him at the entrance of the pueblo, surrounded his party and took away from them 'everything they carried to trade, turquoises and other things'. The confident

A descendant of the Zunis who temporarily interrupted the Spaniards' search for gold

Esteban offered no resistance, not even when the Zunis made prisoners of him and his companions and placed them in a house outside the walls of Hawikuh. They spent the night there without food or water, but Esteban was unworried. The magic of his gourd rattle might have failed him, but this Moorish infidel trusted in the power of the Christian cross, a power which he had seen used many times with unfailing success by his former Spanish masters.

How was it that Esteban (sometimes called Estevanico, Stephen, or simply the Negro) came to be the first man from beyond the Atlantic Ocean to enter the country of the Zunis, the first explorer to venture into what is now Southwestern United States? Ten years earlier this black man who handled himself like a king had been only a faithful servant, a slave taken young from the west coast of Morocco to become the property of Andres Dorantes, gentleman of Spain. In 1528

An inside corner of the walls of the Zuni pueblo

Dorantes and Esteban with Alonzo del Castillo and a remarkable explorer named Cabeza de Vaca were the sole survivors of an expedition shipwrecked by storms on the coast of Texas. For six years these men wandered through Texas, escaping from one Indian tribe only to be captured by another until one day Castillo chanced to make the sign of the cross over some Indians who were suffering great pains in their heads. After Castillo commended them to God, the Indians said that all their pains had left them. From that time the Spaniards were regarded as supernatural beings, rumors of their magical powers running ahead of them so that as they wandered southwestward hoping to find New Spain (Mexico) their progress was impeded by crowds of Indians showering them with gifts and imploring them to cure their ailments. 'In all this time people came to seek us from many parts,' said Cabeza de Vaca, 'and they said that most truly we were children of the sun.'

Among the gifts offered by one of the wandering tribes of western Texas was 'a hawk bell of copper, thick and large, figured with a face'. The Spaniards were greatly excited by this first piece of metal work they had seen since the beginning of their journey. The reason they had come to the New World in the first place was to find gold or other wealth, and here at last was evidence of it. Wherever there was copper there must be gold. When the Spaniards asked the Indians where the hawk bell had come from they were told that it had been brought from the northern direction, from a place of fixed habitations. A few days later, from other Indians they learned that objects such as the hawk bell came from a place far to the north where were buried many plates of the same metal.

The Spaniards were certain now that the hawk bell must have come from the legendary Seven Cities which were filled with gold and silver and precious stones—the Seven Cities where chieftains sprinkled themselves and their women each day with gold dust and rode in chariots of silver.

'We told them to conduct us toward the north,' said Cabeza de Vaca, 'and they answered, as before, that except afar off there were no people in that direction, and nothing to eat, nor could water be found.'

Children of the Sun

When they reached the Rio Grande, the Spaniards turned northward in hopes of finding the Seven Cities of Gold. Everywhere they went now, Indians surrounded them, hailing the strangers as gods and begging only to touch them. The Indians assembled in such numbers that Esteban, the Moorish unbeliever, began to assist his master Dorantes in making the sign of the cross and commending the solicitous Indians to God. The black man quickly became popular with the Indians. They singled him out to receive special favors, including young women for whom he had an appreciative taste. Esteban began wearing feathers in his hair; he joined in the dances of the Indians, learned their chants and a few words of their languages. Of all their gifts, he prized most highly a magic gourd rattle decorated with red and white feathers and a string of tiny bells.

Because he was an excellent ambassador, the Spaniards began sending Esteban ahead of the party, and soon he was meeting Indians who gave him fine turquoises and emeralds said to have come from the mysterious North. By this time the happy blackamoor who had sung and danced his way across the plains of Texas was infected with a desire to find great riches. If he discovered the gold before his master, he could buy his freedom and return to his homeland with the wealth of a king. 'The Negro', said Cabeza de Vaca, 'was in constant conversation; he informed himself about the ways we wished to take, of the towns there were, and the matters we desired to know.' But the riches of the Seven Cities always remained *mas alla*, beyond the horizon, always somewhere far to the north.

And then one day the travelers noticed 'the buckle of a sword-belt on the neck of an Indian and stitched to it the nail of a horse shoe'. They asked the Indian where he had obtained these things. 'From Heaven', he replied, and when the excited Spaniards pressed him further he explained that certain men who wore beards like them had come from Heaven bringing lances and swords and that they had lanced two Indians to death. 'On hearing this,' said Cabeza de Vaca, 'we gave many thanks to God our Lord. We had before despaired of ever hearing more of Christians.'

Their objective now was the nearest Spanish settlement. A few weeks later they reached Culiacán in New Spain, and then in a triumphant procession made up of Spaniards and conquered Indians they entered Mexico City on 24 July 1536. There they were hailed not so much as surviving heroes, but as confirmers of the existence of the legendary Seven Cities and their glittering riches. Antonio de Mendoza, Viceroy of New Spain, was particularly interested, and so was a young friend of his, Francisco Vasquez de Coronado.

For some months the stories of Cabeza de Vaca and his companions were passed around Mexico City, being gloriously embellished with each re-telling. Curiously, none of the adventurers seemed eager to return to the North. Cabeza de

The Zunis were skilled potters: ABOVE an earthen effigy; BELOW an example of their pottery patterns

Vaca and Dorantes, homesick for Spain, declined official invitations to head an expedition to find the Seven Cities. Castillo married a wealthy widow and refused even to consider returning to bare the mysteries of the North. That left only the slave, Esteban, who was transferred as the property of Dorantes to the authority of Viceroy Mendoza.

Even the gold-hungry Mendoza recognized the impossibility of assigning command of an official expedition to a slave. Yet he knew that Esteban's worth to an exploring party into the *terra incognita* of the North was incalculable: the black man was intelligent, had a special gift for dealing with the Indians, and understood their languages.

Viceroy Mendoza eventually solved his dilemma by authorizing the twenty-eight-year-old nobleman, Don Francisco Coronado, to organize an expedition, and then arranging for Esteban and an energetic young Franciscan missionary, Fray Marcos de Niza, to make a preliminary exploration for a route leading to the Seven Cities. In his way Fray Marcos was as much a fortune hunter as Esteban, their difference being that the black man wanted gold for himself while Fray Marcos wanted it for his church.

Early in March 1539 the friar and the black man, with a small band of Mexican Indians, left the town of Culiacán for the North. Along the way other Indian recruits joined them, attracted by the enthusiasm of Esteban who much to the friar's discomfiture kept adding beautiful maidens to his immediate retinue. Esteban promised all who joined him that they would return to Mexico with riches, and they believed him.

Having been charged by Viceroy Mendoza to send back reports on the people he found along the Pacific coast, Fray Marcos halted for Easter week at Vacapa in Sonora Valley and dispatched Indian messengers to the sea by three different routes. They were to bring natives from the coast to see the man from Heaven, Marcos, who wished to question them. During this delay at Vacapa, Marcos decided to send Esteban 'toward the north to see whether by that route, information could be obtained of something important of what we were seeking. I arranged with him that, should he learn of some inhabitated and rich country, something really important, he should not go any farther but return in person or send me Indians bearing the following sign we had agreed upon: If it were something moderate, he should send me a white cross a span in size; if it were of greater importance he should send one two spans in size; and if it were something greater and better than New Spain, he should send me a large cross.'

Esteban went eagerly ahead, and four days later he sent back messengers to Fray Marcos. They were carrying a very large cross the height of a man. 'They told me', Marcos said, 'on Esteban's behalf that I should set out immediately and follow him, because he had met people who informed him of the

A ruined mission, relic of the Franciscans' influence in the Southwest

greatest thing in this world.' Accompanying the cross bearers was an Indian from the north, sent by Esteban to corroborate his story. This Indian told Marcos of so many marvels in his country that the friar admitted he could not believe them until he saw them. This land was called Cibola, the Indian said, and there were indeed seven very large cities filled with turquoises and other evidences of wealth.

As soon as he could complete his business at Vacapa, Fray Marcos started northward, expecting to find Esteban waiting for him. The Moor, however, was so inflamed with gold fever that he could not bear any delay. For the next few days the progress of Marcos and Esteban across what is now Arizona became a race for the golden prize. To make amends for disobeying Marcos's orders to wait for him, Esteban left at each camping place a comfortable shelter with food and water for the use of the friar. He also marked the trail carefully, and once he sent back messengers carrying a cross even larger than the first one.

For several days the friar hurried onward, hoping to overtake Esteban. And then one day he met an Indian running down the trail from the north, one of those who had been with Esteban. The Indian's face and body were covered with sweat, and he was grieving. The people of Cibola, the Indian told Marcos, had slain Esteban and a considerable number of his followers.

One can only surmise what happened to Esteban at Hawikuh. His first error was in assuming that the Zunis would accept him in the manner of the Texas tribes—as a wizard who could make magic with the sign of the cross and a curer of all ailments. The Zunis had never heard of Esteban, but when he presented the gourd rattle they recognized it as a symbol of enemy tribes who sometimes raided the Pueblos—Mescalero Apaches or

Comanches perhaps. Esteban therefore was not to be trusted.

Among the Zunis was a tradition, an old prophecy that bearded men with light skins would come some day from the south and conquer their country. Esteban, however, was a black man–they called him the Black Mexican–and because of his gourd rattle he was a symbol of their old enemies.

In his eagerness for gold, Esteban probably pressed too hard the morning after the Zunis put him under guard in the house outside the walls of Hawikuh. Zuni legend tells of how the chiefs asked Esteban if he had any brothers, and when he answered that he had an infinite number and that they had numerous weapons and were not far away, the chiefs then decided to kill him so he could not reveal the location of Cibola to his brothers.

The fact that the Cibolans had refused entry to their city and then had slain Esteban and other members of his advance party convinced Fray Marcos that there must be gold within Cibola. He knew that if Esteban could not obtain entrance to the city, then no one probably could do so without force of arms. With the boldness that often accompanies fanatical seekers of treasure, however, the friar continued northward, determined to see the city of gold. Whether he came within view of Hawikuh is uncertain, but from a small hill he did describe a pueblo in the distance: 'It has a very fine appearance . . . The houses, as the Indians have told me, are all of stone, built in stories and with flat roofs. Judging by what I could see from the height where I placed myself to observe it, the settlement is larger than the city of Mexico . . . It appears to me that this land is the best and largest of all those that have been discovered.' Marcos promptly named the land for Saint Francis, claiming it for God and the King of Spain, and hurried back to Mexico with his astonishing report.

Fray Marcos believed in the wealth of Cibola because he wanted to believe, just as Esteban had been impelled to believe. And when he took his story back to Mexico it was accepted without question because everyone from the Viceroy down to the lowest laboring Spaniard wanted to believe in a land richer in gold than Mexico or Peru had ever been. Mexico City was filled with young Spanish noblemen who had arrived in the New World too late to share in the pillages of Cortez and Pizarro. Coronado himself was without inheritance, but he had married a young woman of wealth. The news brought by Fray Marcos was exactly what the idle nobility had been waiting to hear, and Coronado had no trouble in assembling an expedition outfitted with arms, horses, and a large number of cattle and sheep for commissary. He and other well-to-do members of the expedition had suits of armor for themselves and their mounts, and they provided themselves with Indian and Negro servants to act as grooms and pages.

In the spring of 1540, Coronado's expedition was marching

The gold pursued by the Spaniards was as false an image as water seen in the desert, a common phenomenon, painted here by Thomas Moran in *The Mirage* (detail).

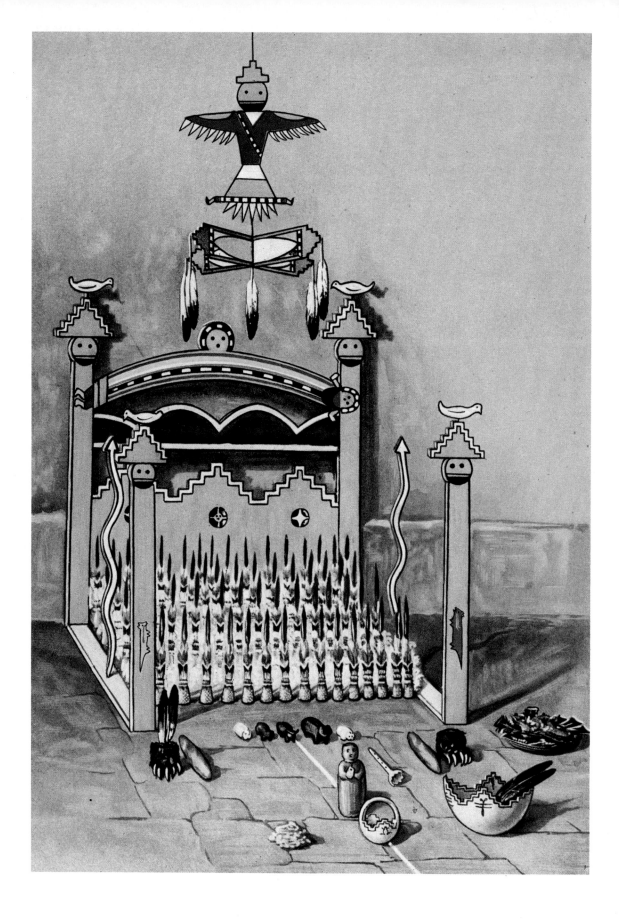

northward – 336 men, a few of their wives and children, and several hundred Indians. At Culiacán, Coronado halted to prepare a base for his slow-moving army; then on 22 April, after selecting eighty well-armed cavalrymen and thirty infantrymen, he set out upon the search for Cibola.

Late in June the Zunis at Hawikuh were receiving reports of strange beasts approaching from the south. Having never seen horses, or men in suits of mail, the Zunis at first believed the cavalrymen were monsters with men's heads and trunks and the bodies of four-legged animals. On 6 July these strange beings, who the Zunis feared might be the brothers of Esteban the Black Mexican, were camped outside the walls of Hawikuh. The Zunis immediately prepared to defend the pueblo, sending their women and children to safety on Thunder Mountain, and collecting heavy stones which they piled on the roofs of the higher apartment levels. Armed with bows and arrows, the warriors assembled in the open outside their pueblo, 'drawn up in squadrons'.

Although the appearance of Hawikuh was disappointing to the gold-seeking Spaniards – 'a small, rocky pueblo, all crumpled up, there being many farm settlements in New Spain that look better from afar' – most still believed that gold was surely inside. As a further impetus for action, the Spaniards were suffering pangs of hunger, the rations they had brought from Mexico being completely exhausted. Coronado sent forward his field-master, Garcia Lopez de Cardenas, to summon the Indians to surrender. In reply the Zunis drew lines of sacred corn meal across the ground and when the Spaniards attempted to cross the lines, they unloosed a volley of arrows upon them, wounding two men.

Eager for both gold and food, Coronado's soldiers held steady, awaiting orders to attack. Dressed in his best armor and wearing a feather-crested gold helmet, Coronado now came forward to view the situation. Hoping to avoid a fight, he brought along some cheap presents, and through an interpreter, he called upon the Zunis to submit peacefully to him as a representative of the King of Spain. The Zunis replied with another shower of arrows.

'When the Indians saw that we did not move,' Coronado said afterwards, 'they took greater courage and grew so bold that they came up almost to the heels of our horses to shoot their arrows. On this account I saw that it was no longer time to hesitate, and, as the priests approved the action, I charged them.' One of those approving the charge was Fray Marcos who shouted, 'Take your shields and go after them!' The friar was so close to entering the city of gold that he could not bear to be turned away now.

When the Spaniards attacked with crossbows and arquebuses, the Zunis fled, some scattering across the plain, others withdrawing into Hawikuh. The latter group hastened to lift their

A Zuni altar with offerings

ladders from the lower apartment levels, and assembled around the rock piles on the higher roofs, preparing for a siege.

'As the hunger which we suffered would not permit of any delay,' Coronado explained later, 'I ordered . . . the attack.' To his dismay, the Spanish bowmen and musketeers were unable to drive the Indians back from the rooftops. He dismounted and rushed forward to lead his men into the narrow crooked entranceway to Hawikuh. The Zunis hurled stones upon their attackers, singling out Coronado in his shining golden armor. 'They knocked me down to the ground twice with countless great stones . . . If I had not been protected by the very good headpiece I wore, I think that the outcome would have been bad for me.' As it was, Coronado's men had to carry him as though dead from the field. When he recovered consciousness he was pleased to hear that the Indians had surrendered. His soldiers, however, had been unable to find any gold in Hawikuh. They could take comfort only in the food they captured. 'We found something we prized more than gold and silver,' admitted one of them. 'Namely, plentiful maize and beans, turkeys larger than those . . . in New Spain.' They also found and freed a young slave, Bartolome, the Indian from Petatlan, who had been Esteban's trusted emissary.

A Hopi Indian painting of a *kachina* (spirit of an ancient)

After their stomachs were filled and their thoughts tended toward gold again, the Spaniards turned upon the Franciscan friar who had spread all those false stories of the Seven Cities of Cibola. 'The curses that some hurled at Fray Marcos were such that God forbid they may befall him', wrote one chronicler of the expedition. As soon as Coronado recovered from his wounds he wrote Viceroy Mendoza: 'I assure you that he [Marcos] has not told the truth in a single thing that he said.' Coronado was not prepared, however, to abandon the idea of 'a wealth of gold and precious stones' being found somewhere in that vast new land. While Fray Marcos with his shattered dreams was returning in disgrace to Mexico (where he died a few years later) Coronado was dispatching a small expedition to the northwest.

From the Zunis, the Spaniards had learned of the Seven Cities of Tusayan, and on 15 July Pedro de Tovar led a detachment of mounted men north from Hawikuh to find out if Tusayan might not be the seven gold cities of legend. Tusayan was Hopi Land, and a few days later the Hopis were alarmed to hear of a band of ferocious men riding about on animals that devoured people. When Tovar's horsemen reached the Hopi mesas, the Indians drew a line of corn meal on the ground as the Zunis had done. After warning the Spaniards not to cross the line, the Hopis boldly ordered them to depart from their mesas at once. Instead of withdrawing, Tovar attacked, killed, and captured several Hopis, and then demanded their obedience in the name of God and King. Overpowered by superior weapons of the fierce mounted men, the peaceful Hopis ceased all resistance and

attempted to appease the Spaniards by presenting them with a few turquoises. These only served to whet the greed of the Spaniards for more riches, but they could find no traces of gold in Tusayan.

In August, Coronado sent another expedition under Lopez de Cardenas directly toward the west. Cardenas's mission was to verify stories told by the Indians of a mighty river and a canyon inhabited by giants. 'When they had marched for twenty days they came to the gorges of the river, from the edge of which it looked as if the opposite side must have been more than three or four leagues away by air . . . it was utterly impossible to find a way down, either for horses or on foot . . . Although the men sought diligently in many places for a crossing, none was found.' Cardenas and his horsemen were the first Europeans to look upon the Grand Canyon of the Colorado. Not only did they fail to find a way down or a crossing or the legendary giants, they also failed to find gold. And they were not interested in magnificent scenery.

By late summer, news of the mounted Spaniards and their conquest of Hawikuh had spread through all the pueblos east and west. From Cicuye, the pueblo later called Pecos in New Mexico, a chief journeyed all the way to Hawikuh to see the strange bold men who were camped there. 'He was a tall, well-built young fellow with a fine figure', was the way Pedro de Casteneda, a chronicler of the expedition, described him. Because of his long mustaches, the Spaniards called him Bigotes. He offered his friendship to Coronado and said that if the Spaniards wished to go through his country, then his people, the Pecos Indians, would welcome them. Bigotes would live to regret bitterly this invitation.

In response to Bigotes' visit, Coronado sent Hernando de Alvarado and twenty cavalrymen to accompany the chief back to Cicuye and to explore the country to the east. Alvarado was to investigate the potential food supply in Bigotes' country, especially the great herds of cows [buffaloes] which the chief had told about, and to determine whether or not the country would be a suitable place for the army to spend the winter.

Autumn was approaching when Alvarado reached Tiguex, a group of twelve pueblos built along opposite sides of the Rio Grande near present-day Bernalillo. Tiguex was then the center of power of the great tribe of Tigua Indians, and the arrival of the Spaniards marked the beginning of their downfall which would lead to their almost total extinction. Because they trusted their Pecos neighbor, Bigotes, the Tiguas welcomed the Spaniards on that bright September day. A large party of them marched around Alvarado's tent, one man playing a flute while others presented the bearded white man with gifts of food, blankets and skins. 'The people seem good, more given to farming than to war', Alvarado reported to Coronado. 'They have provisions of maize, beans, melons, and chickens [turkeys] in great abundance. They dress in cotton, cattle skins, and coats made with feathers from the chickens.' In other words, Tiguex would be a good place for the Spaniards to live off the Indians; there was food, shelter, and clothing for the taking.

After his inspection of Tiguex, Alvarado went on to Cicuye (Pecos) with Bigotes, and when the mustachioed chief's people saw their leader returning they came out to welcome him and the Spaniards 'and brought them into the town with drums and pipes something like flutes, of which they have a great many. They made many presents of cloth and turquoises, of which there are quantities in that region.'

Being eager to continue westward to see the buffalo herds, Alvarado asked Bigotes to guide him and his horsemen, but the Pecos chief begged off, pleading weariness from travel and a need to stay with his people. In his place Bigotes offered the loan of two slaves that he had captured while on a hunt in the Plains country. One of these slaves was Sopete, said to be from Quivira. The other was from a land the Indians called Harahey; the Spaniards named him El Turco because his headdress reminded them of those worn by Turks. Sopete was a Wichita, Quivira being the country of that tribe in what is now Kansas. The Turk was a Pawnee, from farther north.

Early in October, with the haltered Turk and Sopete as guides, Alvarado resumed his march toward the east. When they reached the Canadian River the Spaniards saw their first buffaloes, 'the most monstrous beasts ever seen or read about. There is such a quantity of them that I do not know what to compare them with, except with the fish in the sea . . . because the country is covered with them.'

Alvarado and his men had not by any means given up their hopes of finding gold, seven cities of gold, and during the journey they continually questioned both Sopete and the Turk. As the language difficulties lessened and the shrewd Turk learned what the Spaniards wished to hear, he began indulging them with stories of Gran Quivira far to the north, where there was much gold and silver. When Alvarado asked the Turk if he owned any golden objects from Quivira, the Indian replied that he had none but that his master Bigotes had a gold bracelet which had been brought from there. Alvarado was so beguiled by the story of the bracelet from Quivira that he lost all interest in exploring the buffalo plains. He turned back for Pecos to see the bracelet for himself.

Soon after returning to Pecos, where he was again warmly welcomed, Alvarado asked Bigotes if he might see the gold bracelet that had been taken from the Turk. Bigotes expressed great surprise, and replied that he had no gold bracelet. If the Turk had told such a story, then he was lying. Alvarado, however, wanted so desperately to believe there was gold in Quivira that he refused to accept Bigotes' denial.

In the meantime, Coronado had brought all his army up from

Mexico and had begun transferring his headquarters from Hawikuh to Tiguex, where he planned to spend the winter. On learning of this, Alvarado invited Bigotes to go with him to Tiguex for a visit with Coronado, but the suspicious Pecos chief firmly refused to go. Seeing that there was no other way to get Bigotes into Coronado's custody for proper questioning about the gold bracelet, Alvarado invited the chief to his tent one evening and promptly made him a prisoner. Not long afterward, the Spaniards left Pecos bound for Tiguex–with Bigotes, the Turk, and Sopete in close confinement.

For his first meeting with Coronado at Tiguex, Alvarado took along only the Turk, who willingly answered all questions put to him about the riches of Quivira. The country was level there, he said, with a great river filled with fish as large as the horses the Spaniards rode. The chiefs of Quivira traveled in boats propelled by twenty oarsmen on each side, and mounted on the prows of these vessels were great eagles made of solid gold. Every afternoon the chiefs of the Gran Quivira took their siestas under trees ornamented with golden bells which made soft music. When asked if the household objects in Quivira were made of gold, the Turk assured Coronado that even the dishes of ordinary families were made of gold, also their bowls and water jugs.

To make certain that the Turk knew what gold was, Coronado showed him some objects made of tin. After feeling and smelling the cheap ornaments, the Turk said they were not gold. 'I know gold and silver very well,' he declared, 'and care little for other metals.'

Coronado now became as excited as Alvarado about the prospects of gold in Quivira, and he demanded to know more about the gold bracelet which the Turk said Bigotes had taken from him. The wily Turk made a suggestion: If Coronado would let him return alone to Pecos, he was sure he could find the bracelet; Bigotes must have hidden it. Neither Coronado nor Alvarado was willing to trust the Turk on such a mission. Instead Coronado ordered Alvarado to take Fray Juan Padilla and go and question the imprisoned Bigotes once more about the bracelet.

For the inquisition, Alvarado and Fray Juan led the chained Bigotes to a field just outside the pueblo. With them was Pedro de Tovar who had maltreated the peaceful Hopis of Tusayan. Tovar brought along his hunting dogs, and when Bigotes repeatedly denied any knowledge of the gold bracelet, the dogs were unleashed upon Bigotes to force him to confess that he had such a bracelet. Although bitten on his legs and arms, Bigotes still would not 'confess', crying out that the Turk had invented the whole story. The Spaniards, including the man of God, Fray Juan Padilla, were certain that it was Bigotes who was lying. They had to believe in the golden mirage of Quivira.

Winter was now rapidly approaching, with unexpected early

snows. To house his army, Coronado ordered the Tiguas to vacate one of their twelve pueblos. The dispossessed Indians complained because they had to crowd into neighboring pueblos, but as yet they did not dare resist the power of these armored men on four-legged beasts, these gold-mad conquerors of Hawikuh.

Helmets and suits of mail were no protection from the cold of winter. Noting that his men were freezing, Coronado ordered the Tiguas to supply clothing for the three hundred Spaniards. 'The natives were not given time to discuss or consult about the matter', Castaneda recorded. 'There was nothing the natives could do except take off their own cloaks and hand them over until the number that the Spaniards asked for was reached. Some of the soldiers who went along with the collectors, when the latter gave them some blankets or skins that they did not consider good enough, if they saw an Indian with a better one, they exchanged it with him without any consideration or respect, and without inquiry about the importance of the person they despoiled. The Indians resented this very much.'

The Tiguas also resented the molestation of their women by the Spaniards. After one incident of rape, the Indians retaliated by killing some of the soldiers' horses, and driving others into a palisaded court in the pueblo of Arenal. When Coronado sent Lopez de Cardenas, discoverer of the Grand Canyon, to recover the horses, the Indians refused to come out of Arenal even for a parley. Instead they climbed to the high roofs of the pueblo, 'shouted their war cries to heaven and waved as banners the tails of the Spanish horses they had killed'.

Their pride injured, the Spaniards decided they must force submission. They attacked, and after suffering several casualties, managed to reach the terraces of Arenal. The Tiguas, however, refused to capitulate as the Zunis had done at Hawikuh. They remained barricaded within their thick-walled apartments and dared the Spaniards to drive them out.

Next day the soldiers breached the lower walls with battering rams and built smudge fires in the openings. To avoid suffocation, some of the Tiguas rushed out only to be slain by the Spaniards. About three hundred remaining in the pueblo made the sign of the cross, indicating they were willing to surrender if their lives would be spared. Two Spanish officers responded with similar signs. 'They then put down their arms and received pardon', said Castaneda. 'They were taken to the tent of Don Garcia [Cardenas] who, according to what he said, did not know about the peace and thought they had given themselves up of their own accord because they had been conquered.

'As he had been ordered by the general [Coronado] not to take them alive, but to make an example of them so that the other natives would fear the Spaniards, he ordered 200 stakes to be prepared at once to burn them alive. Nobody told him about the peace that had been granted them, for the soldiers knew as little as he, and those who should have told him about it remained silent, not thinking that it was any of their business. Then when the enemies saw that the Spaniards were binding them and beginning to roast them, about a hundred men who were in the tent began to struggle and defend themselves with what there was there and with the stakes they could seize. Our men who were on foot attacked the tent on all sides, so that there was great confusion around it, and then the horsemen chased those who escaped. As the country was level, not a man of them remained alive, unless it was some who remained hidden in the village and escaped that night to spread throughout the country the news that the strangers did not respect the peace they had made, which afterward proved a great misfortune. After this was over, it began to snow . . .'

Never again did the Tiguas trust the Spaniards because Coronado's men had broken their word after accepting the sign of the cross from the warriors who surrendered. During the long cold winter there were other fights and sieges, the Spaniards growing more barbarous with each show of resistance from their unwilling hosts, who fought to the death rather than risk surrender again.

As signs of spring began to appear on the land, the Turk spoke even more glowingly to Coronado of gold in Quivira, 'so much gold they could load not only horses with it but wagons'. And to make certain that the Spaniards would take him to his own country of Harahey, the Turk hinted that Tatarrax the great ruler of Harahey was even richer than the chiefs of Quivira. And beyond Harahey was Guaes, equally as rich in both gold and silver. The greedy Spaniards could scarcely wait to start, but when they did march out of Tiguex on 23 April 1541, they made certain that El Turco and the young Quiviran, Sopete, would not run away. Iron collars with chains attached were placed around their necks.

When the column reached Cicuye (Pecos), Coronado in a conciliatory gesture restored Bigotes to his people. After all, the Pecos chief was of no further use; he had not even produced the mysterious gold bracelet so often mentioned by the Turk.

By early May, Coronado was on the Llano Estacado, meeting with Plains Apaches (Querechos he called them), marveling at their tipis, their dog-drawn travois, and the immense buffalo herds which were their sustenance. Unknown to the Spaniards, the Turk managed to communicate with the Querechos and he persuaded them to help him lead the soldiers out upon the flat grassy plain where they would become lost and confused, thus giving him an opportunity to escape. The Querechos obliged by telling Coronado and his men of rich settlements to the east, and offering to assist the Turk in guiding them there. 'For five days', Coronado later reported, 'I went wherever they led me, until we reached some plains as bare of landmarks as if we were surrounded by the sea. Here the guides lost their bearings because there is nowhere a stone, hill, tree, bush, or anything of the sort.' The guides, of course, were only pretending they had lost their bearings, but during a buffalo hunt one of the Spanish soldiers did become lost and was never found again.

A few days later the column met 'another nation of people called Teyas', who may have been Apaches or Comanches. Upon learning that the Teyas had come from farther east, Coronado questioned them about the rich settlements there. The Teyas replied that there were no cities of gold in the east, but only houses made of straw and buffalo hides and the people who lived in them were very poor, even in maize.

'This information caused me considerable worry.', Coronado said. Not only were the Spaniards traveling in the wrong direction, they were also running out of food, and water was so scarce they had to drink from holes covered with slime. When their Querecho guides deserted them, the Spaniards were left again with only the Turk and Sopete. Sopete tried to inform his captors that they were moving away from Quivira, that it lay to the north, but no one would listen to the young Wichita. El Turco was so convincing that the Spaniards preferred to believe him; indeed he seemed to hold Coronado under some kind of spell.

At last the column came to a great barranca (Tule Canyon) in which another tribe of Teyas was camped. It was here that Sopete chose to create a scene, hoping to force Coronado to listen to him. Sopete 'dropped to the ground and indicated by signs that he would rather have his head cut off' than go farther southward. Quivira, he insisted, was to the north. At this point, Coronado evidently began to believe Sopete, who declared that the Turk had conspired with the Querechos to support his tales of golden cities to the east. Coronado had the good sense to question the Teyas in Tule Canyon before the Turk had an opportunity to communicate with them, and these Teyas also said they knew of no golden cities in the east. Quivira? Yes, Quivira lay far to the north, but no great cities were there, either. The Wichita villages were made of straw houses and they were rich only in maize.

None of the Spanish chroniclers gave any details of how Coronado wrung a confession from the Turk. 'What the Indian said was a lie, except that there was a province which was called Quivira, and that there was corn and houses of straw there', was the way one report put it.

For the next few days, Coronado's confused and starving army floundered about until by chance it came upon Palo Duro Canyon—a remarkable oasis in the vast plain, in some places a thousand feet deep, with perpetual water and grass to attract immense buffalo herds. 'The ravine . . . was a league wide from one side to the other, with a little bit of a river at the bottom, and there were many groves of mulberry trees near it, and rosebushes with the same sort of fruit that they have in France.

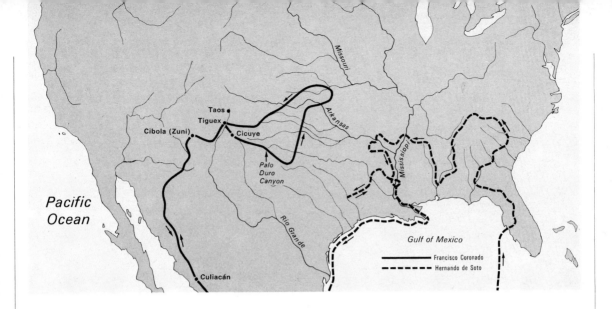

The routes followed by Francisco
Coronado and Hernando de Soto

They made verjuice from the unripe grapes at this ravine,
although there were ripe ones. There were walnuts and the
same kind of fowls as in New Spain, and large quantities of
prunes like those of Castile.'

Palo Duro Canyon, discovered by Europeans on that May
day in 1541, was destined to become a symbolic place in the
history of the American West. Here, three centuries later, the
Southern Plains Indians would make their last stand before
being forcibly confined on reservations. Here would live one of
the last free-roaming herds of buffaloes, and after those shaggy
animals were destroyed Palo Duro would become the site for
one of the earliest cattle ranches on the western plains during
the trail driving days of the cowboys.

Coronado rested his army for several days in the Palo Duro.
The soldiers restored themselves upon the canyon's natural
springtime abundance, dining well on meats, and perhaps they
avoided scurvy by drinking juices of the wild fruits. During this
time Coronado held several councils with his captains. Should
they abandon the search for the golden cities and turn back for
Mexico? Or should they continue to explore this new land?
There were several among the captains who believed that in
the beginning the Turk had been telling them the truth about
Quivira, but then he had changed his story and led them astray
out of fear of what the Spaniards would do when they reached
his golden country. No, it would not do to turn back now without
having seen Quivira for themselves, without one more search
for gold.

Almost every member of the expedition wished to go to
Quivira, but because of the distance and the reported scarcity
of food and water along the way, Coronado chose only thirty
soldiers and Fray Juan Padilla for the journey. The remainder
of the column would return to Tiguex. 'When the men in the
army learned of this decision, they begged their general not to

leave them to conduct the further search, but declared that they all wanted to die with him and did not want to go back. This did not do any good, although the general agreed to send messengers to them within eight days saying whether it was best for them to follow him or not, and with this he set off with the guides he had [a few Teyas] and Sopete. The Turk was taken along in chains.'

(By one of those strange coincidences of history, as Coronado marched north to the upper valley of the Arkansas River, another Spaniard in search of riches, Hernando de Soto, was seeking legendary cities of gold along the lower valley of the Arkansas. De Soto tracked over much of the country which is now the State of Arkansas, following rumors of golden cities far towards the sun's setting, but he never reached the Western Plains.)

Sopete had asked the Spaniards not to bring the Turk along on the journey 'because he would quarrel and try to restrain him in everything that he wanted to do for our advantage'. Coronado, however, thought that El Turco might be of some use. To spare Sopete's feelings, he ordered the Turk kept among the rear guard during the march and out of sight at camping places.

Following fresh buffalo trails northward, the column lived for a month solely on the meat of the animals, cooking it with dried dung from these same animals 'because there is no other fuel in all these plains, except along the arroyos, of which there are few'. In the heat of late June they crossed the Arkansas River at a ford used by Indians and buffaloes for centuries, and that would become well known to Westerners in future centuries. The famed Santa Fe Trail would cross this same ford, and the town to be built here by white men would be named for it—Ford, Kansas.

On 2 July a band of Wichita buffalo hunters sighted Coronado's column moving toward them down the valley of the Arkansas. At the approach of helmeted men riding strange four-legged beasts, the Wichitas 'began to utter yells and appeared to fly . . . Sopete began to call to them in his language, and so they came to us without any signs of fear.'

Great expectations rose again among the Spaniards. These hunters were from Quivira, and the first city of that land of mystery was only four days journey to the northeast. Surely there must be gold or other precious metals in Quivira. After hurrying across the summer-green plains past Pawnee Rock and the Great Bend of the Arkansas, the Spaniards at last sighted a hundred round-roofed buildings glittering golden under the July sun. To this day there is a tradition among the Wichitas that Coronado and his thirty men came in at a fast gallop, shouting and waving their swords in triumph. So convinced were they that what they saw were houses made of spun gold, they refused to believe otherwise until they thrust their swords into the thatching and felt with their hands the texture of the woven grass burned golden by the sun. They were somewhere in what is now Rice County, Kansas.

Although bitterly disappointed, Coronado was not yet ready to abandon all hope. From his hosts, he heard corroboration of the Turk's story about Tatarrax, ruler of Harahey. Coronado did not know that Tatarrax was merely a Wichita word for chieftain, but he did know that Harahey–the Turk's land– might be the last chance for cities of gold. And so Coronado led his men off on another five-days march.

Tatarrax turned out to be a very aged Pawnee with roached hair and a turkey-feather headdress. His total wealth consisted of a copper ornament fastened around his neck. When asked, Tatarrax declared that there was much metal like his neck-piece farther on. The Spaniards, however, found no trace of it during the month they spent in Kansas.

Still kept in chains, the Turk meanwhile was plotting escape by seeking allies among the Wichitas whenever they chanced to come near him. The Turk was aware of a growing resentment toward him from the Spaniards who had swallowed his stories of Quivira the golden, and he began to fear for his life.

From Sopete and other Wichitas, some of Coronado's men learned of the Turk's plots against them. He was whispering to the Wichitas not to give corn to the Spaniards, but instead to kill all their horses and force the Spaniards on foot where they could easily be slain by arrows and war clubs.

Coronado's captains advised him to have the Turk executed before he could do any harm. Somewhat reluctantly, Coronado ordered an investigation; he evidently still clung to a vain hope that the Turk might know the location of a city of gold; surely no simple Indian could have invented all the complicated tales he had told!

The Spaniards recorded few details of their second inquisition of El Turco, the imaginative Pawnee. This time he implicated Bigotes, the Pecos chief, in the original plot to lead the Spaniards astray on the Llano Estacado. Coronado now ordered an immediate and secret execution. When the soldiers assigned to carry out this sentence went to the tent where the Turk was kept prisoner, one of them asked the Indian for the last time: 'Where is the gold and wealth of which you told us at Tiguex?'

'The town having gold and other riches is farther on', El Turco replied. 'I led you by way of Quivira to get my wife in order to take her along.'

But this time the Spaniards refused to believe; they had been lured too many times by *mas alla*; they had crossed too many horizons. This time they placed a garrote around the Turk's neck and twisted it until he choked to death.

A few days later, Coronado erected a cross in the center of Kansas, claiming the land for God and King. After giving the faithful Sopete his freedom, the disillusioned Spaniards turned

All that glisters is not gold–a truism impressed on Coronado and his men by the Wichita grass houses

back for Tiguex. When the thirty weary soldiers reached there in mid-September, their waiting comrades refused to accept the failure of the mission to Quivira. The gold, they were certain, was to be found farther inland.

During the second wintering of the army at Tiguex, Coronado had much time to reflect upon his failures—first at the Seven Cities of Cibola, then at Tiguex, finally in Quivira. He had expended a fortune—his wife's fortune and the fortunes of the men he had asked to join him—yet had nothing to show for it. Most of his men wanted to resume exploration farther inland as soon as spring came, and he promised—but with none of his old enthusiasm—to lead them wherever they wished to go. On Saint John's Day following Christmas, while riding for exercise outside Tiguex, his saddle girth broke. When he fell, a horse's hoof struck his head and for several days he lay near death.

Coronado was never again a vigorous seeker of golden mirages. As he slowly recovered during the winter, his thoughts were mostly of the comforts of home and family. He talked no more of expeditions farther inland in search of great fortunes.

In April 1542, over the opposition of a considerable number of his followers, Coronado ordered a return march to Mexico. Until the very last, sixty men held out, refusing to abandon their dreams of a new kingdom of gold, but in the end they too submitted. Only the friars were permitted to remain in the land of the Pueblos so that they might continue to erect crosses and 'baptize the children whom they might find on the verge of death, thus sending them to Heaven'.

Not long after the dust of Coronado's departing column had settled over Tiguex, Father Juan Padilla—the friar who had made the journey with the soldiers to Quivira—quietly left the Pueblos on the Rio Grande and set out for the north in company with a Portuguese, a Negro interpreter, and a few servants. Ostensibly Fray Juan was returning to Quivira to make converts of the Wichitas to his religion. But when he reached Quivira he did not stop. He went on 'to see with his own eyes' the marvelous land of Harahey. He never reached that mythical country. Along the way a war party of Indians blocked his path, and although the friar fell on his knees and offered prayers to God, the Indians—who may have come from Harahey—filled his body with arrows. In Herington, Kansas, there is a monument to his memory.

Coronado returned to Mexico a non-hero because he brought back no gold, and as details of the expedition became known, he was much condemned for not continuing the march to Harahey to find the golden cities which surely must be there. The Spanish government instituted a public inquiry, but after a long series of hearings, Coronado was absolved of all charges. An embittered man who had ventured everything on a journey of greed, he lived quietly in Mexico for the remaining twelve years of his life, dying 22 September 1554 at the age of forty-four.

Fray Juan was only one of countless zealous missionaries who lost their lives in the New World.

2. To the Western Sea

After Elizabeth I's upstart English seamen defeated Spain's *Armada Invencible* in 1588, the vigor of Spanish conquest began to decline. In 1598 one more futile attempt was made from New Spain by Juan de Onate to find the gold of Quivira. Onate's real mission was to colonize New Mexico and California as a barrier against ventures into the West by the audacious English, but he spent most of his time on exploring expeditions. Had it not been for the Franciscan missionaries, there probably would have been no *Spanish* New Mexico or California. As a result of their energies Santa Fe, the first capital city in what is now the United States, became a symbol of Spanish glory, the farthest outpost of a failing empire.

The Tiguas, the Pecos, and other tribes were treated badly, and in 1680, led by Popé, a Tewa medicine man, the Pueblos rose up and drove the Spaniards out of Santa Fe, killing twenty-one priests and about four hundred colonists from Mexico. The revolutionaries sought out all their tribesmen who had been baptized as Christians and washed them thoroughly with yucca suds to restore their Indianness. They prohibited further use of the Spanish language and destroyed crosses and other religious objects.

Spanish pride and Church zeal could not endure such ignominy. Twelve years later Spanish soldiers and priests returned to Santa Fe to rebuild it, and from that time the city grew into a legend of the West. Englishmen on the east coast of North America knew of and were jealous of Santa Fe; Frenchmen in New France (Canada) heard stories of the great wealth of Santa Fe. The men of Santa Fe, it was said, wore buttons of silver on their trousers, and the women wore slippers of gold. So common were these precious metals that even the tires of carts and carriages in Santa Fe were made of silver and gold.

Frenchmen in the Northeast—like the Spaniards in the Southwest—had long sought concentrated hoards of wealth. Norembega and the Kingdom of Saguenay, the French called their northern El Dorados. They searched for mines of gold, silver and rubies along the shores of the Bay of Fundy, and up the St Lawrence and Ottawa rivers to Georgian Bay. If they could not find Norembega, then they would find a water route across America to the riches of the Orient, to the Indies originally sought by Columbus. The only wealth they found was in the fur trade, and in search of furs they built trading posts and Jesuit missions around the Great Lakes, down the Mississippi, and up its tributaries. At every stopping place they shouted *Vive le Roi* and claimed the land for France.

Not all Frenchmen abandoned the dream of Norembega, of finding quick wealth in one bold effort. Among them were Pierre and Paul Mallet who decided to pursue the mirage all the way from Canada to the golden city of Santa Fe. Enlisting six companions they purchased a supply of knives, awls, axes, and other trade goods and voyaged from the St Lawrence through the Great Lakes and down the Illinois and Mississippi rivers to the Missouri. Two centuries had passed since Coronado's venture into the West, but that land was still so poorly mapped that the Mallet brothers believed the Missouri River would take them to Santa Fe.

Although their journal has been lost, official abstracts from it indicate that by the time the Mallets reached the mouth of the Niobrara, they suspected they were traveling in the wrong direction. Here they turned southward to a stream so wide and shallow that they named it the Platte. No longer able to use canoes or pirogues, they exchanged some of their trade goods for horses from the Pawnees. These Indians were the Turk's people, of course; the French seekers of wealth were in the fabled land of Harahey. During those two centuries since the coming of Coronado, Spanish horses had made a much deeper penetration into the West than the Spaniards themselves. Horses were valuable, yet not so valuable as guns, knives, and other objects of metal.

In June 1739 on the advice of the Pawnees who knew where Santa Fe was, the Mallet party began crossing the plains 'where they could not find enough wood to light a fire . . . where the only means to light a fire consisted of buffalo chips'. Almost every day now they had to ford one of the numerous streams that flow eastward across Kansas. When they reached the Smoky Hill River, it was flooded from June cloudbursts; they misjudged its strong current and lost seven horses loaded with merchandise. Ten days later, 30 June, they were on the Arkansas and found near one of its banks 'stones with Spanish inscriptions'. Because of the lost journal we do not know what these inscriptions were nor who left them–Coronado, the ill-fated Fray Juan Padilla, or Juan de Onate.

Early in June the Mallets came upon a tribe which they called Laitanes–probably Comanches. Among them they met a much-traveled Arikara captive. The Arikara told the Frenchmen 'he had been a slave with the Spaniards and even had been baptized there'. After warning the Frenchmen that the Laitanes 'had some unfriendly plot in mind', the Arikara agreed to guide them to Santa Fe in exchange for his freedom. The next day the

Taos Pueblo, built in 1600

eight Frenchmen and their guide slipped away and 'made ten leagues in order to get away from the Laitanes'.

On 15 July they were outside the pueblo of Taos. One of the Mallets wrote a letter to the Spanish commandant and sent it in by three friendly Pueblos. Not long afterward the bells of the mission began ringing and the commandant, a priest, and 'a great number of people' came out to welcome the first Europeans to cross the unknown territory between the Missouri country and New Mexico.

A week later the Mallets and their companions received an equally warm reception from Governor Gaspar Mendoza and General Juan Hurtado, the alcalde and captain of war in Santa Fe. The Frenchmen were disappointed to find none of the gold and silver they had heard about in faraway Canada, but only a few hundred families in a small city 'built of wood and without any fortifications, the garrison composed of but eighty soldiers, a bad band and poorly armed'.

Although Spanish laws forbade foreign trade in Santa Fe, the people there were so eager to obtain cloth, knives, and other goods that neither the governor nor the general interfered with the Mallets, who were able to sell their merchandise at ten times the prices prevailing in Canada. When the Mallets asked for permission to bring shipments in regularly from New France, the governor replied that he was required to secure permission from the Viceroy of Mexico to grant such authority. For some months the Mallets waited, and then the answer from Mexico was a firm refusal; in fact, the viceroy suggested to Governor Mendoza that he not permit the eight Frenchmen to leave Santa Fe because they had 'spied out the land'. Louis Moreau, a barber-surgeon who had already met and married a Santa Fe woman, and probably one other member of Mallet's party, did remain voluntarily, but Governor Mendoza allowed the Mallets and their remaining companions to leave.

OPPOSITE Captain Meriwether Lewis by Saint-Mémin

Taking an easterly course, the Frenchmen made their way to New Orleans, surprising and pleasing the French governor of Louisiana Territory, Sieur de Bienville. Bienville, who had founded New Orleans, encouraged the Mallets to organize other trading expeditions to Santa Fe. They made two more attempts but each time they approached New Mexico they found that Santa Fe had become a forbidden city. Their goods were seized and confiscated. The ailing Spanish empire was growing more suspicious than ever of foreigners, and to keep his post in Santa Fe the once friendly Governor Mendoza had become quite ruthless. On 30 June 1743 he reported to Mexico City: 'My most pressing task has been the inquiry into the abominable conduct of a Frenchman, one of those who came here in the year 1739 concerning whom I have already reported at length . . . This person, after arriving here attempted with subtle plots to incite the Indians of this kingdom to revolt . . . I sentenced him to death by having his heart taken out through the back.'

Rebuffed by the distrustful Spaniards in the Southwest, the energetic French turned their attention toward the Northwest. Driven by a compulsion as powerful as that which had taken the Mallets to Santa Fe, Pierre de la Vérendrye began a passionate search for the 'Western Sea', a water route across America that would lead him to the riches of China and the real India. Backed by a fur trade monopoly in the Sioux country of Canada, Vérendrye built forts westward from Lake Superior. Wherever he went he constantly queried the Indians for information concerning the Western Sea. To get there, he was told, he must travel until he reached a river in which the water tasted of salt and throbbed back and forth with a frightening noise. In that country were strange men who dressed themselves and their horses in iron.

Learning from the Assiniboines of a tribe called the Mandans who knew much about the Western Sea, Vérendrye with his two sons journeyed to the Missouri River. Before he reached the Mandan villages, Vérendrye's interpreter deserted him and he lost his baggage containing trinkets and other trade goods. Returning to his nearest base, Vérendrye fell ill, and he feared that he would not be able to continue his search for a passage to the ocean.

His two sons, Louis-Joseph and François (Chevalier), had also become fired with their father's quest, and in the spring of 1742 they returned to the Mandan villages, secured a guide there, and set out on horseback to find other Indians who might lead them to the Western Sea. During the summer they visited Crows, Cheyennes, and Shoshones on the Wyoming and Montana plains. Everywhere they went they were told that in the direction of the sun's setting were very high mountains, and beyond these mountains was a great body of salt water. In January 1743, one of the Vérendrye brothers joined a party

of Cheyennes for a horse raid against the Shoshones, and they led him in sight of mountains which were 'well wooded with all kind of timber and appeared very high'. Young Vérendrye was probably in the Big Horns of Wyoming, the closest that he or his brother came to the Pacific Ocean.

Before rejoining their father's fur operations, the Vérendrye brothers properly claimed all the land to the shining summits of the mountains for God and King by burying a lead plate on a high bank of the Missouri. Walking one afternoon near Pierre, the capital of South Dakota, 170 years later, two school children found the six-by-eight inch tablet: 'Deposited by the Chevalier de La Vérendrye, Lo Jos, Louey la Londette, Amiotte, the 30th of March, 1743.'

Louisiana Territory, named for King Louis XIV, was becoming a vast domain, the French claiming most of the land drained by the Mississippi River and its far-winding tributaries. The fate of Western America, however, was tied to the shifting balances of power in Europe with its incessant wars and indolent monarchs who were more interested in mistresses and court etiquette than wilderness lands distant as the moon.

In 1763 at the end of nine years of European war (the British in America called it the French and Indian War), France was forced to relinquish Louisiana west of the Mississippi to Spain, while Great Britain took virtually everything else of French territory in North America.

During the next forty years the world was turned upside down. When the turmoil ended part of the British colonies had won their independence and formed themselves into the United States of America; the French had overthrown their last King Louis and accepted the rule of Napoleon Bonaparte; the Spanish had squandered the last of their American-found wealth in a series of useless European wars. On 1 October 1800 Spain transferred Louisiana back to France.

Five months later an extraordinary man became President of the United States. He was Thomas Jefferson, the only genius ever to achieve political leadership of his people. Not only was he the author of the Declaration of Independence, Jefferson was a scientist, architect, mathematician, linguist, geographer, ethnologist, philosopher, and inventor of many practical machines. He was keenly interested in his country's western frontier and was apprehensive of what the unpredictable Napoleon Bonaparte might undertake in the land beyond the Mississippi. In that day of water transport, and with the rapid settlement of United States territory west of the Alleghenies, New Orleans at the mouth of the Mississippi had become a vital door to the sea. Any foreign government with the power to block the river was viewed by Jefferson as a 'natural and habitual enemy' of the United States. He instructed his minister in Paris to make an offer to purchase New Orleans.

One side of the lead plate buried by the Vérendrye brothers

OPPOSITE Charles Willson Peale's portrait of William Clark, painted a few years after the expedition to the Western Sea

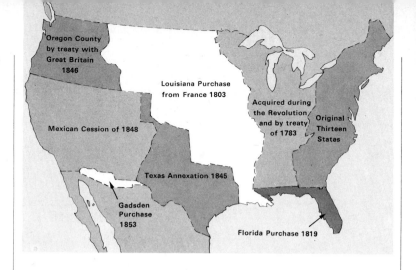

Land acquired by the United States

In the spring of 1803, to Jefferson's surprise, France offered to sell not only New Orleans but the whole of Louisiana Territory. Napoleon was badly in need of money to rebuild his European armies, and he knew little about, and cared nothing for the great wilderness empire in Western America that had been claimed for three King Louis by thousands of resolute French explorers. Jefferson immediately seized the opportunity. For fifteen million dollars he doubled the land area of the United States, acquiring more than five hundred million acres for less than three cents an acre. Even before the transaction was completed, he began devoting much of his energies to thorough and detailed planning for an exploring expedition. He believed that at least ten centuries of time would be spent in filling this territory with farms and towns, and that during this long period the Indian tribes would be absorbed peacefully into the stream of American population. Yet his scientific curiosity was such that he wanted to know what was there in the unknown country of Louisiana Territory. Although the Rocky Mountains marked the westward limits of Louisiana Territory, Jefferson was determined to 'explore the whole line, even to the Western Ocean'. Both Great Britain and Russia claimed the Oregon country between the Rockies and the Pacific, but neither had bothered to establish colonies there.

To lead the expedition to the Western Sea, Jefferson selected Captain Meriwether Lewis whom he had borrowed from the Army in 1801 to serve as his private secretary. Lewis in turn chose William Clark as his partner in discovery, to bear equal rank and responsibility. All three men had known each other for years, having grown up around Charlottesville, Virginia. In 1804 Lewis was thirty, Clark was thirty-four, and they complemented each other well. Lewis was an introvert, preferring solitude; his mind was restless, always inquiring. Clark was a red-haired extrovert–genial, optimistic, practical. Both men were highly intelligent and resourceful, as attuned to the frontier wilderness as modern-day astronauts are attuned to outer space.

They prepared for their journey as carefully as if they were departing for an unknown planet. They had no maps or charts beyond the Mandan villages on the Missouri River – visited by the Vérendryes sixty years earlier in their futile search for the Western Sea. What knowledge there was of the far Rockies was more myth than fact – legends of live mammoths wandering through deep canyons, of solid salt mountains hundreds of miles long, of giants so fierce they killed all intruders upon their domains. Food staples, medicines, and manufactured goods that thirty men would need for two years had to be carried on three small boats. They packed everything with care; for instance they wrapped gunpowder in thin sheets of lead which kept the powder dry and then could be melted to make bullets. Each bale of supplies contained small packets of every article carried, so that if a bale were lost the entire supply of any one item would not be lost.

Months before the journey began, Jefferson prepared a letter of instruction so detailed that there could be no doubt as to the objectives of the mission. No mention was made of finding riches of the Orient, of cities of gold, of Quivira, or Norembega. Lewis and Clark were to ascend the Missouri River, cross the Rockies, and descend to the Pacific by the most practicable river passage. They were to make a thorough survey of a possible water route to the Pacific; they were to study and cultivate friendships with Indians encountered and estimate the possibilities of establishing commerce with them. They were to observe and record all that was noteworthy concerning animals, plants, minerals, soils, and climates. They were to map the sources and courses of rivers, and determine the latitude and longitude of important landmarks.

Routes followed by Lewis and Clark, and Jedediah Smith (see chapter 3)

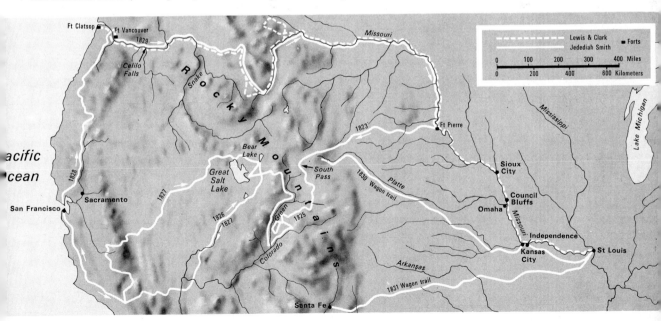

This first scientific journey into the West began on the rainy afternoon of 14 May 1804, a few miles north of St Louis at Wood River opposite the mouth of the Missouri. In addition to Lewis and Clark the permanent party consisted of fourteen soldiers from the U.S. Army and nine recently recruited young frontiersmen from Kentucky. No noblemen or rich men's sons seeking easy wealth were in the group. Their specifications as set down by Meriwether Lewis called for 'good hunters, stout, healthy, unmarried men, accustomed to the woods and capable of bearing bodily fatigue in a pretty considerable degree'. The party also included two French boatmen, Captain Clark's Negro servant York, civilian interpreter George Drouillard, Captain Lewis' Newfoundland dog Scannon, and two horses to be used for towing, hunting and other chores. Additional soldiers and rivermen were to accompany them only as far as the Mandan villages where plans called for the expedition to camp during the winter.

For the first few days of the journey upriver, progress was slow and monotonous. The fifty-five-foot keelboat was equipped with a square sail and twenty-two oars; the two pirogues had six or seven oars, so that there was plenty of work for all. As would be the pattern for much of the journey, Lewis spent much of his time ashore with his dog Scannon, walking and exploring while the boats made their average progress of nine miles per day. Clark remained with the boats, making certain that everything was proceeding according to schedule.

On 21 July after fighting river currents, summer heat, drenching thunderstorms, and mosquitoes, they reached the sandy mouth of the Platte—so named by the Mallet brothers sixty years earlier. Ten days later, twenty-two-year-old Sergeant Charles Floyd wrote in his diary: 'I am verry Sick and Has been for Somtime but have Recoverd my helth again.' Young Floyd was much sicker than he realized, but the excitement of the expedition's first council with Indians took his mind off his ailment.

The Indians were of the Oto, Omaha, and Missouri tribes. Clark ordered 'every man on his Guard & ready for any thing', but he and Lewis managed to keep the meetings on a friendly footing, showing their respect for the Indians but quietly informing them that they were now under protection of a new White Father at Washington who wished them to keep the peace and would soon send them 'traders to supply them with all necessities'. They named the camp where the councils were held 'Councile Bluff, a verry proper place for a Tradeing establishment'. Some years afterward Council Bluffs, Iowa, would be established in the area.

'Serjeant Floyd is taken verry bad all at once with a bilious colic', Clark recorded on 19 August. 'We attempt to relieve him without success.' Medical historians believe that Floyd was suffering from acute appendicitis, and that none of the remedies carried by the explorers could have saved him. He died the next day 'with a great deal of composure'. They buried the young Kentuckian on a high bluff and named a nearby river in his honor.

To replace Floyd as sergeant, the enlisted men were authorized to hold an election. They chose Patrick Gass, a swarthy, black-haired thirty-three-year-old Irishman from Chambersburg, Pennsylvania – a master of carpentry and profanity. Gass was now fourth in command. Sergeant John Ordway, a lanky, loose-jointed New England Yankee, was third in command.

By late August they were well into the Plains country, and Lewis busied himself ashore, collecting and describing animals that he had never seen before – barking squirrels and odd species of goats and foxes. The barking squirrels were prairie dogs; the strange goats and foxes were antelopes and coyotes.

On 24 September five Indians hailed them from the river bank. Clark anchored the boats well out in the river. With George Drouillard assisting, the explorers soon learned by sign language that the Indians were Teton Sioux, and that an encampment of more than a thousand was nearby. They arranged for a council next day with the chief, Black Buffalo.

At sunrise the next morning they had the flag of the United States flying from a staff on the south side of the river (opposite the later site of Pierre, South Dakota, where the Vérendrye brothers had buried their lead plate). By noon the council was under way. 'Captain Lewis proceeded to deliver a speech which we were obliged to curtail for want of a good interpreter.' Perhaps Lewis' phrases were too complex for translation into sign language. He solved the dilemma temporarily by passing out medals and presents to Black Buffalo and the other chiefs. The Indians accepted the red coats, cocked hats, feathers, and tobacco enthusiastically, but made it clear that these were not enough. If the explorers wished to continue farther upriver they would have to make the Sioux a present of one of the pirogues with all its contents. When Lewis pretended not to understand, three warriors seized the cable of one of the pirogues as though to take possession of it, and others had their bows strung and arrows out of their quivers as though preparing for an attack.

For a few moments the fate of the expedition hung in the balance. Lewis who had returned to the keelboat reacted quickly, ordering the men to arms and manning the swivel guns for action. He sent twelve infantrymen hurrying ashore, and when they arrived with rifles cocked, Black Buffalo backed down before the display of firmness, and all hostility seemed to vanish. The chief asked Clark to permit him and three other chiefs to be taken aboard the keelboat for the night. They wanted to ride up to their village next morning and show the wonders of the boat to their people. Clark was dubious, but Lewis thought it might be a conciliatory gesture to take them aboard. That night was a long one for Captain Clark. Distrust-

The view from Floyd's grave

ing the motives of his guests, he kept himself awake until dawn.

Next morning, Indians lined the banks of the Missouri for four miles, and Black Buffalo seemed to enjoy having his people see him riding aboard the white men's keelboat. When they reached the tipi village, Lewis went ashore with the chiefs, handed out more presents, and tried to communicate with his hosts through George Drouillard and Peter Cruzat, one of the French boatmen who knew a few words of the Dakota language.

In contrast to the previous day's hostility, the Sioux were so hospitable that the explorers remained at the village for two days and nights, being entertained with music and dancing, and dining on 'some of the most Delicate parts of the Dog'. On 28 September, however, when they made ready to resume their journey, the Sioux chiefs came aboard and strongly objected.

'They said we might return back with what we had or remain with them,' Sergeant Ordway wrote, 'but we could not go up the Missouri any further. About 200 Indians were there on the bank. Some had firearms. Some had spears. Some had a kind of cutlash, and the rest had bows and steel or iron pointed arrows.' (One reason the Sioux were reluctant for white men to continue upriver was that they had tribal enemies to the west, and feared traders would supply them with rifles and other weapons.)

Lewis asked the chiefs to leave the boat. When they refused to go, he ordered his men to battle stations. Clark took a burning fuse from the gunner and stood ready to fire one of the swivel guns point-blank into the warriors on shore. Black Buffalo stood his ground and demanded a tribute of tobacco. Lewis, who had become very angry, raised his sword as though to cut the mooring rope. The warriors on shore readied their weapons. For the second time, the expedition's fate was in doubt. It was Clark who eased the tension; he presented a large twist of tobacco to Black Buffalo, and the chiefs departed with dignity. 'We then set off under a gentle breeze', Sergeant Ordway noted tersely. That night for the first time in four days Captains Lewis and Clark slept. They had outbluffed the Sioux,

An engraving from Patrick Gass's book about the expedition showing Lewis and Clark parleying with Indians

and the word that these explorers could not be intimidated preceded them up the muddy river.

By 8 October the Arikara village at the mouth of the Grand River had heard about the explorers and received them like visiting heroes. 'All things arranged for peace or war', Clark noted, but the meeting turned out to be quite friendly. Another rumor the village had heard concerned a black man with curly hair. This was York, of course, and he enjoyed the attention given him by the Arikaras. 'Those Indians were much astonished at my Servent', Clark wrote. 'They never saw a black man before; all flocked around him & examined him from top to toe.' The Indians believed that York's black skin was paint; some of the women boldly approached him and tried to rub it off.

In Clark's opinion the Arikara women were handsomer and more amorous than the Sioux women. 'Our men found no difficulty in procuring companions for the night by means of the interpreters', he noted. But they could not linger long among the Arikaras. The autumn days were growing shorter, the nights colder, and they had to press on to reach the Mandan villages before snow began to fall.

It was 27 October when they reached the first village and made the acquaintance of Shahaka (or Sheheke), a fat, good-natured chief who like many Mandans was light-skinned. He was sometimes called Big White. Shahaka offered to share his winter corn supply with the explorers. 'If we eat, you shall eat', he said. 'If we starve, you must starve also.' He taught Captain Clark how to kill buffalo with bow and arrow so that the expedition's ammunition supply could be conserved.

As the explorers visited from village to village, they searched out a good location for their winter camp, to be called Fort Mandan. On 2 November they began felling trees to build cabins, and the winter's work was begun. They built canoes to take them to the Rocky Mountains, dried large quantities of meat, and replaced their worn clothing with apparel made of animal skins. They also gathered intelligence from visiting Indians and French-Canadian traders. As it turned out, the most important visitors to the Mandan villages that winter were an insignificant trader and his female companion. Toussaint Charbonneau was a Canadian who collected young Indian 'wives'. Sacagawea (Bird Woman) was his latest acquisition, a frail sixteen-year-old Shoshone girl who had been captured by the Minnetarees. When the pair arrived on 11 November, Sacagawea was pregnant. During her confinement Lewis and Clark became well acquainted with her, Clark officiating at the birth of her child. 'This was the first child which this woman had boarn,' he recorded on 11 February 1805, 'and as is common in such cases her labour was tedious and the pain violent.'

From Sacagawea the explorers learned that they would have to abandon their boats at the source of the Missouri. To cross the Rockies they would need horses, which they could obtain only from the Shoshones – the Bird Woman's people.

Both Lewis and Clark quickly realized how important Sacagawea had become to the success of their mission. She could speak Shoshone and interpret for them; and she would know something of the country they would have to cross. But to obtain her they would also have to take her lazy rascal of a husband, Charbonneau. 'We called him in and spoke to him on the subject', Clark wrote on 17 March. 'He agreed to our terms.'

By early April wild geese were flying north and ice was breaking up in the Missouri. They packed nine boxes of specimens and reports for President Jefferson, and on 7 April started them back to St Louis on the keelboat with a reduced crew of eight men.

On that same day, Lewis, Clark, and the remaining thirty-one men boarded their six canoes and two pirogues and resumed the westward journey. With them went Charbonneau, Sacagawea, and her son Baptiste, whom Clark nicknamed Pomp.

'We were now about to penetrate a country at least two thousand miles in width,' Lewis wrote,

> on which the foot of civilized man had never trodden; the good or evil it had in store for us was for experiment yet to determine, and these little vessels contained every article by which we were to expect to subsist or defend ourselves. However, as the state of mind in which we are, generally gives the colouring to events, when the imagination is suffered to wander into futurity, the picture which now presented itself to me was a most pleasing one. Entertaining as I do, the most confident hope of succeeding in a voyage which had formed a darling project of mine for the last ten years, I could but esteem this moment of my departure as among the most happy of my life. The party are in excellent health and spirits, zealously attached to the enterprise, and anxious to proceed; not a whisper or murmur of discontent to be heard among them, but all act in unison, and with the most perfect harmony.

Each day the Missouri grew more difficult of ascent, its current running rough and swift. To keep the little boats afloat, the men often had to leap out and swim or wade alongside. Wild game was plentiful enough that they could save their dried meat for the crossing of the Rockies. Lewis' Newfoundland dog, Scannon, became an accomplished hunter; his speciality was trapping antelope, deer, and wild geese in the water and then bringing them ashore. He also outran and brought down a goat. On 19 May, however, a beaver took revenge upon Scannon. One of the men shot the beaver and Scannon swam out to retrieve it. 'The beaver bit him through the hind leg and cut the artery', Lewis recorded. 'It was with great difficulty that I could stop the blood; I fear it will yet prove fatal to him.' Lewis had grown very fond of his shaggy bearlike companion, and tended the animal as carefully as a wounded child. A week later Scannon was ashore again with his master.

For days Lewis had been climbing hills along the river, his eyes searching westward, hoping to see the great Shining Mountains of which he had heard so many tales. On 26 May he saw the high range for the first time 'covered with snow and the sun shone on it in such a manner as to give me the most plain and satisfactory view'.

From the Indians they had heard stories of a giant waterfall thundering out of the mountains. They reached it on 13 June. 'The grandest sight I ever beheld', Lewis wrote, but the falls delayed them for almost a month while they portaged their baggage around it.

On 20 July they sighted signal smokes ahead, but none of the party could interpret their meaning. The explorers were hopeful that they might be Shoshone smokes, and ordered white

Voyageurs by Charles Deas

flags hoisted in the boats to indicate they were on a mission of peace instead of war.

Their next dilemma came a few days later when the Missouri divided into three forks, each of about the same size. After exploring a short distance up each stream, they decided that the branch from the southwest was most likely to take them to the Rockies. In honor of the President they named that branch the Jefferson River; the other two were named the Madison and Gallatin for members of Jefferson's cabinet.

On 30 July the expedition began moving up the Jefferson River. In a short time Sacagawea became very excited. She recognized some of the landmarks along the stream, and then suddenly she saw the very camp site where the Minnetarees had attacked her people and captured her as she tried to escape by wading the river at a shoal. At last, the expedition had reached Shoshone country.

But where were the Shoshones and their horses? Almost every day they found recent evidence of their presence, but the Indians seemed to be deliberately avoiding them (as indeed they were, out of fear of these strange bearded men). On 10 August parties sent ashore found horse tracks only a few hours old. Sacagawea assured them that they were in the heart of her people's country, and pointed out a hill that she remembered from childhood; it was shaped like a beaver's head and was so called by the Shoshones.

Realizing that summer weather would soon end and that time was running out for a crossing of the snow-topped Rockies, the captains redoubled their efforts to find the Shoshones. On the morning of the 11th, Lewis chose three men to accompany him on a long search—John Shields, a reliable Kentucky blacksmith; Hugh McNeal, veteran soldier; and George Drouillard who knew Indian sign language. Two days later they found Shoshones at last, virtually capturing three women. With Drouillard's help, Lewis managed to convince the women that no harm would come to them by showering them with beads, mirrors, and other gifts. 'After they became composed, I informed them by signs that I wished them to conduct us to their camp, that we were anxious to become acquainted with the chiefs and warriors of their nation.'

As they followed the obedient women down a trail toward the river, the explorers sighted the Shoshone chiefs and warriors much sooner than they had expected. Mounted and with weapons ready, about sixty warriors came galloping in a wild charge to rescue their abducted women.

Was this to be the end of the journey, the end of Meriwether Lewis, the end of Thomas Jefferson's dream? All that Lewis could think of to do was to drop his rifle and pull a small American flag from his pack. Facing into the charging warriors, he unfurled the Stars and Stripes, and as he strode forward to meet their fury, he began waving the banner back and forth.

In those few moments that Meriwether Lewis and his three scouting companions awaited the onrush of the mounted Shoshone warriors, they must have prayed for the sudden appearance of Sacagawea to save them from sudden death. Sacagawea, however, was miles away on the river with Captain Clark. It was another Shoshone woman who swung the balance for them, one of the three they had met and treated with kindness. She shouted to the chief that the strangers were friendly white men, and to prove it she held up the presents they had given her.

Dismounting in a single leap, the chief ran forward and embraced Lewis. Pressing his paint-smeared face against the captain's cheek, he said in Shoshone: 'I am pleased! I am much rejoiced!'

From that moment on, the meeting became a spirited celebration, and when Sacagawea arrived later to rejoin her people, the singing and dancing were performed all over again. By a remarkable coincidence, the chief whose name was Cameahwait turned out to be Sacagawea's brother. This of course mightily improved the explorers' chances for obtaining horses to make the crossing of the Rockies.

Trading for horses, however, proved to be a long-drawn-out affair. To obtain the first four animals they bartered a uniform coat, two pairs of leggings, a few handkerchiefs, four knives, and an old checkered shirt. When it became apparent that Cameahwait's band was unwilling to spare any more mounts, parties were sent to neighboring villages in hopes of finding others. Sacagawea's knowledge of the language and her suggestions to the explorers as to how to proceed proved invaluable in these negotiations.

During this enforced delay Captain Clark and Sergeant Gass, using Shoshone guides, made tentative surveys for a route across the mountains. What they observed and what they heard from the Shoshones offered little encouragement. One old man told them the mountains were inaccessible to man or horse, the rivers so filled with rocks and foam that no boat could float upon them, the country so bare of game or edible plants that no Shoshone ever tried to pass across it. The old Shoshone did admit, however, that an occasional Nez Percé crossed from the other side, and Clark was certain that if the Nez Percés could cross, then so could the explorers.

At last on 29 August, the expedition was ready to begin the most difficult part of the journey. With twenty-eight horses, one mule, and six Shoshone guides, they started marching northeastward to the Bitterroot Valley. Sacagawea, Charbonneau, and Pomp were still with them. The young Shoshone woman wanted to go on to see the Great Ocean, and every man in the party welcomed her presence. Captain Clark had fallen in love with her. He nicknamed her Janey and was constantly defending her from the boorish treatment given her by Charbonneau. 'No woman ever accompanies a war party of Indians', Clark said, and he was convinced that the presence of Sacagawea saved them from attack more than once.

The nights were extremely cold now, the trail almost impassable. Sergeant Gass noted with his usual conciseness: 'Fatiguing beyond description.' During the night of 3 September, snow fell upon their camp. 'Our moccasins froze', Sergeant Ordway wrote. 'We have nothing but a little parched corn to eat. The air on the mountains very chilly and cold. Our fingers ached.'

Late that day in a valley now known as Ross's Hole, they came upon a large encampment of Flathead Indians. The presence of Sacagawea and the Shoshone guides insured a friendly council, and as the Flatheads owned an abundance of mustangs, the two captains had no difficulty bargaining for eleven additional mounts.

A week later they started across the Bitterroot Range, following part of the present-day Lolo Trail. By 14 September all their flour and corn was gone, and they could find almost no wild game or fish anywhere along the route. They slaughtered a young horse, and then for several days lived on berries, wolf meat, and crayfish. To keep from starving they had to break out their supply of candles and bear's oil. For water they used snow from the drifts which grew deeper day by day. On 18 September Clark pushed ahead with six men in a desperate search for food. Two days later they met a wandering band of Nez Percés, who were hospitable enough to supply the explorers with dried salmon and camas-root flour.

At last they crossed the Rockies into the valley of the Clearwater, and were now outside the limits of United States territory. The cold, the hard going, the deficient diet had taken their toll. Almost every man was suffering from dysentery. During the last few miles of descent, some fell exhausted beside the trail and had to be carried into camp on pack horses. Lewis was completely debilitated. Although Clark escaped serious illness, he was thrown from one of the Indian ponies, injuring his hip. He took over Lewis' usual surgeon's duties and as soon as a rest camp was made beside the Clearwater, he began dosing everybody with salts, tartar emetic, and jalap. Surprisingly they all recovered, but for three or four days the exploring party was defenseless.

As soon as enough men were able to work, they cut down five large pine trees, hollowed the trunks out by burning, and shaped them into dugouts of sufficient size to carry all members of the party and their remaining supplies. What to do with their thirty-eight horses, which they would need again on their return journey, was a major problem. They solved it by trusting the Nez Percés, giving them presents, and promising them more on their return. Remembering that the horses were the property of the U.S. Army, Lewis had them branded. (The branding iron containing the words 'U.S. Capt. M. Lewis' evidently was lost when the work was finished; almost a century afterward it was found on an island in the Columbia River.)

They spent the month of October in a race to reach the Pacific before winter overtook them. The swift current of the Clearwater swirled the explorers through rapids that came near drowning the crew of one dugout. After surviving one of the roughest of these passages, the terrified Shoshone guides deserted without even asking for their promised payment in trade goods.

When the Clearwater took them into the Snake, the captains were sure they had reached the long-sought Columbia River. (Their camp site that night was opposite the present cities of Clarkston and Lewiston on the Washington-Idaho border.) The river abounded with fish, and they were able to supplement their meager diet.

All their salt was gone now and the tasteless fish diet grew so monotonous that they eagerly accepted stews of dog meat from their Indian hosts. By the time they reached the Columbia River (16 October) they were trading for dogs to be used as meat as casually as they would have traded for wild game had any been available. After refusing to eat dog meat at first, Sergeant Gass finally admitted: 'When well cooked tastes very well.' Lewis declared that dog meat was far superior to horse meat. 'While we lived principally on the flesh of this animal,' he said, 'we were much more healthy, strong and more fleshey than we had been since we left the Buffaloe country.' Through all this time of short rations, no one ever considered sacrificing Scannon the Newfoundland. Every man in the party would have looked upon such an act as cannibalism.

When they reached Celilo Falls on 22 October, they had to portage around the twenty-foot drop of foaming water. Friendly Indians gave their assistance, and a chief warned Clark that the next tribe downriver was hostile and would attack them. 'We therefore examined all the arms', Clark noted tersely. 'Increased the ammunition to 100 rounds.'

Instead of attacking the explorers, however, the tribe below watched with amazement as these mad bearded strangers navigated the Narrows of the Dalles, which Clark described as an 'agitated gut swelling, boiling & whorling in every direction'.

A week later after a rough portage through the Cascades they noticed increasing signs that they were nearing the Pacific. Sea otters appeared in the broadening river. Some of the Indians wore seashells in their noses; others carried articles made of copper and brass, and woven cloth. Then they met an Indian wearing a sailor's pea-jacket and round hat. He spoke a little English. 'Son of a bitch', was one of his exclamations, and the explorers knew that American ships must occasionally touch ashore somewhere near.

The morning of 7 November was cloudy and foggy with a

drizzle of rain. Gradually the air cleared, and then they saw 'the object of all our labours, the reward of all our anxieties'. Captain Clark quickly scribbled in his logbook: 'Ocean in view! O! the joy.'

They had hoped to find a ship, perhaps arrange passage back to the east coast, but all they could find were traces of camp-fires where ship's traders had been. 'They have all sailed away', Sergeant Gass noted with disappointment. With winter coming on, the thought of retracing the four thousand miles to St Louis was something to be put out of their minds.

On high ground about three miles up a small tributary to the Columbia (now called Lewis and Clark River) they built Fort Clatsop, so named for the friendly Clatsop Indians. Cold rains fell almost every day, hindering construction. It was Christmas Eve when they finished the last slab of roofing. Next morning Lewis and Clark were awakened by a salvo of guns fired by the men, 'followed by a song as a compliment to us on the return of Christmas'. It was their second Christmas away from home, and everybody exchanged a few simple gifts, Clark noting that he received a pair of fleece hosiery from Lewis and two dozen white weasel tails from Sacagawea.

There was little to do at Fort Clatsop except hunt and fish, keep a sharp lookout for a visiting ship, and wait for spring-time and the return journey. 'Not any occurrences today worthy of notice', was a repetitious phrase in the daily log. A detail of men was assigned the tedious task of boiling seawater to replace the exhausted salt supply; they produced twenty gallons of salt by the end of February. Indian girls provided the major amusement, but most of the tribes along the coast had been corrupted by visiting traders and seamen, and many of the women were diseased. As Sergeant Gass said, they were also 'much inclined to venery'. Lewis in his role as official surgeon was continually warning the men to avoid infections, but before winter was over he had to administer several doses of mercury, the standard remedy of the day for venereal diseases.

On 23 March 1806 the explorers left Fort Clatsop for the long return to St Louis. Again they suffered hunger and cold during the crossings of the Cascades, but the Nez Percés had faith-fully kept their horses for them and except for a few minor difficulties they again conquered the Bitterroots. In July, Lewis and Drouillard with eight enlisted men left the main party for a venture into hostile Blackfoot territory. The clever Blackfeet came very near taking their horses, weapons, and probably their lives, but the resourceful explorers managed to escape. Before he rejoined Clark, however, Lewis was accident-ally shot by Peter Cruzat who mistook the captain for an elk. It was a buttocks wound—not dangerous but causing Lewis a great deal of inconvenience. He had to lie on his belly in one of the boats for a considerable distance down the Missouri.

The exploring party reached St Louis on 23 September, after

A Blackfoot shirt decorated with plaited quill, grass strips and human and dyed horse hair

Fur Traders Descending the Missouri
by George Caleb Bingham

a journey of two years, four months and nine days—with the loss of only one man by death. Probably the most significant event of the return journey occurred on 12 August when the explorers met two young men traveling upriver by canoe. They were Joseph Dickson and Forrest Hancock of Illinois, heading west to make their fortunes by trapping beaver. The hatters of the world were crying for more beaver skins: the expanding European armies wanted tricorn beaver hats; working men wanted broad-brimmed beaver hats; rich dandies wanted high-crowned beaver hats. The Hudson's Bay Company of Canada could not supply the demand, and Dickson and Hancock saw an opportunity to share in the wealth.

The two young men from Illinois naturally were eager for any information the explorers could give them concerning sign of beaver upriver. John Colter, one of the older enlisted men, had found opportunities to trap a few beaver pelts and evidently was able to supply Dickson and Hancock with more information about trapping expectations than any of the other explorers. When the two west-bound trappers invited Colter to join them as a partner, he immediately applied to Captain Clark for a discharge from his military obligations.

'As we were disposed to be of service to anyone of our party who had performed their duty as well as Colter had done,' Clark noted, 'we agreed to allow him the privilege provided no one of the party would ask or expect a similar permission . . . until we should arrive at St Louis.' Colter's fellow soldiers not only agreed to this arrangement, most of them donated articles essential to him for survival in the wilderness—knives, powder horns, hatchets, and other utensils which according to Sergeant Ordway 'compleated him for a trapping voyage of two years, which they are determined to Stay untill they make a fortune'.

3. Knight in Buckskins

John Colter never made any fortune as a fur trapper. Through those early years of the nineteenth century, fur trading became an international money game, somewhat as petroleum would be in the twentieth century. The Northwest Company, dominated by a group of hardbitten Scots, grew into a rival of the long-entrenched Hudson's Bay Company and extended its operations into Thomas Jefferson's Louisiana Territory. John Jacob Astor founded the American Fur Company, moving westward from the Great Lakes to build a fur-trading post, Astoria, at the mouth of Lewis and Clark's Columbia River. The big companies made deals with Indian tribes, setting tribe against tribe or against trappers of rival organizations. They also controlled auctions and prices. Independent trappers venturing into beaver country–jealously guarded by Indians for one or the other of the big companies–not only risked their lives, they sometimes had difficulty in channeling their pelts into profitable markets.

Colter may have realized his difficult situation by the spring of 1807 when he started down the Missouri in a canoe containing a few beaver skins representing a year's trapping in the wilderness. Sometime during the winter he had parted company

LEFT Beaver trappers followed a hazardous profession: they worked in the cold and wet and were in frequent danger from rivals' attacks.

RIGHT *Presents to the Indians* by Alfred Jacob Miller. A successful trapping venture depended upon the cooperation of the Indians.

with Dickson and Hancock; Colter preferred to work alone. Near the mouth of the Mallet brothers' Platte River, he met a keelboat coming upstream. Among the forty-two men on board was an old friend of the Lewis and Clark expedition, George Drouillard. Leader of the group was Manuel Lisa who had recently organized the Missouri Fur Company, and Drouillard was an associate. Another associate back in St Louis was William Clark who had settled there as commander of the Louisiana Territory militia. (Clark would become governor of the territory after Meriwether Lewis' mysterious death in 1809.)

When Lisa asked Colter if he would like to join the Missouri Fur Company as a trapper, the man from the wilderness did not hesitate a moment. Although he had been absent from white man's civilization for more than three years, Colter quickly transferred his belongings to the keelboat and started westward again.

For the next three years Colter was a valued employee of the Missouri Fur Company, which built forts at the mouth of the Big Horn and at the Three Forks of the Missouri – thus challenging the supremacy of the giant British companies in the Rocky Mountains and on the Upper Saskatchewan in Canada. Just as the British had made the Blackfoot tribes dependent upon them for trade goods, guns, and whisky, so did the Americans involve the Crows. A bloody Indian conflict of long duration was thus engendered by greed for furs. The situation also made life exceedingly dangerous for men like Colter who preferred to trap alone.

In his search for peltry, John Colter was the first white man to see what is now Yellowstone Park, but no one would believe

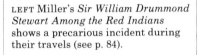

LEFT Miller's *Sir William Drummond Stewart Among the Red Indians* shows a precarious incident during their travels (see p. 84).

RIGHT It was advisable for trappers to befriend local Indians.

Braving the Western wilderness, travelers dig a cache in which to leave provisions for the return journey (many did not survive to retrieve them).

his stories of bubbling hot springs and steaming geysers. Twice he was captured by Blackfeet and twice he miraculously escaped. On one occasion when he and another trapper intruded upon Blackfoot territory, Colter was seized and stripped naked while his partner continued to resist by firing upon the Indians, killing one of their leaders. The Blackfeet in turn killed the trapper, disemboweling him and hurling the man's entrails, heart and lungs into Colter's face. Colter was then challenged to a foot race, the prize to be his own life. Colter won, thus creating one of the great folk legends of the West. After another series of deadly encounters in which several of his friends were killed, Colter staggered into the Missouri Fur Company's fort and announced that he had promised God to leave the Western wilderness. 'If God will only forgive me this time and let me off,' Colter cried, 'I *will* leave the country day after tomorrow – and be damned if I ever come into it again.' Colter kept his vow; he returned to St Louis in a canoe, married, and sired a son. An almost forgotten hero of the Lewis and Clark expedition, he lived on the borderline of poverty, haunted by dark memories of a wilderness that had defeated him until he died three years later at the age of thirty-eight.

In the meantime, Manuel Lisa's Missouri Fur Company struggled to survive. The War of 1812 came and passed, the British seizing the American Fur Company's Astoria on the Columbia River, absorbing it into the Northwest Company and renaming it Fort George. With Blackfoot warriors operating as a mercenary army, Lisa's forts were put under continual siege, the Indians killing off the Missouri company's best men, including George Drouillard, and forcing the Americans to withdraw from the rich beaver country of the Three Forks.

One of the tenacious survivors of this fur war was Andrew Henry. After Lisa died in 1820, Henry was in St Louis where he chanced to meet General William H. Ashley. Ashley had succeeded William Clark as brigadier-general of militia and also was in the gunpowder business, but he was not becoming rich fast enough to suit an ambitious man who had already turned forty. Henry assured Ashley that there were fortunes to be made in beaver trapping if one went about the business in a big way. A handful of men trying to operate from a besieged fort, as Lisa's men had done, could not prosper. A hundred or more men moving with horses in well-armed brigades along beaver-rich streams could make fortunes for their employers.

Ashley had little money but he knew how to obtain credit. He and Henry formed a partnership. On 13 February 1822 they published an advertisement in two St Louis papers, letting it run for more than a month. When one considers the results, the men who were brought together because of it, and what they did, surely no other 'help wanted' advertisement had such far-reaching effects upon the history of the American West.

TO
ENTERPRISING YOUNG MEN
The subscriber wishes to engage ONE HUNDRED MEN, to ascend the river Missouri to its source, there to be employed for one, two, or three years. For particulars enquire of Major Andrew Henry, near the Lead Mines, in the County of Washington, (who will ascend with, and command the party) or to the subscriber at St. Louis.

Wm. H. Ashley

One of the first to appear at Ashley's door in St Louis was a tall, lean, blue-eyed, very serious young man of twenty-three. He gave his name as Jedediah Strong Smith. He told Ashley that he had worked on boats in the Great Lakes and on Illinois rivers, but that his overwhelming desire was to go west and study the ways of the Indians so that he might excel as they did in woodcraft and hunting. Young Smith said that he especially wished to trace the sources of the Columbia River and follow it to the Western Sea as Lewis and Clark had done. And like everyone else, Jedediah Smith also wanted to find his fortune in the track of the western sun.

Smith was probably the best educated of the 150 men employed by Ashley and Henry for their vigorous entry into the fur money game. While young Jed was growing up in Pennsylvania, a country doctor taught him not only how to read and write well, but also gave him a sound foundation in mathematics and Latin. When the boy was fifteen, the doctor presented him with a two-volume set, *History of the Expedition Under the Command of Lewis and Clark* which was published in Philadelphia in 1814. Thus does the printed word affect the course of history; there it must have begun for Jedediah Smith.

Jed Smith, mountain man extraordinary

He was obsessed with a desire to see what Lewis and Clark had seen, especially the Columbia River. When he arrived in St Louis, he was carrying the *History of the Expedition* and a well-worn copy of the Holy Bible. Jed Smith was a religious man, an ascetic, a knight bound upon a mystical quest.

Even before the Ashley-Henry expedition started up the Missouri on 15 April 1822, there were rumors that the Hudson's Bay Company had absorbed the Northwest Company. The giant combine established headquarters at Fort Vancouver on the Columbia River, and was creating a world monopoly of furs. Ashley and Henry's new venture, which they called the Rocky Mountain Fur Company, even with the best of luck would be faced with rougher competition than Lisa's Missouri company.

Their starting luck was bad. On the way upriver, one of the keelboats struck a snag and sank with thousands of dollars worth of supplies and equipment. After the trappers passed the Mandan villages, a hunting party of Assiniboines viewed their fifty horses as fair game for a raid, and swept away most of them. Later on, Arikaras attacked and killed thirteen men, wounding eleven.

These setbacks might have defeated less sanguine seekers of wealth, but Ashley had collected an unusually hardy band of trappers: Jedediah Smith, James Bridger, Thomas Fitzpatrick, James Clyman, William L. Sublette, David E. Jackson, Hugh Glass, Mike Fink, dozens of others whose names are still remembered. They were all young, some of them barely sprouting their first mustaches. In ten years the survivors would be *the* Mountain Men in greasy buckskins, with matted hair and beards, stinking of green pelts, exterminating beaver, exploiting Indians. Jed Smith was the exception. He bathed and shaved regularly, kept his clothing clean, read from his Bible daily, and remained aloof from brawling and fornicating. In less than ten years, after seeing and mapping more of the West than any of his fellows, and at the same time taking his share of fur wealth, Smith would leave the wilderness for reasons that may be too involved in mysticism for most men to understand.

In 1823 Ashley made him captain of a trapping brigade, and it was while leading his party into the unknown country west of the Black Hills that Smith experienced the first of many close brushes with death, his first bitter taste of elemental violence in the garden of the wilderness. One of his men, James Clyman, set it down from memory some years later:

> Capt. Smith being in the advance he ran to the open ground and as he immerged from the thicket he and the bear met face to face. Grissly did not hesitate a moment but sprung on the capt taking him by the head first, pitching sprawling on the earth he gave him a grab by the middle fortunately catching by the ball pouch and Butcher Knife which he broke but breaking several of his ribs and cutting his head badly. None of us having any sugical Knowledge what was to be done one Said come take hold and he wuld say why

Like Smith, this storyteller made a remarkable escape from a grizzly bear which had scalped him.

not you so it went around. I asked the Capt what was best. He said one or 2 go for water and if you have a needle and thread git it out and sew up my wounds around my head which was bleeding freely. I got a pair of scissors and cut off his hair and then began my first job of dressing wounds. Upon examination I found the bear had taken nearly all of his head in his capacious mouth close to his left eye on one side and close to his right ear on the other and laid the skull bare to near the crown of the head leaving a white streak whare his teeth passed. One of his ears was torn from his head out to the outer rim. After stitching all the other wounds in the best way I was capabl and according to the captains directions the ear being the last I told him I could do nothing for his Eare. O you must try to stitch up some way or other said he. Then I put in my needle stitching it through and through and over and over laying the lacerated parts togather as nice as I could with my hands. Water was found in about a mile when we all moved down and encamped, the captain being able to mount his horse and ride to camp whare we pitched a tent the onley one we had and made him as comfortable as circumtances would permit. This gave us a lisson on the charcter of the grissly Baare which we did not forget.

In ten days Captain Smith was well enough to continue westward, but he let his hair grow over his mangled ear and never cut it short again. Along the way they met friendly Cheyennes and Crows, and inquired of them the best route to Green River where by all accounts beaver abounded in multitudes. It was in this way that they found South Pass, which was no steep winding crevice through towering mountains as they had expected but was a broad treeless valley of grass twenty to thirty miles wide. Smith and his trappers were not the first white men to traverse South Pass, but he was probably the first man to recognize its significance to earth-bound travelers. It was a door to the Western Sea; the Rockies were not an

The Westerners

impassable wall, the barrier to land travel and transport that Lewis and Clark had believed them to be. Jedediah Smith knew that wagons could roll through South Pass, but even he did not foresee that in less than a generation the wagons would be there in continuous caravans filled with thousands of men and women wheeling westward in a quest for gold and land.

Green River, known as the Siskadee to the Crows, proved to be rich in beaver. That part of the Rockies where the states of Wyoming, Utah, and Colorado now join became a training ground for Smith, Clyman, Fitzpatrick, Sublette, Bridger, and the others. They learned that successful beaver trappers had to wade for miles in icy waters so as to leave no scent of man, and that the best lure was a bundle of twigs smeared with a beaver's musk glands. They found out that white men could not survive in that country unless they learned everything the Indians knew. They studied the ways of the tribes–hostiles and friendlies–learning to read the meanings of every turned leaf, broken twig, or sudden flight of birds. They concentrated upon the land, its valleys and peaks, its streams and forests. They became the Mountain Men.

In the spring of 1825 Jed Smith and the other captains brought their scattered brigades together at a rendezvous point

Indians at a fur *rendezvous*. The pendants hanging from the Indians' lances, on the left, are enemy scalps, not pelts.

on one of the forks of Green River. Here they met with General Ashley, who had brought supplies for them and trade goods for the Indians. Thus was initiated the first of a series of fur *rendezvous* which grew into annual summer fairs that followed the trappers from one virgin region to another as they exploited successive beaver valleys in the Rockies. Most of the *rendezvous* were held near or in what is now western Wyoming. To describe them, the artist Alfred Jacob Miller used the phrase 'High Jinks', adding that they were 'a species of Saturnalia, in which feasting, drinking, and gambling form prominent parts'. In that day of reticence concerning sexual matters he omitted the orgies which the Mountain Men looked forward to over the long lonely winters. In addition to the debauchery and spreading of white men's diseases, the swindling of Indians through trade was another aspect of the *rendezvous* seldom mentioned by contemporary observers. When Indians brought in beaver skins to trade, they usually received about one per cent of the value of the furs in the form of watered whiskey or cheap baubles. The trading of worthless merchandise to Indians for valuable pelts became one of the most profitable adjuncts of the fur business.

With Ashley and Henry's introduction of the *rendezvous*, no longer would bands of trappers leave the wilderness to expend their time and energies in transporting furs to St Louis. Other men expert at mule-packing and keelboating would do this for them; the Mountain Men would remain in the Rockies for continuous trapping. The fur trade was becoming specialized, more efficient, and exceedingly remunerative for the operators. Ashley and Henry, in fact, made so much money by 1826 that both decided to enter easier fields of endeavor. When their company was put up for sale, Jedediah Smith with William Sublette and David Jackson became the new owners. They divided their responsibilities, Sublette spending most of his time with transportation to and from St Louis, Jackson overseeing field operations, while Smith took on the task of searching out new beaver areas to replace those which were rapidly being trapped out because of the total extermination of the animals.

To see the West, especially those parts of it which no other white man had seen, was the real reason why Jed Smith had ventured there; the amassing of wealth appears to have been only an incidental though not unwelcome concomitant.

After Jim Bridger reported discovering the Great Salt Lake, Smith went to view that inland sea for himself, and it was probably while he was there that he began to wonder what else there might be in the largest blank space still left on maps of the West–the area between the Rockies and California. Smith decided it was time for the Rocky Mountain Fur Company to expand toward California.

In August 1826 he took fourteen of his most dependable men

and left Bear Lake headquarters, heading south along the Virgin River and crossing the Colorado to the Mojave Valley. He was so charmed by the Mojaves with their plentiful supplies of corn, beans, melons, and beautiful bare-breasted women that he stayed with them for several days. The Indians volunteered to guide the Mountain Men across the desert to Mission San Gabriel, and they reached there late in November. The suspicious Spaniards hustled Smith off to San Diego where the governor seized his maps and journals and accused him of being a spy. The governor ordered him to take his party out of California immediately. When Smith asked permission to leave by a northern route so that he might explore for beaver, he received a firm refusal. He was to leave California by the route he had come in.

Smith pretended to obey, but when he reached the lower end of the High Sierras, he turned north as winter set in, looking for pristine beaver streams. He found enough beaver to convince him that California must have an untouched empire of furs in its northern valleys. With the coming of spring 1827, he tried to cross the Sierras for the return journey to Bear Lake. But the snows were heavy that year on the summits, and after five of the party's horses died from exposure, Smith turned back and established a camp on the Stanislaus River. Leaving the main party there with a promise that he would return with traps and other supplies, he took two men, seven horses, and two mules and made a second attempt to conquer the mountains. Thus began another of those ordeals or knightly atonements that Smith seemed deliberately to seek against natural forces. He and his two companions were eight days crossing the Sierras over crusted snow which tore the feet of his horses. Three of the animals died.

When he came down off the mountains, he faced a desert which had to be crossed to reach the Rocky Mountain Fur Company headquarters on Bear Lake. It was June with heat so unbearable that for relief they would sometimes dig holes on the shady sides of hillocks and bury themselves in the sand. When they found holes of water, the liquid was usually too salty to drink. As horses gave out, they ate them. When one of his companions finally abandoned hope and lay down to die, Smith and the other trapper struggled on for miles, finding water and returning with a kettleful of it to bring the dying man back to life. 'In these moments,' Smith wrote, 'how trifling were all those things that hold such an absolute sway over the busy and prosperous world. My dreams were not of Gold or ambitious honours, but of my distant quiet home, of murmuring brooks.'

Among the Paiutes and Gosiutes of Skull Valley, Utah, there is still a tradition of the first white men who came there–three men materializing out of the shimmering Sandy Plain, staggering in rags to a spring where they plunged their heads into its waters. A week later Smith with his two companions was back at Bear Lake in time to celebrate the Fourth of July and to consult with his partners at the 1827 summer *rendezvous*.

As soon as the *rendezvous* ended in July, Captain Smith chose eighteen men to return with him to California. He did not attempt to carry supplies by the direct route across the desert which he had so recently survived, but instead took the roundabout way which by mid-August brought him to the village of friendly Mojaves on the banks of the Colorado. There Smith and his men spent about three days building rafts to carry their supplies across the river.

On the day of the crossing, several hundred Mojaves gathered along the river bank to watch. Smith and eight men went over with the first rafts which were loaded with personal belongings and dried meat. Ten men and the party's horses remained behind on the bank. As soon as Smith and his group were well out in the river, the Mojaves with no warning but a quick war cry attacked the ten men, killing all of them in less than a minute.

Why the 'friendly' Mojaves committed this totally unexpected assault has never been determined. One conjecture is that the

Indians were acting for the Spaniards; another is that a party of trappers from New Mexico had come through a few months before, mistreating the Mojaves so that they had sworn to kill all white men who came there; another is that some of Smith's trappers may have molested the tattooed bare-breasted women.

While their friends were dying with sudden violence, Smith and the eight men watched dumbfounded from the opposite side; then on Smith's orders they quickly discarded most of their belongings and started on foot toward the west. Four or five hundred Mojaves pursued, however, and less than half a mile from the river began closing in on Smith's party. He quickly led his men back to a cottonwood thicket on the river bank, where they hurriedly chopped down enough small trees to form a fragile breastwork.

'Some of the men asked me if I thought we would be able to defend ourselves', Smith later recorded. 'I told them I thought we would. But that was not my opinion.'

By shrewdly alternating the firing of their five rifles, however, the trappers managed to frighten the Mojaves away, and as darkness fell they again started westward into the desert. For the next several days the phrase, 'we suffered much from thirst', was a repetitive entry in Smith's journal. 'We found some relief from chewing slips of the Cabbage Pear, a singular plant . . . verry juicy although frequently found growing on the most parched and barren ground . . .' A veteran now at desert survival, Smith brought his men out of the Mojave to Cajon Pass, and on 18 September 1827 he was back on the Stanislaus to rejoin the men left behind on his first expedition to California. During his absence these men had collected a considerable number of pelts, but they were dismayed to learn of the deaths of their friends and the loss of traps and other equipment at the Mojave village.

Although handicapped by a shortage of traps and horses, Smith was determined to remain in California long enough to explore its northern valleys. While his men gathered more pelts, he went to the coast, got himself arrested by the governor for re-entering California without permission, talked his way out of being sent to Mexico City for a trial, and sold enough beaver skins in San Francisco to buy 250 horses, supplies, and a few more traps.

In January 1828, with a vague promise to the Spanish governor to cross the Sierras and leave California forever, Captain Smith and his men started up the valley of the American River. Even his trappers believed that Smith intended to cross the mountains, and from time to time he did lead them to what appeared to be a pass only to turn back with the verdict that it would be impossible to cross the horses. Although there is no proof of his intentions, Smith probably did not wish to find a route eastward over the Sierras. Six years earlier, when he signed on with Ashley in St Louis, he had told the general that he wanted to see the Columbia River and follow it to the Pacific as Lewis and Clark had done. On the maps which Smith always kept with him—constantly revising as he came upon streams and mountains that no other mapmaker had seen—the Columbia River was plainly marked. The Hudson's Bay Company's Fort Vancouver was on the Columbia, not more than five hundred miles to the north. Jedediah Smith strongly desired to see the Columbia; once there he knew he could take his men up its waters and to the Three Forks of the Missouri as Lewis and Clark had done, and then turn southward to join next summer's *rendezvous*.

Through continual rains, quagmires, and thick forests, they moved on northward, traveling slowly enough to collect beaver pelts almost daily, and packed them on the horses. They crossed the Klamath River and then swung toward the seacoast into what is now southwestern Oregon. On 13 July 1828 they were on the banks of the Umpqua where they met fifty or sixty Indians who called themselves Kelawatsets. The Indians were carrying a few beaver skins intended for trade to Hudson's Bay Company. Smith took them in trade himself, and strapped them to one of his horses.

Next morning Smith and two of his trappers left the other men in camp and went upstream in a canoe to search for a dry route out of the swampy bottomlands of the Umpqua. When they returned, they found the entire camp (except for one man who escaped) killed by the Kelawatsets. Their horses, furs, and equipment—even Smith's maps and journals—were gone. Smith and the two men with him were also attacked near the desolate campsite but managed to escape by dodging into the woods. (In reconstructing the Umpqua massacre, the survivors later decided it had been caused by an incident they had believed minor at the time. An Indian whom they suspected of having stolen an ax in camp had been manhandled by the trappers; they looped a rope tightly around his neck to force him to return the ax. The offended Indian evidently was a chief, and had taken his revenge by leading an attack against the camp the morning Smith was away.)

A few days later Smith and his two companions and the single trapper who had escaped from the Umpqua camp, all reached Fort Vancouver. To Dr John McLoughlin, a giant fierce-visaged Scotsman who ran the Hudson's Bay empire, these four bedraggled Americans did not appear to be much in the way of business competitors. He took them in as guests, sent out an expedition which recovered their furs, horses, and—most fortunately—Smith's maps and journals. McLoughlin later purchased his rival's furs and horses at the going prices. As it was too late in the year to start up the Columbia for a winter crossing of the Rockies, Smith spent the winter at Fort Vancouver, repaying his host with maps and information about California.

The Westerners

In March 1829 Smith at last found his chance to follow Lewis and Clark's route up the Columbia River, but he evidently was in no mood to note his reactions to this fulfilled dream; his record of the journey reveals little of his thoughts or emotions. The violent deaths of so many comrades, first on the Colorado and then on the Umpqua, certainly weighed upon his mind. He was their leader, and it had been his will that had brought them to the places of their deaths. It was in his nature to bear the responsibility.

After rejoining his partners at Pierre's Hole in the summer, he went into winter quarters on Wind River. For Jedediah Smith it was a winter of reflection upon the terrors of life and death. 'I entangle myself altogether too much in the things of time', he wrote one of his brothers in December 1829. 'I have passed through the country . . . to the North Paciffick Ocean, in different ways – through countrys of Barrenness & seldom one of the reverse . . . in Augt. 1827 ten Men, who were in company with me, lost their lives . . . in July 1828 fifteen men, who were in Company with me lost their lives . . .' In another letter he seemed to reach out for expiation: 'It is, that I may be able to help those who stand in need, that I face every danger – it is for this, that I traverse the Mountains covered with eternal Snow – it is for this that I pass over the Sandy Plains, in heat of Summer, thirsting for water, and am well pleased if I can find a shade, instead of water, where I may cool my overheated Body – it is for this that I go for days without eating, & am pretty well satisfied if I can gather a few roots, a few Snails . . . and, most of all, it is for this, that I deprive myself of the privilege of Society & the satisfaction of the Converse of My Friends!'

The following summer Smith attended his last *rendezvous*. His partner, Sublette, surprised everyone by bringing ten wagons from St Louis to Wind River to prove that a natural wagon road ran all the way to the Rockies. 'Smith, Sublette & Jackson are the first that ever took wagons to the Rocky Mountains', commented the St Louis *Beacon*. 'The ease with which they did it, and could have gone on [through South Pass] to the mouth of the Columbia, shows the folly and nonsense of those "scientific" characters who talk of the Rocky Mountains as the barrier which is to stop the westward march of the American people.'

Jed Smith, however, chose this time to turn his back on all of it. When he informed his partners that he wanted to dispose of his share of the company, they also decided to sell out. After transferring ownership of the Rocky Mountain Fur Company to Jim Bridger, Thomas Fitzpatrick, and three other trappers, Smith and his partners returned to St Louis with the wagons which were loaded with thousands of dollars in furs.

At the age of thirty-one and wealthier than most men, Jed Smith was at loose ends in St Louis. It is possible that he envied twenty-six-year-old Jim Bridger who had taken over Smith's duties and was still out in the Western wilderness. Bridger could not read or write, but he had learned to accept the muck and slime of primitive existence, had made himself a part of the violence and pain and blood, inflicting death and accepting the inevitability of it for himself, taking the daughters of the country into his blankets and never imagining himself to be a civilized man corrupting the innocence of nature.

Jed Smith had not returned to St Louis encompassed by horrors as John Colter had done, but he evidently had accepted the belief that he could not keep himself a worthy knight in the sight of his God if he remained in the West. He feared that he would sink back into that state of natural bestiality which civilized man had succeeded in covering with a thin gloss of religion, honor, courtesy. Perhaps he also felt that he had been an instrument in the violation of nature. Did he wish to leave the awesome beauty of the West as he had found it, untouched by civilized man? If a few hundred men could destroy most of the beaver in the Rockies in less than a decade, what could a few thousand, or a few million do?

Mountain men

He remembered leading a brigade of trappers on horseback into an Indian village in the Rockies where no white man had ever been; the frightened Indians fled, a young girl falling down dead in her terror. Jim Bridger would have been mildly amused by the incident, but Smith brooded over it. 'Could it be possible that we who call ourselves Christians are such frightful objects as to scare poor savages to death?'

Because of Smith's reputation as an explorer, a young man from Connecticut who had come to St Louis to mend his health visited him one day for advice about going on to the Rockies. 'If you go into the Rocky Mountains,' Smith told him bluntly, 'the chances are much greater in favor of meeting death than in finding restoration of health. If you escape the former and secure the latter, the probabilities are that you would be ruined for anything else in life than such things as would be agreeable to the passions of a semi-savage.'

To escape succumbing to the passions of a semi-savage, Smith decided to emulate Lewis and Clark and write a book about his Western explorations. While this work was in the planning stage–employing a clerk, assembling and copying his journals–he began to hear much talk from friends and acquaintances about fortunes to be made in trade with Santa Fe. Trader William Becknell had already marked off a wagon route between St Louis and Santa Fe, and the Mexican

Early travelers on the Santa Fe Trail

authorities there welcomed goods from the United States, Mexico having recently won her independence from Spain.

When his former partners, Sublette and Jackson, proposed to Smith that they join in organizing a wagon train for the spring of 1831, Smith yielded to the old lure of Santa Fe. It was not so much that he wanted to profit from such a venture, he told himself, it was because the Southwest was the only part of the West that he had not seen and if he was to publish a book about the West then he must go to Santa Fe. He asked Governor William Clark for a passport to New Mexico and instructed his clerk to begin studying Spanish.

The wagon train left St Louis on 10 April 1831—twenty-two mule-drawn wagons and seventy-four men, including Smith's brother Austin. Late in May they reached the arid plain below the Arkansas River; a spring drouth had made it much drier than the year Coronado crossed it three centuries earlier. On the 27th, after three days of traveling without water, the train was halted and men sent out in several directions to search for a water hole. Smith headed south with a companion and they found a hole with a mud-encrusted bottom. Leaving the man there to dig for water, Smith went on, crossed a small rise, and vanished forever.

After a futile search for him, his partners took the wagons on to Santa Fe. A few days later a band of Comancheros—Mexicans who traded with the Comanches—rode into town. They carried a rifle and a pair of silver-mounted pistols for sale, and when Smith's brother Austin saw the weapons he recognized them as belonging to the missing Jedediah. The Mexicans said they had obtained the weapons in trade from a band of Comanches who had killed Smith at a water hole.

Several versions of Smith's death as told by the Comancheros have survived in legend: Of how he approached the Indians fearlessly, of how when he turned away they hurled lances into his back, of how he resisted and died fighting to the end. Austin Smith described it this way in a letter to their father: 'The Spanish traders who trade with those Indians informed me that he saw the Indians before they attacked him, but supposed there could be no possible chance of an escape, he therefore went boldly up, with the hope of making peace with them, but found that his only chance was defence, he killed the head Chief. I do suppose that then they rushed upon him like so many blood-hounds; the Spaniards say the Indians numbered from fifteen to twenty.'

Jedediah Strong Smith had been a Westerner for less than ten years, and no one can be certain whether at his final leave-taking he hated the West, feared it, loved it, or regarded it impassively as a knight's testing ground for endurance. Although he never could accept its savage earthiness, certainly no man had seen more of the West or had been more of a Westerner than he.

4. Medicine Paint Catlin

In the spring of 1830, while Jedediah Smith was preparing to leave the Rocky Mountains forever, a Byronically handsome young man in his early thirties – blue-eyed, dark-skinned, black-haired – arrived in St Louis intent upon venturing into the West for a purpose quite different from that of the usual traveler. He was George Catlin of Pennsylvania, former lawyer and self-taught artist who had become proficient enough in the latter endeavor to be accepted as a member of the Philadelphia Academy of Fine Arts. For the past six years, Catlin had been earning his living as a painter of portraits of the famous and well-to-do, but he had grown dissatisfied with the meaning of his life.

'My mind was continually reaching for some branch or enterprise of the art, on which to devote a whole lifetime of enthusiasm,' he explained, 'when a delegation of some ten or fifteen noble and dignified-looking Indians, from the wilds of the "Far West", suddenly arrived in the city, arrayed and equipped in all their classic beauty, – with shield and helmet, – with tunic and manteau, – tinted and tasselled off, exactly for the painter's palette!'

George Catlin's interest in American Indians had been with him since earliest childhood when his mother fascinated him with stories of her adventures while a captive of the Iroquois during the Revolutionary War. Somewhat symbolically he bore a scar on his cheek from a tomahawk thrown carelessly by a boyhood playmate with whom he often played at Indian games. In Philadelphia he had spent a great deal of time in museums making drawings of tribal costumes, weapons, and ornaments – a considerable number of which had been brought back from the West by Lewis and Clark.

Catlin began his half-formed plan of recording American Indians on canvas by visiting reservations in New York State, and even after taking on the responsibilities of marriage in 1828 he frequently rejected generous commissions for portraits in order to hurry off to an eastern reservation to add the face of an Indian to his collection. Painting acculturated tribesmen such as Red Jacket of the Senecas and John Quinney of the Mohegans only served to whet his determination to paint

OPPOSITE George Catlin's *Pawnee Warrior Sacrificing His Favorite Horse*

70

Indians 'unrestrained and unfettered by the disguises of art'. To do this he knew that he must go far into the West. 'The history and customs of such a people, preserved by pictorial illustrations, are themes worthy of the lifetime of one man,' he said, 'and nothing short of the loss of my life, shall prevent me from visiting their country, and of becoming their historian.'

Although he received no support whatsoever from his family or friends, once his mind was made up Catlin never wavered in his purpose. 'I broke from them all–from my wife and my aged parents,–myself my only adviser and protector.' When he called upon William Clark in St Louis, he was well armed with letters of introduction from important Easterners as well as a selection of paintings and drawings of Eastern Indians. At that time Clark was sixty years old and was serving as both Governor of Missouri Territory and Indian Agent for the Territory of the Upper Louisiana. The latter office gave him complete authority in all matters concerning Western Indians, and he could have dissolved Catlin's dream right there in St Louis. Clark, however, was intrigued by the artist's grandiose scheme; after all, it was no more impossible an objective than had been Clark's endeavor with Meriwether Lewis only a quarter of a century before. And although the governor was probably not at all impressed by Catlin's fine letters of recommendation, he did admire his Indian portraits.

At Clark's invitation, Catlin set up his easel in the governor's office, and almost daily the artist had an opportunity to sketch visiting Indians from the West who came regularly to St Louis to trade and discuss treaty matters with their Red Headed Chief (Clark). When Clark went up the Mississippi to Fort Crawford in July to meet with the Sauks and Foxes, he took Catlin along. In the autumn the two men–who had now become close friends–journeyed up the Missouri to Cantonment Leavenworth and then overland into Kansas. Among the notable portraits done by Catlin during these journeys was that of Tecumseh's brother, the famed Shawnee Prophet.

Catlin returned to Pennsylvania to be with his wife for Christmas, but he was back in St Louis early in 1831. Governor Clark, no doubt suspecting that his young protégé was in need of funds, posed for a full-length portrait–and then encouraged his prosperous St Louis friends to follow his example. (Whether Catlin met Jedediah Smith who was busily preparing for his ill-fated Santa Fe journey at this time is uncertain. No one has yet found a Catlin portrait of the Knight in Buckskins, but if one exists it should be worth a large fortune.) After earning enough money to pay his keep for a while, Catlin joined Major John Dougherty, special agent to the Pawnee, Oto, Omaha, and Missouri tribes, for a summer's journey up the valley of the Platte.

For the first time the artist had an opportunity to view Plains Indians 'in their natural simplicity and beauty'. Those who

OPPOSITE A portrait by Catlin: *The White Cloud, Head Chief of the Iowas*

A Pawnee chief and two warriors

especially took his fancy were the Pawnees, the people of Coronado's long-ago Harahey, of El Turco who tantalized the Spaniards until they garroted him to death. Catlin saw Pawnee warriors with shaved heads and painted bodies, bedecked in scarlet and blue blankets, galloping about on their spirited horses. He saw bows and arrows put to real work in buffalo hunts; he saw Pawnee women drying meat and packing it into parfleche cases, cultivating corn, weaving baskets; he saw the dome-shaped earthen lodges of the Pawnee villages. He still continued to paint only portraits, but he began taking notes and making quick little sketches of background objects and scenery.

For George Catlin those first two years of working in and out of St Louis were only preliminary exercises. They gave him an opportunity to learn what to look for among Western Indians, to discover ways and means of persuading his subjects to pose naturally, to accept them as representatives of 'a truly lofty and noble race'.

After a second winter in Pennsylvania–where he showed off his work to friends and sold a few copies to obtain much needed funds–he returned again to St Louis. This time he arranged with Pierre Chouteau of the American Fur Company to travel aboard the *Yellowstone* as far up the Missouri as the vessel would go. It was a significant voyage; the *Yellowstone* was the first steamboat to penetrate the Western wilderness. In a few years, Indians who lived along the river would be complaining because the trees which grew on its banks would all be cut down for burning in the boilers of a continuing procession of steamboats.

The *Yellowstone* left St Louis on 26 March 1832. To earn

money during his year in the far West, Catlin had arranged with the New York *Commercial Advertiser* to dispatch, whenever opportunity offered, travel letters for publication—a method still in use by literate but underfunded adventurers for paying the expenses of their journeys.

As the *Yellowstone* chugged upriver, Catlin occupied himself with sketching scenes along the way. Whenever the boat stopped at an Indian village, he hurried ashore to make notes and hasty drawings. About mid-May, several miles below Fort Pierre, the steamboat buried its prow in a sandbar. After a vain attempt to get it afloat again, Pierre Chouteau informed Catlin that he could remain with the crew until higher water lifted the boat free, or he could join a group of trappers going overland to the fort, a two-hundred-mile journey on foot. 'I packed on the backs and in the hands of several men, such articles for painting as I might want,' Catlin noted in his journal, 'and with my sketchbook slung on my back, and my rifle in hand, I started off with them.'

They were six days crossing a sea of green grass and wild

The *Yellowstone* steaming past St Louis

Catlin and an Indian companion stalked the herd in wolfskins, not only to shoot buffaloes point-blank but also for a close view for the artist's ever-present sketchbook.

flowers. 'We saw immense herds of buffaloes, and although we had no horses to run them we successfully approached them on foot, and supplied ourselves abundantly with fresh meat . . . Amused with many pleasing incidents and accidents of the chase, we arrived, pretty well jaded at Fort Pierre.'

Catlin immediately set up his easel, and the novelty of what he was doing there in the midst of the wild Sioux country attracted so many curious Indians that the painter was forced to place them in lines to await their turns as sitters. He now began to develop a shorthand method of pictorial recording. It was somewhat like the pictographs which his subjects drew on buffalo skins to record their winter counts and calendars. If the camera had been invented then he would have been snapping a shutter continuously, hoping for perhaps one good shot out of

A self-portrait of Catlin painting a Mandan chief, Mah-to-tah-pay

ten, but because there was no camera he had to invent a technique of rapid drawing somewhat similar to that of the rapid shutter-snapping of a news photographer. He worked frantically, like a man privileged to visit a strange planet for a brief hour; he felt compelled to record everything he saw in that fresh and teeming West.

Sometimes he would hurriedly draw a landscape and then splash figures of Indians across the background. Because he was constantly in motion he brushed paint thinly on unstretched canvas so that it would dry quickly enough to be rolled up and stored in the tin tubes he used to protect his work. Some years later when his illustrated books were published, the crude printing processes of the day reproduced his line drawings with lithographed colors. Catlin's contemporaries who knew his art only through reproductions in books rather than from viewing the finished paintings in his gallery tended to dismiss him as a primitive, a reputation which has clung to his name. His field sketches and his perfected oil paintings, however, are as different as amateur snapshots and studio photographs.

On 31 May the *Yellowstone* arrived at Fort Pierre on the crest of melting snow water which had suddenly filled the Missouri. A month later the steamboat with Catlin aboard reached its destination – Fort Union at the mouth of the river for which the vessel was named. This was field headquarters of millionaire John Jacob Astor's American Fur Company which had become a dynamic enterprise under the direction of Pierre Chouteau. The American Fur Company had recently won the loyalty of the formerly hostile Blackfeet away from Hudson's Bay Company, and would shortly force Jim Bridger and his partners of Jed Smith's old Rocky Mountain company to become subservient to American Fur in the final boom years of the trade.

Catlin wasted no time in sketching Crows, Assiniboines, and Blackfeet encamped around the fort, and then he set off in a

'Flathead' Indians (probably Chinooks) fishing. These Indians sometimes bound their babies' heads for a similar flattened effect.

Bear Dance of the Plains Cree

canoe to visit Cheyenne, Gros Ventre, and Cree villages in the area. His admiration for the Indians apparently was reciprocated; the only trouble he had was from a band of grizzly bears that invaded his camp and chewed up some of his precious oil paints. Because colors were important and sometimes sacred symbols to all Indians, Catlin earned a special place in the eyes of these people who loved bright paints and admired skill in their uses. They soon named him Medicine Paint, or White Medicine Painter.

'No man's imagination,' he wrote in one of his letters from Fort Union, 'with all the aids of description that can be given to it, can ever picture the beauty and wildness of scenes that may be daily witnessed in this romantic country; of hundreds of these graceful youth, without a care to wrinkle or a fear to disturb the full expression of pleasure and enjoyment that beams upon their faces; their long black hair, mingling with their horses' tails, floating in the wind, while they are flying over the carpeted prairie and dealing death with their spears and arrows to a band of infuriated buffaloes.'

The observant artist clearly saw that the fur traders were debasing the Indians; he well understood the meaning of that first steamboat moored at the juncture of the Missouri and the Yellowstone:

I have . . . contemplated the noble races of red men who are . . . melting away at the approach of civilization; their rights invaded, their morals corrupted, their lands wrested from them, their customs changed, and therefore lost to the world, and they at last sunk into the earth and the plowshare turning the sod over their graves; and I have flown to their rescue, not of their lives or of their race (for they are *doomed* and must perish), but to the rescue of their looks and their modes, at which the acquisitive world may hurl their poison and every besom of destruction, and trample them down and crush them to death; yet, phoenix-like, they may rise from the 'stain on a painter's palette', and live again on canvas and stand forth for centuries yet to come—the living monuments of a noble race.

Late in the summer Catlin left Fort Union in a canoe, accompanied by two trappers bound for St Louis. From Jean Batiste and Abraham Bogard, Catlin learned a great deal about the ways of the West, some of such a bawdy nature that it shocked both his romantic attitude and his Wesleyan Methodist philosophy. The trappers' stories helped to prepare him for the pagan rites and torture ceremonies of the Mandans. When they stopped at those Mandan villages where Lewis and Clark had wintered a quarter of a century earlier, the inhabitants were preparing for their *O-kee-pa* ceremonies. Catlin was one of the first white men ever given an opportunity to view the four-day ordeal, and he was the only one to record it in pictures.

'The strange country that I am in,' he wrote from the Mandan villages in July, 'its excitements, its accidents and wild incidents, which startle me almost every moment, prevent me from any very elaborate disquisition upon the above remarkable events at present.' He had his drawings, however, some of which could not be publicly exhibited during that age of Victorian modesty, and later. he wrote most of it down for his book *O-Kee-Pa*, including an amusing description of the central figure of the performance, a Mandan dancer with a giant penis carved of wood and painted a glaring vermilion. The torture ceremony was a variation of the Sun Dance, skewers being run beneath the breast muscles of the participants. 'There were then two cords lowered down from the top of the lodge . . . which were fastened to the splints or skewers, and they instantly began to haul him up; he was thus raised until his body was suspended from the ground, where he rested until the knife and splint were passed through the flesh or integuments in a similar manner on each arm below the shoulder, below the elbow, on the thighs, and below the knees. Each one was then

Mandan ceremony of voluntary torture

instantly raised with the cords until the weight of his body was suspended by them, and then, while the blood was streaming down their limbs, the bystanders hung upon the splints each man's appropriate shield, bow and quiver . . .'

The Mandans disturbed and fascinated Catlin; in one letter his Methodism prevailed over his artistic detachment: 'These people *can be saved*', he wrote, and then recommended that missionaries come there to introduce the plowshare and prayers so that the Mandans could become 'civilized and Christianized (and consequently *saved*) in the heart of the American wilderness'. There was nothing that Catlin or anyone else could do to *save* the Mandans in any sense of the word; five years later ninety-five per cent of them were dead from the most lethal scourge brought by the white men – smallpox. The survivors were taken in by their cousins, the Hidatsa, and that was virtually the end of the Mandans as a tribe.

Much later than they had planned, Catlin and his trapper companions reached St Louis in their tiny boat, which was packed with paintings, Indian costumes, sketches, and note-books. Catlin had completed the most fruitful expedition of his life. In three months of hard traveling and constant work he had created a collection of sixty-six Indian portraits, thirty-six scenes of Indian life, twenty-five landscapes, and hundreds of rough sketches. He had also written a series of long travel letters. Some of his work had already been sent down to St Louis 'by steamer and other conveyance, about twenty boxes and packages at different times . . . and I have, on looking them up and enumerating them, been lucky enough to receive and recognize about fifteen of the twenty, which is a pretty fair proportion for this wild and desperate country.'

Certain now that his three years in the West had produced enough material for a museum, Catlin hurried back to Pennsylvania to prepare his exhibits. According to the Pittsburgh *Gazette* of 23 April 1833, most of the paintings were 'in an unfinished state, he only having had sufficient leisure to secure correct likenesses of the various living subjects of his pencil and the general features of the scenery which he had selected, the backgrounds and details being reserved for the labours of a future time'.

Coincidentally in that same spring of 1833, Charles Bodmer, a twenty-seven-year-old Swiss artist, was traveling up the Missouri with a wealthy German, Prince Maximilian of Wied-Neuwied. While stopping briefly in St Louis, Bodmer had an opportunity to view several of Catlin's paintings owned by Indian Agent Benjamin O'Fallon and may have been influenced in his choice of subject matter by them. Bodmer was a schooled artist, and because he was not pressed for time or funds, he produced more finished work than Catlin. Unfortunately, Bodmer's portraits and scenes of the West would remain buried and almost unnoticed for years as accompaniments to the

Catlin, with a sketchbook under his arm, studying Indian burial customs. He aimed to record all aspects of Indian life–and death–before it disappeared.

expensive book of travels published by his patron. (Frederic Remington who carefully studied the work of early frontier painters did not discover Bodmer until 1892.)

Catlin on the other hand was determined that the whole world must *see* the American West through his pictures. After a rather indifferent reception in Pittsburgh, he and his wife Clara took the collection down the Ohio to Cincinnati. Here they worked for days at finishing and framing his paintings, and the Cincinnati exhibition with accompanying lectures by the artist attracted moderate crowds and favorable notices. 'A collection of paintings which we consider the most extraordinary and interesting that we have ever witnessed . . . His gallery now contains about 140 pictures, and we are informed that he has in his possession an equal number in an unfinished state.'

After another exhibition at Louisville, the Catlins had enough money to go on a leisurely winter trip through the South. When George returned to St Louis in the spring of 1834, Clara accompanied him, and while he went on what was to be his last productive journey into the West she remained with friends in nearby Alton, Illinois.

'In the spring of 1834 I obtained permission from the Secretary of War', Catlin said, 'to accompany the First Regiment of Mounted Dragoons, under the command of Colonel [Henry] Dodge, to the Comanches and other southwestern tribes.' The dragoons, a mounted infantry force, had recently been organized and this was their first march into Indian country. The mounted men and their splendid horses and uniforms were meant to impress upon Western Indians the power of the United States; as more and more wagons began to roll on trails to Santa Fe and

A display of Plains Apache archery at the gallop, a skill Indians used with success against white soldiers

Oregon, more and more tribes were inclined to resist this intrusion of their lands.

For Catlin the military expedition offered a convenient and safe way to paint Indians he had not yet seen – Comanches, Kiowas, Osages, Wichitas, Wacos, Arapahos, and Jicarilla Apaches. 'I am going farther to get *sitters*, than any of my fellow-artists ever did,' he wrote from Fort Gibson in June, 'but I take an indescribable pleasure in roaming through Nature's trackless wilds, and selecting my models, where I am free and unshackled by the killing restraints of society . . . Though the toil, the privations, and expense of traveling to these remote parts of the world to get subjects for my pencil, places almost insurmountable, and sometimes *painful* obstacles before me, yet I am encouraged by the continual conviction that I am practising in the *true School of the Arts* . . . I have learned more of the essential parts of my art in the three last years, than I would have learned in New York in a lifetime.'

During that hot summer journey across the plains of the Southwest, many dragoons sickened and died, and although Catlin himself suffered from 'a slow and distressing bilious fever', he brought back some of his finest portraits and scenes to add to his collection – views of wild horses and buffalo, massed ranks of Comanches and dragoons, a unique depiction of a Wichita grass house village which must have been somewhat the same as those found by Coronado three centuries earlier.

'One of the most thrilling and most beautiful scenes I ever witnessed', was the way Catlin described his meeting with the Comanches. When the dragoons formed in three columns with a line front outside a Comanche village, the warriors rode to meet them, wheeling their horses, forming into line, and dressing their ranks like well-disciplined cavalry.

> The two lines were thus drawn up, face to face, within twenty or thirty yards of each other, as inveterate foes that never had met; and to the everlasting credit of the Comanches, whom the world had always looked upon as murderous and hostile, they had all come out in this manner, with their heads uncovered, and without a weapon of any kind, to meet a war-party bristling with arms, and trespassing to the middle of their country. They had every reason to look upon us as their natural enemy, as they have been in the habit of estimating all pale faces; and yet, instead of arms or defences, or even of frowns, they galloped out and looked us in our faces, without an expression of fear or dismay, and evidently with expressions of joy and impatient pleasure, to shake us by the hand, on the bare assertion of Colonel Dodge, which had been made to the chiefs, that 'we came to see them on a friendly visit'.

Catlin spent the next two summers rounding out his collection, but neither of these journeys took him very far into the West. In 1835 he visited the Ojibways and the Santee Sioux in Wisconsin and Minnesota, and in 1836 he returned to Minne-

An everyday scene in a Sioux camp

sota for the purpose of finding and painting the Indians' sacred red pipestone quarry on the Coteau Des Prairies somewhere west of Fort Snelling. According to tradition, no white man had ever seen the quarry where Indians in the West came to obtain claystone for making ceremonial pipes.

On the way there, Catlin was stopped by a band of Sioux who ordered him to turn away from the quarry. His ability as a persuader stood him in good stead now. His boldness combined with his brushes, bright-colored paints and canvases served as passports to the pipestone quarry. In addition to sketches and paintings, he brought back samples of the red pipestone for scientists to examine. Its uniqueness gained Catlin another sort of immortality: a mineralogist named it *catlinite* and so it is called to this day.

During the winter of 1836–7 Catlin gathered up his various collections–which were scattered from St Louis to Pennsylvania–and settled temporarily in his wife's hometown of Albany, New York. There he put together what he was to call his 'Indian Gallery'. Tallying up he found that he had 494 paintings representing forty-eight tribes. For convenience in storage and transport he had kept most of the oils uniform in size: 28 × 23 inches. During the spring and summer of 1837 he held trial exhibits, first in Albany and then in Troy.

(In this same year, Alfred Jacob Miller went West with a wealthy Scotsman, Captain William Drummond Stewart, and brought back three hundred scenes of the Plains and the Rockies that no other artist had yet recorded. Miller later painted several large canvases from his sketches for Stewart and other private collectors, but most of his work remained buried for almost a century. Unlike Catlin he was not a showman.)

In the New York *Commercial Advertiser* of 23 September 1837 appeared this notice:

> CATLIN'S INDIAN GALLERY. *Opens for exhibition on Monday Evening, the 25th instant and will be continued each evening . . . In the lecture room of Clinton Hall. There will be several hundred Portraits exhibited, as well as Splendid Costumes–Paintings of their villages–Dances–Buffalo Hunts –Religious Ceremonies, etc. Collected by himself, among the wildest tribes of America, during an absence from this city of seven years. Mr. Catlin will be present at all of these exhibitions, giving illustrations and explanations in the form of a Lecture . . . Each admission 50 cents.*

The exhibition was an immediate success, so many people coming to pay their half dollars that he was forced to move to a larger hall in the Stuyvesant Institute on Broadway. For the first time, Easterners could *see* the American West in all its color, romance and grandeur, and Catlin was eager to explain his paintings to them. 'His manner of speech was quick and earnest,' one of his listeners commented, 'and his lectures pleasing and entertaining.' Although the gallery was still attracting large audiences in December, Catlin suddenly closed it then in order to travel to South Carolina to investigate the mistreatment of Osceola and to paint the Seminole leader's portrait.

Sometime during that winter he evidently made up his mind that his gallery should become a museum, owned by the people of the United States and located in Washington. To give Congress and other government officials an opportunity to see what it consisted of, Catlin opened his exhibition in Washington on 9 April 1838. While there he won the support of Henry Clay, Daniel Webster, and William H. Seward in his campaign to make the gallery the nucleus of a national museum. Although a resolution was introduced in the House of Representatives to acquire 'Catlin's collection of Indian portraits and curiosities', no further action was taken.

After Congress adjourned, Catlin and his show moved on to Baltimore and Philadelphia. On 16 August, when he opened in Boston, he was somewhat dubious about the reception he would receive in America's center of learning. So many Bostonians came, however, that he had to move to Faneuil Hall. 'Mr. Catlin admires the Indians,' said one critic, 'and speaks of their high qualities, and of the cruel injustices with which they have been treated by the Americans . . . The pictures, as works of art, are deficient in drawing, perspective, and finish; but they convey a vivid impression of the objects, and impress the mind of the spectator with a conviction of their fidelity to nature which gives them an inexpressible charm.'

To jog Congress into action on the acquisition of the gallery for a museum, Catlin announced to the press that if the United States government did not want his paintings, then he would take them to Europe and either sell to a European government or dispose of the collection piecemeal to private collectors. Catlin did not actually want to take his gallery abroad, yet even with the support of many leading newspapers who wished to keep the collection in America, he failed to secure any action from the government. It was no help to his cause that Congress was in an Indian-hating mood in those years, and Catlin had been labeled an Indian-lover.

When the 1839 session of Congress adjourned, Catlin decided to carry out his threat and take the gallery to Europe. In the fall of that year he opened in London's Egyptian Hall, expecting to stay only a few days. The exhibition was so popular, however, that he remained in England for almost five years, gradually converting the gallery into a Wild West show—with live Indians, tipis, buffalo skins, bows, arrows, and other trappings. In 1841 his *Letters and Notes on the Manners, Customs and Conditions of the North American Indians* was published in London, bringing him fame but not much fortune.

When the crowds of English visitors began dwindling, Catlin moved the gallery to Paris, leasing a large hall in Rue St

Honoré. The poet Baudelaire was 'particularly struck by the transparency and lightness' of the skies in Catlin's paintings, and said that his use of color held 'an element of mystery which delights me more than I can say. Red, the color of blood, the color of life, glowed so abundantly in his gloomy Museum that it was like an intoxication; and the landscapes–wooded mountains, vast savannahs, deserted rivers–were monotonously, eternally green.' King Louis Philippe was a visitor, and he became so enthusiastic that he arranged for Catlin to transfer the exhibition to the Louvre. All this time the artist had kept in close touch with friends in Washington, and he was still hopeful that the United States government would purchase the gallery for a museum.

Louis Philippe commissioned Catlin to paint a series of historical events relating to the French in North America, but before the assignment could be completed, revolutionaries overthrew the king and forced him to flee to England. Catlin never received any money for this work which had taken months of his time, and because of his close association with Louis Philippe, he also had to leave France, but he managed to bring his gallery intact to London.

In an effort to raise money enough to take care of himself and his children–his wife had recently died–he opened his gallery again to the English public. This time there were few visitors. Indian paintings were out of phase with the times; the new technique of photography suddenly was all the rage. Even in prosperity Catlin had been unable to handle his money matters; in adversity he borrowed funds and then went bankrupt. Suddenly he was surrounded by creditors, and his gallery probably would have been dispersed to dealers and collectors all over Europe had not a wealthy boiler-maker of Philadelphia, Joseph Harrison, come forward with money to pay off Catlin's debts. Harrison took over the gallery and had everything crated and shipped to Philadelphia, leaving Catlin with neither money nor a gallery with which to earn money.

In 1852 Catlin was living alone in Paris, despondent and destitute, after his children had been sent back to America to be brought up by his wife's family. Always a visionary, it did not require much persuasion on the part of a Parisian acquaintance for him to join in a quixotic journey to Brazil in search of fabulously rich gold mines. They found no gold, but Catlin found South American Indians and painted them. During the next five years, he made two other long journeys into the jungles and mountains of South America, and then up the west coast of North America to Alaska. As time carried him past the age of sixty, he seemed to be fighting a battle against his own physical dissolution. Like young Jedediah Smith, the aging George Catlin set up difficult obstacles in the natural world and then attempted to overcome them. He too felt bound to ascend Lewis and Clark's Columbia River, to visit the Great

Falls, to conquer the roaring waters of the Snake. With a fugitive slave named Caesar Bolla as companion, he crossed the Rocky Mountains eastward to the Colorado River, and then traveled on to the Rio Grande. For eight hundred miles, Catlin and Bolla lived in a small dugout canoe, paddling their way down the Rio Grande to Matamoros.

In 1870, when he was seventy-four years old, George Catlin returned to the United States, bringing with him about four hundred oils done on cardboard, many of them being copies of the original works which Joseph Harrison still kept stored in his Philadelphia boiler works, refusing to allow them to be redeemed. In addition Catlin had many new paintings of South American Indians, as well as the historical series he had done for the bankrupt Louis Philippe. 'Catlin's Cartoon Collection' was the advertised name of the new gallery. The Indian wars in the West were daily in the news, and as Catlin had prophesied thirty years earlier the magnificent tribes he had visited then were now being converted into 'a basket of *dead game* – harassed, chased, bleeding, and dead; with their plumage and colours despoiled . . .'

Not many New Yorkers were interested in seeing Catlin's Cartoon Collection, and he had to pack everything into storage. The following year he received an unexpected invitation to exhibit the Cartoon Collection at the Smithsonian Institution. Old and ill, he knew that this was his last chance to persuade the government to acquire his pictorial record of a West that was passing forever. He prepared his exhibit with great care, had a ninety-nine-page catalog printed to explain each painting, and waited for the government to act.

Congress in 1872 was more concerned with appropriating funds to the War Department – to pursue Apaches and to put down Red Cloud's defiant Sioux – than in furnishing money to buy pictures of dead Indians. In October, Catlin packed his paintings for the last time and went to Jersey City, to die before the year's end.

In 1879 the indifferent government received what was left of the original gallery as a gift from the heirs of Joseph Harrison, the boiler-maker. Through the years the collection had endured moths, two fires, and water damage; the robes, costumes, masks, moccasins, and tipis had rotted away; many of the paintings were darkened by smoke. The Smithsonian packed the paintings away, keeping most of them in storage until well into the twentieth century. In 1912 one of Catlin's surviving daughters sold the Cartoon Collection to the American Museum of Natural History in New York. The man whose paint brush brought an entire generation of millions of people their only visual impressions of the American West lay in a Brooklyn cemetery, as forgotten as the Indians he had tried to rescue from oblivion, 'a basket of dead game – harassed, chased, bleeding, and dead'.

5. Parkman and the Year of Decision

In the late summer of 1838, when George Catlin opened his Indian Gallery in Boston, one of those who eagerly paid the fifty cents admission charge was fifteen-year-old Francis Parkman, Jr. A descendant of New England divines and wealthy Boston merchants, Francis Parkman, with his insular notions and aristocratic leanings, seemed an unlikely candidate to become a Westerner. The influence of Catlin's pictures and lectures upon young Parkman must have been considerable. Six years afterward, when Parkman took time out from his senior year at Harvard to make a grand tour of Europe, he noted in his journal upon arriving in London: 'I went immediately to Catlin's Indian Gallery. It is in the Egyptian Hall, Piccadilly ... The portraits of the chiefs, dusty and faded, hung round the walls, and above were a few hunting shirts, and a bundle or two of arrows; but the rich and invaluable collection I had seen in Boston had disappeared ...'

Not long after becoming a student at Harvard, Francis Parkman had made up his mind that he was going to become a historian—not of Europe but of America. He often imagined himself to be a character in one of James Fenimore Cooper's novels, and whenever he went for a walk in the woods outside Boston he always carried a rifle—as did Hawkeye or Chingachgook. One of his classmates said that Parkman had 'Injuns on the brain'. By 1846, the year after he graduated from Harvard, he knew that he must travel to the West and live for a time with the Indians. The reason for this, he explained, was that no history of America could be written without a thorough knowledge of primitive Indians. Because the Indians in the East had either been exterminated or forced to adopt the white man's culture, Parkman felt that it was necessary for him to go and see George Catlin's Indians on the Western Plains.

With his cousin Quincy Adams Shaw—another aristocratic and well-to-do Bostonian—Parkman arrived in Independence, Missouri, early in May 1846. At nearby Westport they obtained horses and mules for their journey across the Plains to the American Fur Company's base at Fort Laramie. Parkman promptly named his riding horse Pontiac, after the great Ottawa chief who was to play a leading role in his first histories of the

Platte River, Nebraska (detail) by Albert Bierstadt. The Mallets had given the river its French name because it was wide and shallow; Parkman referred to it as 'a thin sheet of water'.

LEFT A detail from *Encampment on the Plains* by Worthington Whittredge. By the time Parkman and Shaw took to the trail there was already a steady stream of emigrants moving West.

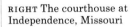
LEFT A detail from *Encampment on the Plains* by Worthington Whittredge. By the time Parkman and Shaw took to the trail there was already a steady stream of emigrants moving West.

RIGHT The courthouse at Independence, Missouri

American frontier. At Independence, Parkman and Shaw had an opportunity to look over the Santa Fe traders and Oregon-bound emigrants. 'Among them are some of the vilest outcasts in the country. I have often perplexed myself to divine the various motives that gave impulse to this migration; but whatever they may be, whether an insane hope of a better condition in life, or a desire of shaking off restraints of law and society, or mere restlessness, certain it is, that multitudes bitterly repent the journey, and, after they have reached the land of promise, are happy enough to escape from it.'

To accompany them on their venture into the West, Parkman and Shaw employed two French Canadians who had formerly worked for fur companies. Henry Chatillon, a man of about thirty, was their guide and intermediary with the Indians. Deslauriers, whose first name was not recorded, served as a muleteer, driving their supply cart which contained provisions, camping gear, and ammunition. Because of the declining fur trade, many of the Mountain Men were now reduced to such means of earning their livings; in 1846 Jim Bridger was hunting buffalo for their hides.

Being credulous tenderfeet, Parkman and his cousin accepted all the frontier fantasies concerning 'dangerous armed hordes of polygamous Mormons . . . lawless Kentucky fellers from the barbarous border country', and 'thieving, murderous Pawnees on the Plains'. To gain added security against these perils they decided to join up with a trio of Englishmen who were heading West for adventure and sport.

At Fort Leavenworth, Parkman and Shaw stopped to call on Colonel Stephen Watts Kearny, whom they had met in St Louis. Kearny regaled them with tales of the march of his dragoons the previous year to Fort Laramie and Bent's Fort – a show of force for the benefit of Indian tribes growing resentful over the invasion of their lands. Here Parkman received his first inkling that 1846 was to be a year of decision in the West. The American expansionist movement, Manifest Destiny, was driving hard for Oregon, Santa Fe, and California. As the young Bostonians and the colonel sat sipping Madeira at a white-clothed table in Fort Leavenworth, skirmishes between United States and Mexican troops were already beginning along the Rio Grande. Within a few weeks Kearny would be a general, leading the Army of the West in its conquest of New Mexico and California. Within a few more weeks, the Oregon country would be taken from the British by the mere formality of a treaty signing.

On 23 May Parkman, Shaw, and their British companions started westward across the Plains. That evening they encamped near the 'trail of the Oregon emigrants'. This was the closest Parkman had come to using the name 'Oregon Trail'. It had appeared in print for the first time only the previous year.

A few days later Parkman realized that Captain Bill Chandler of the British Army was a rank amateur when it came to leading an expedition into the American West. Time seemed to hold no meaning for the Englishman. Departures were delayed; horses were allowed to stray; bad weather kept him under shelter. On 10 June Parkman and Shaw decided to part amicably with Chandler and his two fellow countrymen, and they then joined a small wagon train of emigrants who were traveling on a fast schedule for Oregon by way of Fort Laramie.

Parkman's attitude toward his emigrant companions varied with his moods. One day he would dismiss the women as being 'damned ugly', and the men as rude and ignorant. The next he would depict them with all the delight that Chaucer showed in his Canterbury pilgrims; for instance, a pretty girl with a parasol riding on horseback alongside a young man. 'The girl and her beau apparently found something very agreeable in each other's company, for they kept more than a mile in advance of their party, which H. [Henry Chatillon] considered very imprudent, as the Sioux might be about.' Parkman never abandoned his fear of the 'much-dreaded Mormons', avoiding all contact with them, and his ire always arose when any emigrant tried to invade his Yankee privacy. 'They demanded our names, whence we came, whither we were going, and what was our business.' The last query was especially painful to Parkman. He wearied of trying to explain to the emigrants the purposes of his journey westward. 'Traveling in that country', he wrote, 'from any other motive than *gain*, was an idea of which they took no cognizance.'

As they were traveling along the Platte, which he described as 'a thin sheet of water', he tried to analyze the meaning of the flood of emigrants. 'They are not robust, nor large of frame, yet they have an aspect of hardy endurance. Finding at home no scope for their energies, they have betaken themselves to the prairie; and in them seems to be revived, with redoubled force, that fierce spirit which impelled their ancestors, scarcely more lawless than themselves, from the German forests, to inundate Europe, and overwhelm the Roman empire.'

Ten years earlier the Reverend Samuel Parker and Dr Marcus Whitman, who wanted to Christianize the Indians of the West, had come this same route. After they crossed South Pass, Reverend Parker noted: 'There would be no difficulty in constructing a railroad from the Atlantic to the Pacific.' At the Green River *rendezvous* that summer, Dr Whitman proved his surgical skill by removing an arrowhead that had been driven into Jim Bridger's back years before by a Blackfoot warrior loyal to the British-owned fur companies in the Oregon country. Dr Whitman returned to the East that winter, and the next spring brought back a beautiful blonde bride, Narcissa Prentiss Whitman. Traveling with them in a wagon from Westport Landing on the Missouri was another pair of newlyweds, Henry and Eliza Spalding. Narcissa and Eliza were the first white women to cross the Rocky Mountains, and with their husbands they were the first Americans to attempt to reach the Columbia River in an overland wagon.

Although they abandoned their wagon at Snake Fort on the Boise River, they had opened a trail to Oregon, or as Parkman called it, the Oregon Trail. In 1840 fur-trader Joe Meek brought three wagons across the mountains to the Columbia. In the summer of 1841, seventy Americans banded together at Independence, Missouri, for a wagon journey westward over the trail to Oregon. The next year a hundred men, women, and children followed their example. In 1843 a thousand made the wagon journey, and at Champoeg in spite of British claims to the territory, they established a provisional Oregon government 'until such time as the United States of America extend their jurisdiction over us'. In the year that Francis Parkman traveled over the trail, the number of Americans in Oregon passed ten thousand.

On 14 June young Parkman met his first 'real' Indians, Old Smoke's band of Oglalla Sioux who were also traveling to Fort Laramie. Some years earlier Henry Chatillon had taken a wife of that tribe, and he boldly led his young Bostonians into the tipi village on Horse Creek for a visit with Old Smoke. 'Warriors, women, and children swarmed like bees; hundreds of dogs, of all sizes and colors, ran restlessly about; and, close at hand, the wide shallow stream was alive with boys, girls, and young squaws, splashing, screaming and laughing in the water.' One of the young warriors with these Oglallas was Old Smoke's nephew, Red Cloud, who twenty years later would become famous for his stubborn defense of the Powder River country. In 1846 Red Cloud was in his early twenties, but if Parkman met him he made no note of his name. At that time the Oglallas were divided into two factions, one led by Old Smoke and the other by Bull Bear, son of the elder Bull Bear (whose magnificent face was painted by Alfred Jacob Miller in 1837). The elder Bull Bear had been killed in 1841 during an intertribal fight over a woman, and Red Cloud was the principal assailant. Parkman's interest in these matters was intensified because his guide, Chatillon, was married to one of Bull Bear's daughters.

From the Oglallas, Parkman received his first intimation that the Plains Indians were disturbed by the swarms of oxen and wagons passing through their country over what they called the Great Medicine Road. 'They could scarcely believe that the earth contained such a multitude of white men', he said. 'Their wonder is now giving way to indignation; and the result, unless vigilantly guarded against, may be lamentable in the extreme.' Yet like George Catlin before him, Parkman in that summer of 1846 could see no way of averting the doom portended for the Indians in the long trains of emigrants 'dragging on in slow procession by the encampment of the people whom they and their descendants, in the space of a century, are to sweep from the face of the earth'.

Next day Parkman and his companions rode up to the gate of Fort Laramie where they were received 'by no means cordially' by James Bordeaux, acting for the American Fur Company. Parkman handed Bordeaux a letter from Pierre Chouteau which they had obtained in St Louis. It served as a magical passport; the lack of cordiality turned into a warm welcome. As Parkman noted, the fur company held absolute sway in the West. 'The arm of the United States has little force . . . the extreme outposts of her troops are about seven hundred miles to the eastward.' Bordeaux assigned Parkman and his party a large apartment inside the fort where they spread their blankets on the floor. 'From a sort of balcony we saw our horses and carts brought in, and witnessed a picturesque frontier scene. Conversed and smoked in the windy porch. Horses made a great row in the *corale*. At night the Inds. set up their songs.'

On the following morning Old Smoke's Oglallas came splashing across Laramie Creek, horses and dogs dragging big and little travaux filled with tipi skins, utensils, children, and puppies. It was a scene of utmost confusion, noise, and whirling color, but after a few moments each Oglalla family with its horses and equipage filed off to a plain at the rear of the fort, and within half an hour, sixty or seventy tipis were ready for occupancy. 'Their horses were feeding by hundreds over the surrounding prairie, and their dogs were roaming everywhere. The fort was full of warriors, and the children were whooping and yelling incessantly under the walls.'

Parkman could not resist drawing a contrast between the vivacious friendliness of the Indians and the grim churlishness of a group of Oregon-bound emigrants who camped at Fort Laramie on that same day. 'Tall awkward men, in brown homespun; women, with cadaverous faces and long lank figures . . .

An early photograph of under-
standably dour emigrants

They seemed like men totally out of their element, bewildered and amazed, like a troop of schoolboys lost in the woods . . . for the most part, they were the rudest and most ignorant of the frontier population; they knew absolutely nothing of the country and its inhabitants; they had already experienced much misfortune, and apprehended more.'

A few days later Parkman met a large group of prosperous and more knowledgeable emigrants bound for California. They had recently deposed their captain and 'split into half a dozen pieces'. One of these pieces eventually was led by two brothers named Donner who against the advice of the Mountain Men at Fort Laramie took a cut-off route to California. As Parkman later phrased it, the Donner party was 'interrupted by the deep snows among the mountains, and, maddened by cold and hunger, fed upon each other's flesh!'

Francis Parkman had not traveled so far, however, to waste his time with westward-seeking white emigrants. 'I had come into the country chiefly with a view of observing the Indian character. To accomplish my purpose it was necessary to live in the midst of them, and become, as it were, one of them. I proposed to join a village, and make myself an inmate of one of their lodges.'

Thanks to Henry Chatillon, Parkman was able to fulfill his dream. Shortly after their arrival at Fort Laramie, Chatillon received news of the illness of his wife, Bear Robe, who was living with her brother's (Bull Bear the younger's) band of Oglallas. On 20 June Chatillon, Parkman, Shaw, and Deslauriers with two French traders, Raymond and Reynal, and two young Oglallas, Hail Storm and the Horse, set out for Bull Bear's village. The Horse, much admired by Parkman, was Man-Afraid-of-His-Horses, who later married the daughter of Chatillon and Bear Robe. During the Sioux Wars of the 1870s he became both a rival and a lieutenant of Red Cloud.

For this journey Parkman and his cousin acquired red flannel shirts, fringed outer jackets, pantaloons of dressed deerskin, and Sioux moccasins, all made by Indian women at Fort Laramie. Half a century later, Parkman still had his buckskin shirt when he supplied Frederic Remington with full details of his and his companions' costumes for the illustrations which the artist drew for the deluxe 1892 edition of *The Oregon Trail.*

As they rode westward from Fort Laramie, they left the emigrants' trail for the first time. Parkman knew he was in primeval Indian country when he saw a herd of two hundred elk emerge from a thicket and come out upon an open plain, 'their antlers clattering as they walked forward in a dense throng'.

Shortly after Chatillon reached his Indian wife, she died. A horse was slain for her, and food and household implements provided for her last journey to the spirit world. It was soon obvious to Parkman that Bull Bear's Oglallas were without real leadership. The younger Bull Bear's authority was challenged by Whirlwind (sometimes called Tunica) and also by the Horse and two or three older men. Among the latter was Red Water, more than sixty years old, and when Parkman learned that his band was planning a hunting venture into Shoshone country, he arranged to join them.

For three weeks in July he lived with the Oglallas and made himself 'an inmate of one of their lodges'. He shared the tipi of Red Water's son, Big Crow, as the tribe moved leisurely into the Laramie Mountains, which were then called the Black Hills because John C. Frémont had so marked them on his map–a copy of which Parkman had in his possession. This was the high point of Francis Parkman's Western experience, if not of his entire life.

Although afflicted with dysentery and other ailments, the young man from Boston forced himself to keep going. (His cousin Quincy Shaw returned to Fort Laramie to recover from a severe skin eruption diagnosed as poison ivy.) Every day was a new adventure, and with Reynal along to serve as interpreter, Parkman absorbed the Sioux legends, folklore and culture that abounded around him. He collected a vast amount of information about Indian attitudes, costumes, weapons, language, food, ways of hunting, and their daily routines. As he put it, everything was 'daguerreotyped' upon his memory.

Like Jed Smith, however, there were times when he realized he was an intruder upon a world of which he could never be a part. He was disturbed when Indian children screamed in terror at first sight of his white face, but they soon overcame their fear so that on cool nights some of them would come into Big Crow's tipi and snuggle into the strange white man's warm blankets. One cannot help but wonder if Crazy Horse might have been among the children on this hunting expedition; he would have been four or five years old.

Having learned to eat dog meat, which he rated as delicious, Parkman decided to give his hosts a feast of the dog. With a few beads and a gaudy handkerchief he traded a fat dog from an old woman who killed and singed the animal for him and boiled up two kettlefuls of meat. With bread, tea, and sugar from his supplies, Parkman spread quite a banquet in Big Crow's lodge. Red Water was the guest of honor, of course, and after the dinner was over the old chief walked around the camp singing a song in praise of the feast. Parkman was delighted.

Next day he was ill again and dosed himself with opium – the popular remedy of the times. 'I became like a man in a dream', he said. 'I lay down in Big Crow's lodge and slept, totally unconscious till the morning. The first thing that awakened me was a hoarse flapping over my head, and a sudden light that poured in upon me. The camp was breaking up, and the squaws were moving the covering from the lodge.' He could barely mount his horse, but a day or so later when the Oglallas found a buffalo herd, he plunged into the hunt with renewed zest.

At the end of the hunts there were feasts and celebrations. To add his bit to the festivities, Parkman ripped pages out of his copy of Frémont's *Exploring Expedition to the Rocky Mountains* and rolled them around gunpowder and charcoal to produce firework squibs which when lighted whizzed and sputtered through the air to the astonishment of the Sioux. 'From that time forward I enjoyed a great repute as a "fire-medicine".'

They were now in Shoshone country, enemy country, and Parkman completely forgot his illness when the Oglallas began talking of a war party. The warriors could never make up their minds, however, and it must have been during this week of buffalo feasting, story telling, and merriment that Parkman shedded the last of the romantic notions about Indians which remained from his boyhood reading of James Fenimore Cooper. The Indians he was living with began to assume the shapes of flesh-and-blood individuals. Because of his Puritan heritage he could not help being squeamish over their frankness about sex, and he could never quite accept their beliefs in the powers of 'medicine' which he should have recognized as being akin to the beliefs of ancient Greek and Roman warriors. Yet he did learn to see them as real human beings instead of as gods or devils.

The Westerners

The young warrior White Shield, for example, made a great display in his full war dress as he paraded around the camp one day to stir up enthusiasm for a war party to avenge the death of a brother. But like any other human being, White Shield fell victim to a sore throat and a bad cold–and called off the raid. Then there was old Red Water, always moving with the great dignity of a chief, measuring his words and actions carefully. On the one day of the hunting journey that his leadership was in demand because of a violent quarrel in camp, Red Water strode majestically from his lodge, gun and bow in hand, only to trip and fall sprawling on his face while his weapons flew scattering in every direction.

Yet the more Parkman came to see them as human beings like himself, the wider seemed the gulf between him and his new friends. 'As the pipe passed the circle around the fire in the evening,' he noted on 29 July, 'there was plenty of that obscene conversation that seems to make up the sum of Ind. wit, and which very much amuses the squaws. The Inds. are a very licentious set.'

A week later he was happy to be back in Fort Laramie, conversing with Quincy Shaw and reveling in the licentious poetry of Lord Byron. On 4 August the travelers began their roundabout return journey. Parkman wanted to see Bent's Fort, which was as important a station on the mountain branch of the Santa Fe Trail as Fort Laramie was for the Oregon Trail. On their way southward across what is now Colorado, they were impressed by the beauty and magnificence of the Rockies which towered to the west.

For two weeks the travelers saw no other human beings, but Quincy Shaw remarked that country so beautiful must soon be invaded by farmers and stockmen, and that settlements and towns would soon drive out the Indians. 'We condoled with each other on so melancholy a prospect', Parkman was to recall a quarter of a century later–during which brief span of time strikes of gold and silver changed the face of the mountains and brought in hordes of wealth seekers to fill new cities. 'We did not dream how Commerce and Gold would breed nations along the Pacific, the disenchanting screech of the locomotive break the spell of weird mysterious mountains, woman's rights invade the fastnesses of the Arapahos, and despairing savagery, assailed in front and rear, vail its scalp-locks and feathers before triumphant commonplace.'

On 20 August at a crude trading post which later became the town of Pueblo, Colorado, they heard their first news of the Mexican War that had begun during the summer. Trade from Taos south was suspended while General Kearny assembled his Army of the West for the capture of Santa Fe. Five days later Parkman and his companions were at Bent's Fort. 'A man on the road', he noted, 'told us that the Spaniards would evacuate Santa Fe without fighting.' This is precisely what happened,

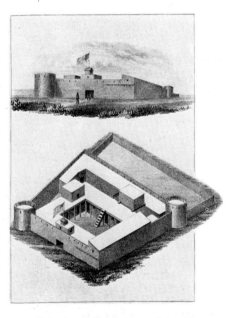

A plan of Bent's Fort, Colorado

and if Parkman had arrived at Bent's Fort a few days earlier he would have met nineteen-year-old Susan Shelby Magoffin whose husband Samuel and his brother James were involved with a mysterious satchel of gold and a fifth-column plot which made it possible for General Kearny and Manifest Destiny to possess Santa Fe without firing a shot.

Unfortunately Parkman missed an acquaintanceship with the high-spirited Susan, but on the Santa Fe Trail late in August he met a fourth member of that money-making family of traders, William Magoffin. William was bound for Santa Fe with a long train of wagons filled with goods. He warned Parkman's small party of travelers to beware of prowling Plains Indians who seemed to be aroused by the long lines of soldiers trooping westward through their country.

Parkman and his companions encountered only one large group of Indians—Arapahos who gave them no trouble, 'having been well frightened lately by the threats of Gen'l Kearny . . . All along the road we met detachments of troops and military stores passing to Santa Fe.' Most of the troops were scattered companies of Colonel Sterling Price's regiment, 'long-legged Missourians, in homespun, over which they slung their powder-horns, bullet pouches, etc. There were a few regulars following a little behind, in regulation uniform that would hardly pass inspection.'

They also met the Mormon Battalion, five hundred young men of that persecuted faith, who had enlisted solely for the purpose of obtaining pay, subsistence, and a passage to

The Mormon Battalion resting at a stream

the West. General Kearny had promised to discharge them in California as soon as that land was safely secured for the United States. 'There was something very striking', Parkman said, 'in the half-military, half-patriarchal appearance of these armed fanatics.' Two years later a small group of these California-bound 'fanatics' would be instrumental in the discovery of gold in California–an occurrence which would unleash a torrent of rapacious humanity upon the American West.

Francis Parkman himself was to play a role in inspiring that mighty migration which would desolate the civilization of the Indians of the West. As soon as he returned to Boston, he began preparing the story of his great adventure for *Knickerbocker Magazine*. The first instalment under the title, 'The Oregon Trail: A Summer's Journey Out of Bounds', appeared in February 1847. Easterners were eager for just such an authentic account of the nation's new Western Empire, and the circulation of *Knickerbocker Magazine* soared with each succeeding episode. The editor shrewdly stretched 'Oregon Trail' out through 1848 into 1849, in which year George Palmer Putnam published it as a book. Because of the discovery of gold which had created a sudden demand for information about trails to California, Putnam changed the title to *The California and Oregon Trail*. 'A sly publisher's trick', Parkman called it, but he must have been pleasantly surprised at the book's popularity. Only a decade earlier, Washington Irving had published three Western books in quick succession, but the nation was not ready for them then. Parkman's *Oregon Trail*, in fact, drew more attention to Irving's earlier accounts of the West than they had received on publication, and new illustrated editions of Irving were brought out after Parkman's book appeared to satisfy the demand for information about that romantic land.

How many Americans became Westerners after reading *The Oregon Trail*, no one can say. Edition after edition of the book followed through the years until there was no longer a Western frontier, and in the 1970s four editions were still in print. How many hundreds of other books about the West derived from *The Oregon Trail*, borrowed from it, stole from it, no one can say, either. For more than a century, Parkman's descriptions of Indian life–costumes, customs, beliefs, habitations, hunting methods, arts, weapons–have filtered into the continuing literature of the West, lifted by travel writers, by book-writing Indian-fighters and their wives, by serious chroniclers and dime novelists for their accounts of the West. It is safe to say that one cannot read a Western book or view a Western film without finding something in it of Francis Parkman's *Oregon Trail*.

In 1847, while Francis Parkman was sending chapters of *The Oregon Trail* to *Knickerbocker Magazine*, more than four thousand emigrants followed the trail itself to Oregon Territory.

The half-title page of the book produced from Parkman's magazine articles

THE
California
&
OREGON TRAIL.

Darley Del.   CHILD SC

ALVORD, PRINT. N. Y.

At the western end of the trail, Marcus and Narcissa Whitman had completed construction of a mission at Waiilatpu and were hard at work Christianizing the Cayuse Indians.

In the summer of that year Narcissa wrote in her diary: 'The poor Indians are amazed at the overwhelming numbers of Americans coming into the country. They seem not to know what to make of it.' Narcissa believed that the Cayuse people loved her and Marcus. She sang hymns to them, and Marcus cured their ills. In the beginning, the Indians regarded Narcissa as a blonde goddess and Marcus as a powerful *te-wat*, or medicine man.

But everything went wrong during the summer and fall of 1847. Marcus set out poison to kill animals that annoyed him; he was probably the first of many Westerners to use this method of destroying wildlife, a practice which continues to this day. Either he or some of the white men who worked at the mission also put strong cathartics in some of the melons in the mission field to discourage thefts by the Indians. Several Cayuses became deathly ill from eating poisoned meat and baited melons. A rumor spread among them that Dr Whitman was poisoning the Indians in order to get their land and horses.

In that summer the swarms of emigrants brought an epidemic of measles to the Cayuse country; the Indian children began to die like the poisoned wildlife. When the white children at the mission also were made sick with measles, Dr Whitman cured them, yet for some reason he did not cure the Cayuse children. The Indians knew nothing of immunity; all that they knew was that the once powerful *te-wat* was letting their children die. If Whitman, a white man, could not or would not cure one of his own diseases, then he himself must die.

On 29 November Marcus Whitman helped to bury three children of a Cayuse chief, all dead of measles. Later that day, the Indians attacked the mission. They killed Marcus and Narcissa, and seven other white people, and then took into captivity fifty-one women and children, including Jim Bridger's half-blood daughter, Mary Ann. In the hope that they could frighten all the white people into returning over the Great Medicine Road to the place from whence they had come, the Indians burned the mission buildings, tore down the fences, and uprooted the fruit trees that had been planted by the blonde goddess and the once powerful *te-wat*. This was the beginning of the Cayuse War which, instead of driving away the white men, virtually extinguished the Cayuse tribe.

6. Josiah Gregg and the Wandering Princess

Josiah Gregg

Traveling a few days behind Jedediah Smith on his ill-fated journey toward Santa Fe in the summer of 1831 was twenty-five-year-old Josiah Gregg. Young Gregg had been sickly all his life, and in that year while he was struggling to become a lawyer in the community around Independence, Missouri, his health broke completely. A physician diagnosed Gregg's ailment as 'consumption', and told him the only way he could recover would be to travel with a wagon train to Santa Fe; the salubrious air of the Plains would either cure or kill him.

Although Gregg was almost certain that he would die before reaching Santa Fe, he made arrangements to join a wagon train leaving Independence on 15 May 1831. Unable to mount a horse, he started out in a light carriage. Within a few days to his great surprise, Gregg was able to ride, to stand his turn at guard watch, and he also acquired an insatiable appetite for the coarse food of the wagoners. He began to take a keen interest in every detail of the wagon journey, and among other things learned that the recent wagon tracks they were following belonged to the train of Jedediah Smith. And then one day they met a Mexican buffalo hunter who told them the 'most melancholy news' of the death of a man traveling with the wagon train just ahead. 'From his description we presumed it to be Capt. Smith . . . he was pierced by the arrows of a gang of Comanches who were lying in wait for him!'

The journey to Santa Fe not only restored Gregg's health, it convinced him that in spite of the constant dangers and physical discomforts of heat and cold and thirst, a man could grow richer much faster in the Santa Fe trade than in practicing law on the Missouri frontier. Each year for the next eight years he took a wagon train of goods to Santa Fe. In 1843, at thirty-six, he retired to Van Buren, Arkansas, and to occupy his time began writing a book about his experiences. The book which he called *The Commerce of the Prairies* was published in two volumes in 1844. Gregg never expected any popular acceptance of his book; in fact, his contract with his New York publisher allowed him a considerable number of sets at cost for presentation to friends and relatives. He was not aware of the sudden upsurge of interest in the West, however, and was amazed

Samuel RIGHT and Susan Magoffin

when two other editions had to be published in rapid succession to supply the demand.

On 1 July 1846, at Little Cow Creek on the Santa Fe Trail, eighteen-year-old Susan Shelby Magoffin consulted one of her volumes of *The Commerce of the Prairies* and wrote in her diary: 'According to the calculation of Mr. Gregg, a gentleman who made several expeditions across the Prairies and who wrote a history of the trade &c, we are 249 miles from Independence.'

Because 1846 was the Year of Decision, Susan's honeymoon in New York City with her wealthy forty-five-year-old husband, Samuel Magoffin, had been interrupted. This pert and pretty black-haired teen-ager was already pregnant, but Samuel Magoffin could not bear to leave her in Independence. When his older brother James summoned him to join a secret mission to Santa Fe, Samuel outfitted for the use of his bride the most luxurious carriage ever seen in the West. It was cushioned with numerous pillows, and at Susan's hand were books, medicines, wines, and the feminine necessities of the times. The accompanying tent for use at night was carpeted and fitted with a dressing

Josiah Gregg and the Wandering Princess

BELOW An engraving of 'Camp Comanche' from Gregg's *Commerce of the Prairies* which Susan constantly consulted

table and folding chairs. She and Samuel slept between silk sheets and their wants were attended by a maid named Jane and two male Mexican servants.

James and Samuel Magoffin of Kentucky had been in the Santa Fe trade for several years, and had grown much wealthier than Josiah Gregg. They not only dominated the Santa Fe market but extended their business far down to Chihuahua and were so well liked in the Mexican circles which they frequented that they were known as Don Santiago and Don Manuel. James had married Maria Valdez, a cousin of Manuel Armijo who happened to be the governor of New Mexico at Santa Fe.

To Senator Thomas Hart Benton of Missouri and President James K. Polk, who were planning to add New Mexico and California to the United States, the Magoffin brothers had all the attributes of useful secret agents. By careful planning and the use of a popular slogan, 'Fifty-four Forty or Fight', Oregon had been won with the scratch of a pen. Perhaps with cajolery and bribery, New Mexico could be won as easily from within. Senator Benton took James Magoffin to Washington, and after a secret meeting with President Polk, James set out in that portentous summer of 1846 to overtake his brother Samuel on the Santa Fe Trail. Their mission was to enable General Stephen Kearny's Army of the West to capture Santa Fe without resorting to arms. Just how they were to accomplish this was probably never put into writing. Legend has it that James carried a satchel filled with gold coins, but no one has yet found documentary proof of this. Exactly what Samuel Magoffin's role was to be in the mission is not known, either. If Susan knew, she did not reveal it in her diary. She was too busy enjoying the journey. 'Oh, this is a life I would not exchange for a good deal! I breathe free without that oppression and uneasiness felt in the gossiping circles of a settled home . . . It is the life of a wandering princess, mine.'

Susan made most of her diary entries during the daily 'noonings' when the wagon train stopped to rest and water the animals. After lunch, she and Samuel—her pet name for him was *mi alma*—would recline on a buffalo skin in the shade of a wagon, sipping wine or 'a little *toddy* with water'. Her writing style was obviously influenced by Josiah Gregg's, even to tossing in a few Spanish words and phrases.

As for Gregg in that summer of 1846, he also had been recruited by President Polk and the planners of America's Manifest Destiny. 'I received communication from some of my friends in Washington City,' he wrote in July, 'requesting me if practicable, to join the division of our army destined for Chihuahua, or some other point in Northern Mexico . . . I am willing to undergo any privations and labor, which my physical powers can endure, where there is even a remote chance of serving my country.' Thus was Gregg swept up into the expansionist fever of the frontier. He attached himself to an

The trails of emigrants and soldiers increasingly trespassed on Indian lands. OPPOSITE A detail from *A Buffalo Hunt on the Southwestern Prairie* by John Mix Stanley

Arkansas cavalry regiment, and as he was starting across Texas to conquer Mexico, Susan Magoffin was camped in her luxurious tent near the Arkansas River. She was beginning to suffer homesickness, along with the first illnesses that often accompany pregnancy. The dark waters of the Arkansas reminded her of the Mississippi. 'It makes me sad to look upon it.–I am reminded of home.'

It did not occur to Susan that in leaving her home she had invaded the home of the Plains Indians. Neither she nor Josiah Gregg ever made note of the fact that the Santa Fe Trail crossed territory belonging to Indians. Even within the young lifetime of Susan Magoffin a 'permanent Indian frontier' had been established by act of Congress along the line of the 95th meridian, west of which no white persons were to be permitted to trade without a license or to claim land for settlement. All this had been forgotten in the mad hunger for territory, in the rush to fulfill the nation's destiny by expanding it by any means to the shores of the Western Sea. The Indians along the way were a constant annoyance, a danger to be avoided or eliminated.

At Pawnee Rock on the Fourth of July, Susan recorded that the high mound was named for the Pawnee Indians, a 'most treacherous and troublesome tribe'. She had never seen a Pawnee, and it never entered her head that the tribe had a reason to be disturbed over the constantly increasing procession of traders and soldiers passing through their hunting lands. She celebrated the holiday by climbing up to carve her name 'among the many hundreds on the rock and many of whom I know'.

That afternoon when the train resumed its westward passage, the driver of her carriage was careless in crossing a dry creek bed. Susan's carriage overturned, collapsing the top and sides. It was rough treatment for a pregnant woman. 'I was considerably stunned at first,' she said, 'and could not stand on my feet.' Her husband carried her to the shade of a tree and brought her back to consciousness by rubbing her face and hands with whisky. Although she complained of lingering pains in her back and sides, she was more concerned over what had happened to her books and bottles, baskets, bags, and boxes.

Next day at Pawnee Fork, the Magoffin train was overtaken by a government courier. They were to halt and await the arrival of General Kearny's troops for the final stage of the entry into Santa Fe. During the delay, Magoffin and some of his men organized a successful buffalo hunt and Susan was treated to hump ribs which she said were superior to any meat to be found in the best hotels of New York or Philadelphia.

On 8 July the first companies of Kearny's soldiers caught up with the train, bringing Samuel Magoffin orders to proceed to Bent's Fort. He was to wait there for the arrival of his brother

OPPOSITE A detail from *Crossing the Rocky Mountains* by George Douglas Brewerton

James and General Kearny who were several days behind on the trail.

At the start of the 180 remaining miles to Bent's Fort, Susan foolishly decided to ride horseback instead of in her broken carriage. After a few hours of this, the pregnant eighteen-year-old began to long for her 'younger days' when she did not mind being on the back of a jolting steed. The next morning she was quite ill and joined her maid Jane in a springless canvas-roofed Dearborn wagon.

Samuel was now evidently worried about Susan's condition, and became so eager to get her into Bent's Fort that he quarreled with his drivers when they refused to keep the wagons moving through a moonlit night. Next day was Sunday, and Susan forgave the men for disobeying her husband when they marked the holy day by substituting hymn singing for their usual blistering profanity.

On 17 July Susan was so ill that Samuel decided to send for a doctor who was traveling with a small train of Mexico-bound emigrants a few miles ahead. The doctor was Philip Masure, a Belgian with sandy hair and beard, a polite man of 'lively address and conversation' who assured the Magoffins that he was professionally capable in all branches of 'physic, surgery and midwifery'.

The doctor's presence seemed to reassure Susan, but a night or so later a thunderstorm struck the Magoffins' tent, flinging the center pole down upon her. Before Samuel could reach her, she was rainsoaked. He rolled her into blankets and stowed her away in the Dearborn wagon to dry out.

At last on 26 July they reached Bent's Fort, and William Bent hastened to clear a room for the ailing bride of his old friend, Samuel Magoffin. To Susan the fort's thick adobe walls and its single guarded entrance gave it the feeling and appearance of an ancient castle. The earthen floor of her room had to be sprinkled continually to keep down the dust, but there were opposite windows from which she could view either the Colorado plain or the busy interior patio.

Next morning she felt well enough to take a short walk along the bank of the Arkansas River and she could not help but contrast the wildness of the scene with her strolls from Spring to Wall Street while she and Samuel were honeymooning in New York City. She continued taking the medicines prescribed by Dr Masure who amused her with his admonishments to Samuel to remove his young wife from the rigors of the West and travel with her through Europe so that she might regain her health. (On this day Josiah Gregg and the Arkansas cavalrymen were preparing to ford Red River for their journey across Texas. At San Antonio they would join the Army of the Rio Grande for an invasion of Mexico that was meant to divert the attention of that nation from the imminent seizure of New Mexico and California.)

The presence of a pretty teen-aged white girl in Bent's Fort was such a novelty that practically every trader and military officer in the vicinity took the time to visit her and pay their respects by drinking a toast to her health and beauty.Thirtieth July was a special occasion, her nineteenth birthday, but Susan was too ill to celebrate. Instead she complained of noises from the fort's patio—mules braying, farriers shoeing horses, children crying, and men shouting.

Next day she suffered a miscarriage, and a week passed before she was able to write in her diary: 'In a few short months I should have been a happy mother and made the heart of a father glad, but the ruling hand of a mighty Providence has interposed and by an abortion deprived us of the hope, the fond hope of mortals!' While she lay semi-conscious, General Kearny and her brother-in-law James Magoffin arrived at Bent's Fort. James undoubtedly came to her room to reassure the worried Samuel, but both brothers were busily involved now in conferences to further the plot to capture Santa Fe.

That same day General Kearny addressed a proclamation to the citizens of New Mexico, informing them that he was entering their country 'with a great military force with the object of seeking union and to ameliorate the condition of its inhabitants; he does all this by instructions of his government by which he will be efficaciously sustained in order to carry into effect its views'. Kearny did not explain what the conditions of the inhabitants were that needed ameliorating, but went on to recommend that the New Mexicans remain tranquil, warning them if they took up arms to resist conquest they would be looked upon as enemies and treated accordingly.

On 1 August James Magoffin, accompanied by Captain Philip St George Cooke and a detachment of dragoons left Bent's Fort bound for Santa Fe. Magoffin probably was carrying the legendary satchel of gold coins; he certainly was carrying a copy of the proclamation and a letter from General Kearny addressed to Don Manuel Armijo, Governor and Commanding General of New Mexico—and Magoffin's relation by marriage.

Among other things the letter from Kearny informed Armijo that the Rio Grande from its delta to its source was now the boundary between the United States and Mexico. 'I am coming by order of my government to take possession of the country over a part of which you are presiding as governor. I come as a friend . . . I come with a strong military force, and a still stronger one is following me as a reinforcement . . . I advise you to submit to fate . . . if you should make up your mind to make resistance and oppose us, with such troops as you may be able to raise against us, in that event, I notify you that the blood which may be shed, the sufferings and miseries that may follow shall fall upon your head, and, instead of the blessings of your countrymen you will receive their curses.'

A few hours after James Magoffin and his escort left Bent's

Fort, General Kearny started the first units of his Army of the West marching down the same trail toward Santa Fe. For three days the daily departures of soldiers disturbed the sleep of Susan Magoffin—the blare of bugles, the rattle of swords, the jingle of spurs, the clanging of blacksmiths' hammers, the shouts of sergeants issuing commands. As she lay in her convalescent's bed she meditated upon the follies and wickedness of man who allowed himself to sink to the level of beasts 'waging war with his fellow man . . . striving for wealth, honour and fame to the ruining of his soul . . .'

(About that same time, far away in Massachusetts, Henry David Thoreau was returning to Walden Pond after spending a brief time in the Concord jail. Thoreau had been sentenced to jail for refusing to pay his poll tax—a gesture of protest against the Mexican War. 'When a whole country is unjustly overrun and conquered by a foreign army and subjected to military law,' he said, 'I think it is not too soon for honest men to rebel and revolutionize.' He was convinced that the war was the work of slaveholders bent upon expanding slave territory.)

On 7 August Samuel Magoffin received clearance to resume the movement of his wagon train toward Santa Fe. He transferred Susan from her bed in Bent's Fort to the cushions of her repaired carriage. Soon after crossing the Arkansas River, they were in Mexican territory. If brother James succeeded in his mission to Santa Fe, this land would become a part of the United States before the wagon train reached that city.

As the wagons rolled across the sagebrush plain toward Raton Pass, Susan saw her first mirage, and was pleased to find in Mr Gregg's *Commerce of the Prairies* an explanation for its occurrence. 'False ponds', Gregg called them, and went on to say they had deceived many travelers on the arid plains. He believed they were the result of the sun's reflection upon gases emanating from the sun-scorched earth. While Susan Magoffin was reading Gregg, the author himself was approaching San Antonio where an invasion column was gathering to join General Zachary Taylor on his march to Monterey.

By mid-August the Magoffin train was into the rocky passes north of Santa Fe. One morning during a delay, Dr Masure brought Susan two freshly killed jackrabbits. 'So we have lain here in the hot sun with the tent windows raised,' she wrote, 'and eating roast-hare and drinking wine.'

Meanwhile in the Governor's Palace at Santa Fe, James Magoffin and Captain Cooke were meeting secretly with Governor Armijo, a portly man with a taste for splendid costumes. For the meeting on 12 August, Armijo received his visitors in 'a blue frock coat with a rolling collar and a general's shoulder straps, blue striped trousers with gold lace, and a red sash'. What threats and promises were made at that meeting will probably never be known. A few days later Governor

Armijo with a small escort prepared to leave Santa Fe. As he was mounting his horse in front of the Governor's Palace, a small crowd of loyal Mexicans gathered to block his departure. From his coat pockets, the governor drew handfuls of coins which he tossed into the air, and while the crowd scrambled for the gold and silver, Armijo set spurs to his mount and galloped away on the south road for Chihuahua.

In Raton Pass north of Santa Fe about that same time, Samuel Magoffin received a message from his brother that negotiations were going smoothly. Samuel was to continue bringing forward the rich train; if anything should go wrong, he would receive sufficient warning to turn back for Bent's Fort. General Kearny's advance units were already camped near the ruins of Pecos pueblo, only a day's march from Santa Fe.

On 27 August a messenger brought to the wagon train the astounding news that the Army of the West was in possession of Santa Fe. Without firing a shot, General Kearny had marched into the plaza on 18 August and raised the flag of the United States. Samuel immediately urged his drivers to speed the progress of the train; if Susan had not been present, he would have mounted his fastest horse and raced into Santa Fe to join the celebration.

The train made its last camp at Pecos pueblo, the once prosperous Cicuye, where three centuries earlier the friendly mustachioed Bigotes had welcomed Coronado's gold-mad Spaniards, and had suffered at their hands because the Turk told them a fanciful story about a gold bracelet which never existed. When the Spaniards came there, Pecos was a thriving city of four-tiered structures, more than a thousand solidly built apartments containing several thousand people. Because they refused to accept the slavery imposed by succeeding waves of invading Spaniards, the Pecos Indians were reduced to 152 survivors when a count was made in 1790. Only eight years before Susan Magoffin came briefly to Pecos, the seventeen survivors of Bigotes' people abandoned their ruined town and crossed the mountains to Jemez, to be absorbed into that pueblo, to disappear as a people. With them they carried live coals from the sacred fire which their ancestors had promised to keep burning until the last of the white men were driven from the Pueblo country.

Susan had never heard of Bigotes or the great pueblo of Pecos, but she was sensitive enough to recognize that pride and power had once been there in that place of desolation where now stood as a kind of symbol only an abandoned church. 'We got off our horses at the door and went in, and I was truly awed.'

Next day in the excitement of entering Santa Fe, the somberness of Pecos was forgotten. Brother James had a house waiting for her—four rooms with plank ceilings and white-washed walls. James also had managed somehow to obtain a supply of oysters, and the Magoffins celebrated their reunion with oysters and

Santa Fe in 1846

champagne. When they entertained General Kearny, Susan delighted the commander by engaging in a running flirtation. She confided to her diary that although Kearny was small in stature, he was very agreeable in conversation and manners and could receive and return compliments with ease.

The Magoffin brothers evidently had received Kearny's support in a plan to proceed south to Chihuahua to see if another coup could be accomplished as easily as the one in Santa Fe. If more territory was there for the taking, why not take it? Just thinking of Manifest Destiny made James livelier than ever; he cracked jokes and spun yarns and drank champagne with more than his usual gusto. On 1 September Susan recorded that James was going south to prepare for General Kearny's coming, but she was not fully informed. Kearny's destination was California, where a zealous American major,

John C. Frémont, was attempting his own private conquest. In Chihuahua, James was to prepare the way for Zachary Taylor's Army of the Rio Grande.

With all this enthusiasm for conquest bubbling around her, Susan somehow managed to keep her head and was probably the only American in Santa Fe who had any misgivings about her warlike male compatriots. Kearny's officers all seemed eager for a fight even if they had to provoke one.

In October the Magoffin train was ready to roll for Chihuahua. Samuel once again packed Susan into a carriage to resume the life of a wandering princess. Marching ahead of them was Colonel Alexander Doniphan's slow-moving column of Missouri cavalrymen. Not until the last week of December did the troops drive the Mexicans from El Paso in what one of the officers described as a 'Christmas frolic'. The Year of Decision, 1846, ended before the Magoffins could leave El Paso for Chihuahua. Ugly rumors were coming back from there that brother James had been arrested and was on trial for his life, and Samuel did not dare risk a journey deeper into Mexico.

Late in the winter they heard that James had been executed as a spy, and that the armies of the United States had suffered terrible defeats. Neither rumor was true. Brother James possessed the money and the charm to talk his way out of any scrape, although when Colonel Doniphan's Missourians neared Chihuahua, the Mexican authorities hastily whisked him away to Durango. Perhaps they feared the wealthy American might buy Chihuahua as he had bought Santa Fe. As for the armies of the United States, they were marching victorious across northern Mexico, taking one town after the other. Chihuahua fell early in March.

With James held in Durango–during his confinement he purchased 2900 bottles of champagne which he shared with his jailers–Samuel had to manage the entire Magoffin enterprise. On 14 March Susan, although pregnant again, bravely joined his train as it began jolting southward from El Paso over the rough road to Chihuahua. During the next few months, the wandering princess saw most of the captured cities of northern Mexico–Chihuahua, Saltillo, Monterey, Cerralvo, Matamoros.

She also saw the swaggering leaders of her country's military forces, the volunteer officers more drunk on power than the West Pointers. A few men in the ranks were dying from fevers and dysentery, but hardly anyone ever got shot. War was a glorious experience, especially for the officers. For another decade they would revel in memories of exotic Mexico and when a chance came in 1861 to bring back the flags and bands and cheering crowds, the booming guns and power of command, they could hardly wait to get started again even though it meant fighting each other.

Old Zachary Taylor played his role of Rough and Ready to the hilt, exchanging his resplendent uniform for a faded gray sack coat, a blue bandanna, striped cotton pants, and a broad-brimmed Mexican sombrero. On one occasion the general—who as a reward for conquest was soon to become President of the United States—learned that young Mrs Magoffin was to be present for a cake and champagne reception. He hastily donned his regulation uniform, but the observant Susan noted wrinkles in his blouse and trousers and guessed that he had not unpacked them since leaving the United States.

As in all wars, the enlisted men occasionally attempted to dispose violently of officers they considered more of a menace to them than to the enemy. A prime target was Major Braxton Bragg. According to Susan, some of Bragg's men placed a slow-fused shell in his tent and blew up his trunk and cot, but the major escaped alive. The men tried once again later, but Bragg was destined to survive to become one of the most incompetent generals on the Confederate side of the Civil War—a fact which offers some proof that enlisted men can be excellent judges of poor leadership.

It was on the road to Saltillo that Susan in her second pregnancy suffered the most uncomfortable and perilous journey of her short life. For three weeks a Magoffin train of thirty wagons bounced over rocks and ditches, through heat and suffocating dust, sometimes halting only an hour or so before resuming travel for the night. Susan could get little sleep, and she lost her zest for recording events in her journal, abandoning it entirely for almost three months.

On 11 May Private John T. Hughes of the First Missouri Mounted Volunteers, marching ahead of the Magoffin wagon train, noted in his diary: 'Report of McGoffin being attacked by a Banditti.' Susan, Samuel, and the wagons were rescued, however, by Lieutenant George Gordon and a detachment of sixty horsemen who galloped to the scene of ambush. Susan made no record of this exciting event.

Nor did she mention Josiah Gregg, who was traveling with this same column of Missourians, although she surely must have met her favourite author. Less than a week after the narrow excape from banditti, Samuel offered Gregg a partnership in the Magoffin import business. At Saltillo on 23 May the offer was repeated. 'Today,' Gregg wrote, 'Saml. Magoffin renewed an offer of co-partnership (mercantile—he to furnish the means). After due reflection . . . I concluded to embrace his offer, and leave for the U.S. . . . and buy perhaps near $40,000 worth of merchandise.'

Susan recorded neither of these important incidents, a sure indication that she was ailing, or as she would have phrased it 'burdened with trials and woes'. Early in August, before Samuel took her to Matamoros to await the birth of her child, she wrote: 'I do think a pregnant woman has a hard time of it, some sickness all the time, heart-burn, head-ache, cramp, etc. after all this thing of marrying is not what it is cracked up to be.' She was on the edge of revolt, but she never quite took the final step. Her son, born at Matamoros while she was suffering from yellow fever, lived only a brief time. For eight more years she followed Samuel in his restless search for riches and power in Western America. After producing for him two daughters, she died in St Louis, worn out at the age of twenty-eight.

As for the author she so highly esteemed, Josiah Gregg, he also was doomed by the Western mirage of quick wealth. After returning to the United States to buy goods for his new partnership, he received a message from Samuel Magoffin advising him to curtail his purchases. Conditions in Mexico were chaotic, and apparently the United States government had no intention of annexing territory below the Rio Grande.

Bitterly disappointed, Gregg decided to go to Washington and see President Polk. He hoped to persuade Polk that northern Mexico should be made United States territory; at least he could ask Polk to give him an official appointment in Mexico to work toward that end. On 31 July 1847 Gregg wrote in his journal: 'I was so astonished at the evident weakness of Mr. Polk, that I then felt I would not accept anything at his hands–and departed accordingly. It is remarkable that a man so short of intellect should have been placed in the executive chair!'

Gregg made his way back to Mexico where he set up a profitable practice of medicine in Saltillo. (He had studied medicine a few months in Louisville, Kentucky, after his first retirement from the Santa Fe trade.) 'I have long been of opinion that the Anglo-Saxon race is destined to govern the entire American continent, at no very distant period.' But while Gregg waited for Manifest Destiny to come to him in Mexico, a significant event occurred in California. Another former Santa Fe trader, a ne'er-do-well Swiss who was always in debt, had journeyed there from New Mexico and secured a grant of fifty thousand acres of California land from the Mexican government. On 24 January 1848 gold was found in his millrace on the American River. The former Santa Fe trader's name was John Sutter. On 30 August 1849 Josiah Gregg arrived in San Francisco to join the Gold Rush.

7. The Road to El Dorado

Present at the moment of discovery of gold in California was Henry W. Bigler, a member of that battalion of Mormons met by Francis Parkman in September 1846 on their march to Santa Fe. 'The Mormons were to be paid off in California, and they were allowed to bring with them their families and property', Parkman noted. He went on to surmise that these 'religious fanatics' would probably found a Mormon empire in California.

The Mormons planned no empire in California; the place of refuge they had chosen was somewhere in the Great Salt Lake Basin. After the assassination of their founder Joseph Smith in 1844, they had been driven from Illinois and scattered from Missouri across Iowa and into Nebraska. As most of their land, houses, and other property had been confiscated or destroyed, they were without resources to emigrate beyond the Rockies. The recruitment of the Mormon Battalion, therefore, was mutually advantageous to the United States government which needed military manpower for its conquest of California, and to the Mormons who needed passage to the West and money which was to be paid the members of the battalion.

After reaching Santa Fe in October 1846, the Mormon Battalion marched on to California with General Kearny. For several months they performed garrison duty at San Diego and Los Angeles. At the latter village of some three thousand inhabitants, the Mexicans were extremely fearful of the battalion because they had been told that Mormons were cannibals, especially fond of eating children. In July 1847, after Kearny praised the battalion for helping make California a part of the United States, the men were released from military service. By this time, advance units of Mormon emigrants had arrived in the valley near Great Salt Lake and were already planting potatoes. 'This is the place where I, in vision, saw the ark of the Lord resting', declared the church's leader, Brigham Young. As soon as members of the Mormon Battalion learned of this, they began organizing parties to turn back east across the Sierras to join their people in the Promised Land. The Mormon leaders at Salt Lake, however, sent messengers to California advising the battalion members to remain where they were. The Salt Lake colony did not have sufficient food supplies to carry additional members through the winter. 'Remain in California and labor during the winter, and make your way to Salt Lake Valley in the spring, bringing your earnings with you.'

One party of nine, including Henry Bigler and Ira Willis, found employment with John Sutter, that former competitor of Josiah Gregg in the Santa Fe trade. A bankrupt emigrant from Switzerland, Sutter had entered the trade in 1835 by obtaining a wagonload of old pistols, cheap trinkets, and second-hand clothing on credit from St Louis pawnshops. Joining a train to Santa Fe, he turned his wagonload of junk into a profit. By 1838 Sutter had enough money to go to California where he hoped to obtain a land grant from the Mexican government. He arrived there just in time to find the failing Russian colony at Fort Ross preparing to sell out and depart California by order of the Czar. After securing a large land grant at the junction of the Sacramento and American rivers, Sutter made a credit deal with the Russians for their 1700 cattle, 940 horses and mules, 9000 sheep, numerous agricultural implements, and an arsenal of French weapons which the Russians had collected a quarter of a century earlier in the wake of Napoleon's army during its disastrous retreat through the snow from Moscow.

Sutter moved everything to his land grant, which he called New Helvetia. He built a fort with twenty-four of Napoleon's guns mounted on the ramparts, and began construction of a ranch house, workshops, and mills. By the time that Henry Bigler, Ira Willis, and the other discharged members of the Mormon Battalion came there to work for him, Sutter was

Sutter's Fort on the Sacramento

ruling his domain like a benevolent feudal lord. Scores of white men worked in his fields and tended his herds, and several hundred Indians considered themselves to be his subjects.

Upon employing the Mormons, Sutter assigned them to James W. Marshall who was building a sawmill on the south fork of American River about fifty miles northeast of the fort. On 24 January 1848, Henry Bigler—a very poor speller—noted in his diary: 'This day some kind of mettle was found in the tail race that looks like goald, first discovered by James Martial, the Boss of the Mill.' Marshall took the bright metal particles down to the fort and showed them to Sutter. Neither man knew how to test for gold, but Sutter owned an encyclopedia and in it they found instructions which they followed until they were assured that what Marshall had found was indeed gold.

For several days, Marshall, Sutter, and the few Mormons at the mill kept the gold find a secret. Sutter, who was far-sighted enough to realize that a gold rush might destroy his peaceable kingdom, begged his employees not to reveal the discovery to anyone else. Because the men were uncertain as to whether they could gain more at gold prospecting than from the wages which Sutter was paying them, they continued working at the sawmill. On Sundays, however, Henry Bigler began slipping away on the pretext of hunting for game. In February he found a seam of gold in a rock outcropping and in one afternoon took out more gold than Sutter paid him in a week. The other Mormons joined him on his weekend excursions, and Bigler passed the news up to Sutter's grist mill where his friend Ira Willis and two other former battalion comrades were working. When the sawmill was completed on 11 March all the Mormons began prospecting for gold. In that month a madness swept through New Helvetia, and John Sutter found himself abandoned in his fort as his workers joined the gold rush, leaving 'only the sick and lame behind'.

Rumors of gold reached the small town of San Francisco, and in April a newspaper editor journeyed up to Sutter's Fort to investigate. He reported that he was not able to find enough gold to buy a drink. In May a Mormon elder named Samuel Brannan visited the sawmill on American River. Brannan had traveled by ship around Cape Horn to determine whether or not California might offer a better place to found a Mormon colony than the Great Salt Lake Basin. While awaiting reports from Salt Lake, Brannan established himself in San Francisco. When he went up to Sutter's sawmill, his fellow Mormons there evidently let him in on the secret that they were finding gold in quantity. Brannan returned to San Francisco on 8 May with a bottle of gold dust, and convinced everyone that fortunes could be dug out of the American River.

Prospector's Departure by J. J. Ray. In many towns afflicted by gold fever those who left far outnumbered those who stayed.

From that day the gold rush truly began, first as a trickle of curious searchers, gradually increasing to a stream of wealth seekers until it finally became a flood of greedy gold hunters, the greatest mass movement of human beings from every corner of the earth since the Crusades to the Holy Land. The news traveled slowly at first, mainly by word of mouth, the telling and re-telling increasing the magnitude of gold discoveries. Three weeks passed before the word reached Monterey, only a hundred miles down the coast from San Francisco. 'Our town was startled out of its quiet dreams today, by the announcement that gold had been discovered on the American Fork', wrote the Reverend Walter Colton, Monterey's alcalde, on 29 May. 'The men wondered and talked, and the women too; but neither believed.' The rumors became so persistent, however, that on 6 June Reverend Colton dispatched a trusted messenger to the American Fork. Two weeks later the messenger returned with several specimens of gold; there was no longer any doubt in Monterey of the great discovery.

'The excitement produced was intense,' Colton said, 'and many were soon busy in their preparations for a departure to the mines. The family who had kept house for me caught the moving infection. Husband and wife were both packing up; the

blacksmith dropped his hammer, the carpenter his plane, the mason his trowel, the farmer his sickle, and the baker his loaf, and the tapster his bottle. All were off for the mines, some on horses, some on carts, and some on crutches, and one went in a litter. An American woman, who had recently established a boarding house here, pulled up stakes, and was off before her lodgers had even time to pay their bills. Debtors ran, of course. I have only a community of women left, and a gang of prisoners, with here and there a soldier, who will give his captain the slip at the first chance.'

Colton was quite right about the soldiers. Within a few months after the gold rush started, forty per cent of the enlisted men stationed in California deserted to dig gold, and on many occasions details of soldiers sent in pursuit of deserters also deserted. A young lieutenant stationed at Monterey commented that practically everybody had 'gone to work for the filthy stuff, none remain behind but we poor damned officers. All have their pockets full of gold . . . save those in the employ of the government – we are the sufferers.' The lieutenant's name was William Tecumseh Sherman.

Almost every town in northern California was emptied of its inhabitants, who in a few weeks founded new shanty towns of canvas along the Sacramento and its tributaries. By midsummer of 1848, two-thirds of the houses in San Francisco stood empty,

Sutter's Fort expanded into the city of Sacramento in less than ten years.

al frame house erected Jany 1st 1849 by S. Brannan   Lith & Publd by Britton & Rey. S Francisco   Present population estimated at 20,000 June 1st 1850

SACRAMENTO CITY.

and all hotels and stores were closed. Sutter's Fort meanwhile had become Sacramento City, and John Sutter was driven half-mad by an invading army of ten thousand trappers, soldiers, sailors, farmers, lawyers, clerks, carpenters, and schoolteachers turned gold seekers. He retreated to Feather River, leaving his feudal empire in dissolution.

By that time the news was beginning to reach the Eastern United States, but most newspapers there were skeptical. Even before the rumors of gold, the West had become a mythical place, everything too wondrous to be believed. On 29 August, Reverend Colton sent a letter from Monterey to a friend in Washington, D.C., but it was three months getting there. A Washington newspaper printed it on 11 December 1848: 'At present the people are running over the country and picking gold out of the earth here and there, just as a thousand hogs let loose in a forest would root up the ground-nuts.'

During that same month specimens of California gold were received by the Secretary of War in Washington, with a report of men finding fifty dollars a day with a pick, shovel, and pan. In his annual message to Congress, President Polk transformed the fabulous gold-strike stories from rumor to fact, and the East was stirred into mass excitement. Before the December holidays ended, hundreds of eager gold seekers bought passage on ships bound around Cape Horn for San Francisco. Newspaper

Before overland travel became tolerably quick, the best way from the East to the West coast was by ship round the Horn.

accounts switched rapidly from skepticism to exaggeration: *California gold is inexhaustible. A man willing to work can dig out a thousand dollars of bright yellow metal in a single day, and there is room in that vast area for a hundred thousand miners.*

Eighty thousand went to California in that first gold rush summer of 1849, the majority traveling overland, most choosing the Oregon Trail route. At every jump-off town along the Missouri River and the 95th meridian—that forgotten line once chosen as a protective barrier for the Indian people—the successors to Francisco Coronado assembled their wagon trains. At Council Bluffs, St Joseph, Fort Leavenworth, Independence, and Fort Smith, traders in oxen, mules, and wagons made greater fortunes than most of the fortune hunters would ever find—the Fools of Forty-Nine, the folk ballad called them, bound for Californ-i-o.

That first wave of gold seekers was a masculine migration. Of the eighty thousand, less than five thousand were women and children. Among the few women making the overland journey was Sarah Royce. With her husband Josiah and two-year-old daughter Mary, she crossed the Missouri at Council Bluffs, Iowa, on 8 June 1849 in search of El Dorado, the land of gold. Here, less than half a century earlier, Lewis and Clark had held their first council with Plains Indians. Here, less than a dozen years in the future, at the landing point on the western bank where the Royces saw nothing but a log house and a blacksmith shop, construction would begin on the first trans-continental railroad. Around the busy railroad shops which were to make wagon travel obsolete would rise the city of Omaha.

Sarah Royce's home for five months was a rolling covered wagon drawn by three yoke of oxen. For the first month, in company with several other wagons, the Royces followed the Platte River route, much of it so well described by Francis Parkman. Beyond Fort Laramie, however, Parkman's new book was of no help as a guide. Sarah Royce had a copy of Captain John C. Frémont's report on his explorations, and on 21 July she noted that they had reached Sweetwater River 'so named by Frémont and his men, on account of its water being so much better than any they had tasted for several days before'. On 4 August they reached South Pass—Jed Smith's door through the Rocky Mountains—and at the point where Frémont described the continental divide, 'the culminating point', as being between two low hills Sarah left her wagon and per-formed a silent ceremony of farewell to the East. No longer would the streams flow eastward to the shores of her childhood, and she wondered if she would ever again return.

A week later they were at Jim Bridger's fort, where the former fur trapper now maintained a fully equipped black-smith shop for repair of emigrants' wagons. Here the Royces must decide which route to follow to California. They could turn north to Fort Hall and then go west again around the upper end of Great Salt Lake, or they could continue straight west toward Salt Lake City and skirt the lower end of the lake. The Fort Hall route was easier to travel, but was considerably longer. Both routes ultimately followed the dreaded Humboldt Valley with its alkaline waters and forbidding deserts. As the season was growing late, the Royce party decided to take the shorter route by way of the Mormons' City of the Saints.

In 1849 the trail between Bridger's Fort and Salt Lake City was so poorly marked that the U.S. Corps of Topographical Engineers ordered Captain Howard Stansbury into the area to locate a route specifically for use of California-bound emigrants. Stansbury and his surveying party of eighteen men reached Bridger's Fort two days before the Royces, and he was there when they arrived.

During his journey from Fort Laramie to Bridger's Fort, Captain Stansbury was appalled by the disorganized condition of the emigrants that he was following. He passed numerous graves of cholera victims, and at one ferry crossing was told that twenty-eight travelers had drowned there. The road was strewn with articles that had been discarded. Broken wagons and dead oxen lay along both sides of the trail. 'Immense quantities of white beans which seemed to have been thrown away by the sackful, their owners having become tired of carrying them farther, or afraid to consume them from danger of cholera. The commanding officer at Fort Kearney had forbidden their issue at that point on this account. Stoves, gridirons, moulding planes and carpenters' tools of all sorts, were to be had at every step for the mere trouble of picking them up.' Bar-iron and steel, blacksmiths' anvils and bellows, crowbars, drills, augers, gold-washers, chisels, axes, lead, trunks, spades, ploughs, grindstones, baking-ovens, kegs, barrels, harness, clothing, boxes, bonnets, and bacon littered the route of Stansbury's surveyors. All the debris of nineteenth-century man began to clutter the Garden of the West; in three generations it would become an avalanche of discarded wastes fouling highways, rivers, and deserts.

Bridger's Fort, said Stansbury, was 'built in the usual form, of pickets, with the lodging apartments and offices opening into a hollow square protected from attack from without by a strong gate of timber'. While the captain waited for his wagons to be repaired, the Royces, disdaining any need for a military escort, departed for Salt Lake City. The going was rough through the Wasatch range, but like many thousands of others who took this route they were overwhelmed by their first view of Great Salt Lake Valley through the remarkably pure and transparent atmosphere of that time. 'We paused to take breath,' Sarah later recalled, 'and faced each other with mutual looks of wonder, we agreed that we did not know each other; and it was not until after free use of the pure valley waters, aided in some instances by the hot mineral springs, that we recovered our identity.'

Salt Lake City had already become a second staging area for California-bound travelers. Here they traded for better oxen and horses, refitted their wagons, and reorganized trains for what they had been told would be the most grueling experience of the long journey. Most of the emigrants in the Royce party decided to join their wagons to a group organizing to follow a southern route–the trail Jed Smith had used around the lower end of the Sierras to avoid early snows. The Royces boldly decided to strike out across the salt desert, straight toward the west. Captain Frémont's map, however, was of no further use to them. Between the blue markings of Great Salt Lake and John Sutter's New Helvetia, the captain had left a vast blank space which he labeled 'The Great Basin, surrounded by lofty mountains, but believed to be filled with rivers and lakes which have no communication with the sea, deserts and oases which have never been explored, and savage tribes which no traveler has seen or described.'

In Salt Lake City the Royces happened to meet a former member of the Mormon Battalion–none other than Ira Willis, one of the nine men who had been working for John Sutter at the time of the gold discovery which had brought the Royces to the West. After rejoining his people at Salt Lake City, Willis discovered a keen demand from passing travelers for a guide to the gold mines which he had left behind. He decided to supply the demand, and titled it *Best Guide to the Gold Mines, 816 Miles* by Ira J. Willis, Great Salt Lake City. 'The little pamphlet was wholly in writing,' Sarah Royce said, 'there being at that time no printing press in Salt Lake.'

J. Goldsborough Bruff, captain of another train traveling behind the Royces, reported meeting Willis outside Salt Lake City on 29 August. Upon seeking information about routes to California, Willis 'took out of his pocket a sort of Guide book, formed of a sheet of paper folded small, miserably written, and worse spelling, which he said was the last he had, & I might take it for 50 ¢, but that he had sold a number to emigrants for $1 each. I purchased it more for a curiosity than any idea of its serving me en route.'

Armed only with this fragile guide, Sarah and Josiah Royce, their infant daughter Mary, and one unnamed elderly man, set out from Salt Lake City on 30 August, determined to cross Frémont's Great Basin in their single wagon. They had been unable to persuade any other wagon to join them, and the man who volunteered to accompany them owned only one ox, which they added to the team. A few days later they overtook two young men who were attempting to make the crossing on a horse and a mule. The new recruits offered to spend their time hunting for game in exchange for some of the Royces' flour. It was a poor arrangement, game being virtually non-existent on the alkali flats.

One day when the hunters were absent, a band of armed Indians blocked the wagon, and apparently wanted payment of some kind for the privilege of crossing their country. After about an hour, Josiah grew impatient over the endless palavering. He raised his whip and rushed the oxen into motion. The astonished Indians did not bother to pursue. Perhaps they realized the Royces had practically nothing to give them.

Two days later they met several Mormons returning to Salt Lake City after digging gold during the summer. At the Royces' request one of them traced out in the sand a map of the route from the Sink of the Humboldt to Carson River, told them where to watch for turns in wagon tracks, and where water holes could be found.

Neither Ira Willis' handwritten guide nor the Mormons' sand-drawn map kept them from getting lost in that Western wasteland where capricious winds can suddenly cover tracks and water holes. Traveling by night to avoid the heat of the sun, the Royce party evidently missed every guide point, and during the first days of October they floundered helplessly on the desert, with only three quarts of water to share among five adults and a child. Yet somehow they found their bearings and survived to reach the trees and cool waters of Carson River.

Reuben Shaw who was traveling with a train a few days ahead of the Royces described the approach to the river:

> On the last twenty miles of our march we passed the skeletons of many animals which had perished before they could reach the water. Oxen died with their yokes still on them, while horses and mules lay dead in their harness, and property of all kinds, even bedding, was scattered along the road. Wagons, from which their canvas tops had not been removed, were shrinking in the hot sun, with the tires ready to fall from the wheels. Oxen, after making a desperate fight for their lives, perished within a mile of the river, while everything along the road gave evidence of there having been terrible suffering by both man and beast.

When the Royces reached the river, the first snows of autumn were swirling on the high Sierras which lay between them and California's El Dorado. The only food they had left was small amounts of mouldy bacon and parched corn meal. Just as they were about to abandon their wagon for the mountain crossing, two men who had been sent from Sacramento City to rescue late travelers met and guided them over the Sierras. And so late in October of 1849, Sarah Royce brought her two-year-old daughter by muleback over steep ridges, past drifts of snow, and down deep canyons to the sunlit valley of the Sacramento. In the handwritten guidebook which Sarah still carried, she found that Ira Willis had labeled the place 'Pleasant Valley Gold Mines'. The few miners who still remained there in tattered tents reported the 'diggings pretty much worked out'.

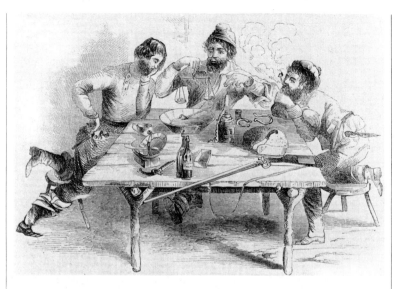

The amount of gold extracted was absurdly small compared to the effort exerted and hardships endured to find it.

But somewhere over the horizon—*mas alla* as Coronado's men had cried again and again—surely there was gold to be found, great quantities of gold.

A few did strike it rich, but if one adds up the wealth in dollars taken out of California earth during the years of the Great Rush and divides by the number of men who sweated to find it, the individual enrichment comes to about one dollar a day, 365 dollars a year if a man worked on Sundays. Back East that might have been a tolerable income for those times, but in California's El Dorado, as Sarah Royce discovered, baked potatoes cost seventy-five cents apiece, single onions one dollar.

One of the searchers, a man whose name is now forgotten, slaved for three years to dig out a quarter of a million in gold. He worked such long hours that he could scarcely find the time to scratch a note to the Pennsylvania sweetheart for whom he was toiling, a maiden who had promised to wait for his return. On his part, the man had sworn to bring her a fortune, and he did, but in the meantime she had grown impatient of his return and married another suitor.

Disillusioned, the rich man drifted down to Alabama and put his fortune into black slaves and cotton land, which made him even richer. He married a Southern Belle, and when the Alabama land was exhausted he took his wife west to the Red River Valley of Texas and established a plantation on virgin soil. It was as large as John Sutter's New Helvetia.

When the Civil War came, this former Pennsylvanian who had founded his fortune on California gold was rich in greenbacks and bank credit. As demand for his cotton increased, he grew even wealthier, but because he was a Yankee and refused to take his wife's side in the war, preferring to remain a fortune-

The tangle of deserted ships in San Francisco harbor

building neutral, she left him and returned to Alabama. At the war's end, Federal troops freed his slaves and drove him off his plantation because he had supported the Confederacy with his cotton. The man still possessed hundreds of thousands of dollars, his original fortune having changed in a decade from gold to U.S. greenbacks, and then to Confederate notes. He left this worthless paper money in Texas and returned to Pennsylvania where he died a pauper.

Josiah Gregg, who had dreamed of becoming a merchant prince in Mexico, grew impatient of waiting for Manifest Destiny to come to him in Saltillo. Learning of the gold strike, he made his way to Mazatlan and took a steamship up to San Francisco, determined to replenish his fading fortune. When he arrived there on 30 August 1849 he found the harbor filled with an 'immense forest of masts'. The crews of most of the vessels had abandoned ship and rushed off to the gold mines.

Gregg remained in San Francisco several days, recovering from a minor surgical operation and picking up as much information as he could about locations of recent gold discoveries. Rumors were coming in of a rich strike on Trinity River, more than three hundred miles to the north. In the early autumn, Gregg went up to Rich Bar on the Trinity in company with several other venturesome gold hunters. They soon found that the best gold veins had already been claimed; they also found that the weather in this part of California was quite different from that of the lower Sacramento Valley. Rains fell almost every day, changing to snow as winter approached. From Indians in the vicinity of Rich Bar, Gregg learned that the Pacific Ocean lay only about eight days' travel to the west.

As there were insufficient stores of food in camp to supply Rich Bar through the winter, Gregg organized an expedition to travel to the coast and then proceed southward back to San Francisco. Eight men including Gregg formed the party which left Rich Bar on 5 November. A week later, after an arduous journey through continuous rain, over rugged mountains and deep canyons, their food was exhausted. When they entered the redwood forests, their progress was slowed to seven miles a day, and they existed on what game they could find–eagles, ravens, fish. On 7 December they reached a body of water which they named Trinidad Bay, and Gregg carved upon a tree the latitude, the date, readings from his barometer and thermometer, and his name. As they struggled southward along the eastern edge of Humboldt Bay, Gregg's strength began to fail. On Christmas Day a member of the party found a dead elk in the brush and they roasted its head in the ashes of their campfire for a holiday feast. Early in January 1850 the group split in half. Because they were making such slow progress along the rugged coastline, Gregg and his three companions turned inland, hoping to reach a mining camp in the Sacramento Valley. For several days they could find no food except acorns and roots. Late in February, somewhere near Clear Lake, Gregg became too weak to stay in his saddle. 'He fell from his horse,' a member of the party reported afterward, 'and died without speaking–died of starvation.' His three companions dug a hole with sticks and buried Josiah Gregg, his scientific instruments, and his journals beneath a pile of rocks. The others survived to tell the tale.

James Marshall, who discovered the yellow metal that lured fortune hunters from all over the world, watched helplessly while these invaders overran his 640-acre land claim. They stole his horses, his saddles, and his mining tools. When he tried to drive them away by force, the encroachers hired armed guards to keep him off his own property while they took out what gold they could find there, and then they sold part of his land for town lots at bonanza prices. Marshall sought reparations through the courts, but the trespassers sat as judge and jury and even his attorney became a hireling of his enemies. Eventually he lost his half interest in the sawmill he had built for John Sutter. Although everyone believed him to be richer in gold than any other man in California, he was finally reduced to the clothes on his back and twenty pounds of China rice for food.

When Marshall crossed the mountains in a try for another

gold strike, crowds of miners followed him. Because he had found the first gold, they believed he possessed powers of divination which would lead them to a new fountainhead of riches. Wherever Marshall stopped to dig, he was surrounded by eager claim hunters, and one group of men grown as ruthless as Coronado's Spaniards threatened to hang him if he did not find a rich lode for them.

For seven years Marshall eked out an existence by panning for gold; then he gave up and returned to Coloma–the town that had grown up around his lost mill. There he kept himself alive by digging gardens, sawing wood, or doing any odd job which the good citizens would offer him. He scraped together a few dollars and bought a small piece of the land that had been taken away from him ten years earlier. On this land he began growing grapes, and built a small winery to demonstrate that the Sacramento Valley was equal to any wine-producing area in the world. The California law-makers, however, put such a high tax on Marshall's wine that he was driven into bankruptcy. Once again he took up his pick and his pan and went out prospecting, but his luck turned no better.

In 1871 at the age of sixty-one Marshall was persuaded to go on a lecture tour. He was an awkward speaker, but enough curious people paid admission fees to guarantee his travel expenses. In Salt Lake City he was taken to meet the great Brigham Young, but when Marshall was introduced as the man who discovered California gold, Young declared him to be a liar. It was in the records of the Church of Jesus Christ of Latter-day Saints that members of the Mormon Battalion had found that gold.

When Marshall returned to California his brief period of fame evidently induced the legislature to appropriate money for a small pension to be paid him for his contribution to the greatness of the Golden State. Two years later the law-makers discontinued the pension on the ground that Marshall spent too much of it on alcoholic liquors.

For another decade, however, Marshall managed to survive by working as a carpenter and carving objects out of wood, selling them for whatever he could get. When he died in August 1885, his body had to be packed in ice to preserve it while a long debate ensued between the Society of California Pioneers and the Native Sons of the Golden West over a proper burial place. The instant that James Marshall died he had become a great and important person. They finally decided to bury him on a hill overlooking the place where he had discovered gold. Not long afterward, the Californians who had been unwilling to sustain James Marshall in life spent thousands of dollars for a glorious monument and appropriated a monthly stipend for a caretaker to clean bird droppings from the metal figure of the dead man, to raise and lower each day a United States flag on a staff, and keep the surroundings neat for tourists.

John Augustus Sutter, former Santa Fe trader, founder of New Helvetia, builder of Sutter's Fort, wanted only to cultivate his land and increase his livestock herds. When he sent James Marshall up the American River to build a sawmill, Sutter was enjoying the best days of his life. And then the gold-hunters came in a swarm across New Helvetia, slaughtering his prized cattle and sheep for food, stealing even the cannon off his fort. When he appealed to the courts for restoration of his land, the title was declared invalid because it was a Mexican grant. Three years after gold was discovered, Sutter was bankrupt, and for a while lived almost as penuriously as Marshall.

Eventually the California legislature appropriated $250 per month as a suitable pension to Sutter for his part in the discovery of gold and as partial compensation for the loss of his vast tract of land. The money enabled him to go to Washington where he spent his days lobbying for federal reparation. He first asked for $125,000, and year by year, as Congress failed to act he gradually reduced the amount, hoping for whatever they might give him for the empire that had been swindled away from him. In 1880, John Sutter died, ignored and forgotten, in a cheap hotel in Washington, D.C. It was too much trouble and expense for the Pioneers and Native Sons to pack his body all the way back to the West. He ended up in a little Moravian cemetery at Lititz, Pennsylvania. After the name of Sutter became important in history, the Californians rebuilt his vandalized fort so that tourists might see it when they came to Sacramento.

Henry Bigler, Ira Willis, and other members of the Mormon Battalion carefully hoarded the gold they dug from the American River. In the year when it seemed that everyone else in the world was hurrying westward to California, the battalion members turned eastward to Salt Lake City. When they reached there, in obedience to the laws of their church they gave one-tenth or more of their gold to the Church of Jesus Christ of Latter-day Saints. Most of them prospered in the new State of Deseret, so named for the Land of the Honeybee in *The Book of Mormon*.

Without the gold brought from California, Deseret might well have collapsed in its first months of existence for lack of funds to obtain necessities for development of the colony. With gold in hand, the church's Council of Fifty felt emboldened to claim for Deseret boundaries extending to Oregon on the north, the Rocky Mountains on the east, Mexico on the south, the Sierra Nevadas and that part of the Pacific Ocean coastline which contained the town of Los Angeles and the port of San Diego on the west. Ruler of that enormous empire was the President of the Twelve Apostles, Trustee in Trust for the Church, Governor of the Kingdom of God, husband of seventy wives–the Lion of the Lord, Brigham Young.

RIGHT A watercolor by Thomas Moran of South Dome in California's Yosemite

OVERLEAF The Forty Niners: *Mountain Jack and the Wandering Miner* by E. Hall Martin

8. An Angel of Light, A Goblin Damned

Brigham Young's roots were in Vermont where he was born in the second year of the nineteenth century. As a young man growing up in the hard times of that era he drifted westward across New York State, working as a carpenter, painter, and glazier. In 1830 he was living in a frontier village near Rochester, married to a frail wife who had borne him two daughters and then become an invalid whom he had to lift out of bed each morning after he had fed and dressed the children. His hands were calloused, his shoulders broad and muscular; he was clean-shaven and fairly handsome with auburn hair worn over his ears in the fashion of the times.

Along with most of his neighbors, Young had accepted a kind of backwoods Wesleyan Methodism, but he was forever challenging the faith because for him it held no answer to the riddle of life.

In adjoining Ontario County, seventeen-year-old Joseph Smith had been visited by Moroni, a messenger from Heaven who revealed to the boy the presence of a sacred record engraved upon plates of gold. Smith dug these golden plates from a hill called Cumorah and translated them into a style of English somewhat imitative but without the poetic power of the King James version of the Holy Bible. The plates contained accounts of prophets who had come to America from Israel. Some of their descendants were American Indians, but as the centuries passed their practices had become corrupt, the evil tribes triumphing over the good until at last only Moroni was left.

By the time Smith finished translating the golden plates—which were then returned to Moroni's keeping—he had made believers of some of his neighbors. Eleven of them later testified they had seen the plates and lifted them in their hands. One of them sold his farm to pay a printer in Palmyra, New York, the cost of five thousand copies of the *Book of Mormon* as translated by Joseph Smith.

When one of these copies of the *Book of Mormon* reached Brigham Young, he read it with interest. A visit from missionaries of Joseph Smith's new Church of Jesus Christ of Latter-day Saints was all the persuasion he needed to switch

C. C. A. Christensen's *Journey to Nauvoo* shows Mormons making their way to Illinois after their expulsion from Ohio.

137

from Methodism to Mormonism. He was especially drawn to the Mormon doctrine that happiness is the normal expectancy of life, and he was fond of quoting from the Second Book of Nephi, Chapter Two, Verse 25: 'Men are that they might have joy.' Young had not found much joy in frontier Methodism. Apparently a considerable number of other restless, westward-moving Americans felt as he did. Within a few months the new church had attracted several thousand members, but because of continuous persecution they had to leave New York State. Their new haven was Kirtland, Ohio, the inflow of Mormons first doubling, then tripling the population. It was here in 1832 that Brigham Young first met Joseph Smith and spoke to him in the gift of tongues. 'I wanted to thunder and roar out the gospel to the nations . . . It burned in my bones like a fire pent up.' Young afterwards claimed that Smith prophesied then that a day would come when Brigham Young would preside over the church.

That day came twelve years later, after jealous followers of other creeds drove the Mormons to the bank of the Mississippi at Nauvoo, Illinois. Here on the frontier of the Indian lands, these people who knew how to work with their hands made a New Zion. Around a temple they built a city of solid brick and stone, the largest city in Illinois, with converts streaming in daily from the east. Brigham Young went on a mission to England to preach the message and he recruited hundreds from among the downtrodden of Liverpool and Manchester–anywhere in Britain where he could find callous-handed working people who would listen to him. Many made their way to Nauvoo, and the Illinois politicians came to woo their votes. Chicago was then only a village; the Mormons of Nauvoo held the balance of power between Whigs and Democrats. In the end this power of the Mormons proved disastrous to them because the politicians came to fear it; other churches striving for converts on the Western frontier hated it and wanted to destroy it.

When Young returned from England, Joseph Smith informed him that a revelation had come from God instructing the Mormons to introduce polygamy. Celestial marriage, Smith called it, and declared that the more wives a man took the greater would be his glory in Heaven. Young later said that when Smith first told him of the new manifestation he was filled with revulsion. Nevertheless, both he and Smith began taking additional wives, Young marrying four between June 1842 and May 1844, the fourth being a fourteen-year-old girl. This practice of polygamy was meant to be kept secret within the church, but several members were so violently opposed to it that they renounced Mormonism. Wild rumors of licentiousness at Nauvoo began spreading throughout Illinois and Missouri. On 7 June 1844 two apostates published a newspaper filled with attacks upon the church for its advocacy of polygamy. Joseph

An Angel of Light, A Goblin Damned

Smith and his Council of Twelve immediately ordered the press destroyed, an act which gave the church's enemies the excuse they had been waiting for to break the growing power of Nauvoo. Smith was arrested by state authorities and jailed in nearby Carthage. On the afternoon of 27 June an armed mob from the Mormon-hating countryside invaded the jail and shot Smith to death. He was the first religious leader in America to die by assassination.

The shattered church that Joseph Smith had founded probably would have vanished had it not been for the strong will of Brigham Young. Although fragments did break away, Young managed to hold the majority of believers together. Before abandoning Nauvoo to the mobs, he added several of martyred Joseph Smith's widows to his collection of wives, and then led his people off to the West.

It was evident now to Young that the Mormons could not live in peace unless isolated from a government which seemed determined to prevent them from worshipping God in their own way, instead of offering protection as guaranteed by its constitution. He knew that he must find a land so undesirable that no others would covet it. On maps of the early explorers he found what he was looking for in territory then claimed by Mexico, the worthless desert of the Great Salt Lake.

In the summer of 1847, Young led the first company across the Plains – 143 men, 3 women, and 2 children in 73 wagons. On 28 June at Big Sandy he met Jim Bridger, who was on his way to Fort Laramie. As Young had been looking forward to meeting Bridger at his fort and obtaining information from him about the Salt Lake basin, he invited the veteran Mountain Man to camp with the Mormons for the night. Bridger accepted, and in his usual blunt manner told Young that it would not be prudent to bring large numbers of people into the Salt Lake basin; it was little more than a desert. When the Mormon leader replied that he was being divinely guided, Bridger reportedly derided him and offered a thousand dollars for the first bushel of corn raised in the basin. A coolness developed between them; about all that the two men had in common was a liking for plural wives.

On 24 July Brigham Young reached the place he had seen in a vision and he remained there until he died thirty years later, a ruler absolute over his followers, fusing church and state, dictating their religion, their economics, their politics, even their social activities. He forced his people to overcome droughts, insect plagues, scarcity of timber, early frosts, lack of markets and transportation. He showed them how to bring water from melting snows on the surrounding mountains down into the drab valleys, turning them green and increasing their herds of grazing livestock. He built theaters for dancing and joy, schools because he believed it was impossible for a man to be saved in ignorance, and temples for marriages,

ABOVE Brigham Young, the Lion of the Lord

BELOW Mormon baptisms are performed by a member of the Aaronic priesthood.

baptisms, and the preaching of his message.

After the Mexican War, when the Salt Lake basin became United States territory, Young petitioned for admittance of his State of Deseret into the Union, but was refused on grounds that Deseret contained too small a population. To increase the population, he dispatched missionaries throughout the states and to several foreign countries. New converts came by the hundreds, riding in dilapidated wagons and pulling handcarts on foot. But it was not lack of population that kept the Mormon state out of the Union. The real reason was polygamy which aroused the fierce and bitter jealousy of the Puritan establishment, although only about five per cent of Mormon families were involved in the practice. Deseret became land-locked Utah Territory, considerably reduced from the enormous area originally claimed by Young. He was permitted to remain as governor, but it galled him to have to accept rulings from federal judges, one of whom he described as 'a baby-calf who ought to go home to his mammy straight'.

Ignoring the geographical boundaries of Utah Territory, Young and his council established Mormon outposts far to the north and south as well as to the Pacific coast. They sought strategic locations to control travel routes in and out of Utah, among them being Jim Bridger's fort. On the pretext that Bridger was selling arms to Indians and inciting them to war, a paramilitary force of 150 Mormons drove Bridger and his family into the mountains. They stripped his trading post, gutted the buildings, and took away his livestock. After this was done they established their own trading posts along the trail junctions.

Meanwhile a wave of anti-Mormon feeling was sweeping the country. Tales of harems, of young girls forced into wedlock, of bestial behavior, of plots for territorial expansion, of mistreatment of non-Mormons filled the Eastern press. The Mormons naturally reacted by becoming xenophobes, suspicious of every move made by the Federal government, a situation which only strengthened Young's hand in his battle for absolute power. He defied the courts which charged him with administering a 'priestly government . . . despotic, dangerous, and damnable'. Again the deepest reason for pressure against Young was probably polygamy. In 1857 President James Buchanan declared Brigham Young and his followers to be in a state of rebellion against the government of the United States, and in May of that year ordered an army to march from Fort Leavenworth to invade the Kingdom of the Saints. Jim Bridger volunteered to serve as a guide for the expedition, reoccupied his fort, and leased it to the Army for a supply base. On 15 September Young announced that he would stand up and fight with the sword of the Lord. He declared martial law in Utah, ordered his people to begin evacuating their towns to the countryside, and began a guerrilla war.

This contemporary cartoon shows Young with his wives and offspring confronting Ulysses S. Grant. The Mormons did not abolish polygamy until 1890.

A Mormon emigrant train, following the route of the telegraph poles to Salt Lake City

As in most of its encounters with guerrillas throughout history, the U.S. Army fumbled through a series of fiascos, chasing an invisible enemy, losing supply trains, and coming close to starvation and freezing during the winter. Young meanwhile thundered denunciations and became a national celebrity. He talked of moving his entire colony to Mexico or to Russian Alaska in order to escape the 'armed mercenary mob' which had been sent against him. Behind the scenes, negotiations proceeded between Young's representatives and those of the United States. In April 1858 hostilities ended with a stalemate. Young agreed to halt resistance and accept the rule of a Gentile (non-Mormon) governor. The United States agreed to withdraw its troops after marching them through Salt Lake City as a symbol of the supremacy of the Republic. Actually nothing was changed. Brigham Young continued to rule the church–which was Utah–and he ignored all diatribes against polygamy. In fact after the burdens of the invasion were ended, he added several more wives to his assemblage, and his children became so numerous that he had to build a private school for them.

141

He had become a world figure now, often visited by fellow celebrities passing through Salt Lake City. Horace Greeley interviewed him and reported that he was a 'rather thick-set man of fifty-five seeming to enjoy life, and to be in no particular hurry to get to heaven'. Sir Richard Burton who had come from Britain expecting to find a hedonist enjoying seraglios equal to those in Araby found instead a 'gentleman farmer' in gray homespuns. 'His favorite food is boiled potatoes with a little buttermilk, and his drink water . . . He has the plain simple manners of honesty. His followers deem him an angel of light, his foes a goblin damned.' Burton tried to read a copy of the *Book of Mormon* which was presented to him. 'Surely there was never a book so thoroughly dull and heavy; it is monotonous as a sage-prairie . . . In one point it has done something. America, like Africa, is a continent of the future; the *Book of Mormon* has created for it an historical and miraculous past.'

And so the Lion of the Lord flourished, but he strove in vain to gain the admittance of Utah Territory into the Union as a state. Not until long after he was dead and polygamy abolished was Utah welcomed as a state, in 1896.

Inevitably it was a woman who came nearest to breaking Brigham Young's spirit. Wife No. 19, she called herself, but she was much farther down the list than that, No. 51 by some accounts. Her name was Ann Eliza Webb, but she was barely into her teens the year that Young stalemated the Army of the Republic, and she did not appear upon the public scene until much later–during the time of the Women's Rebellion in the West.

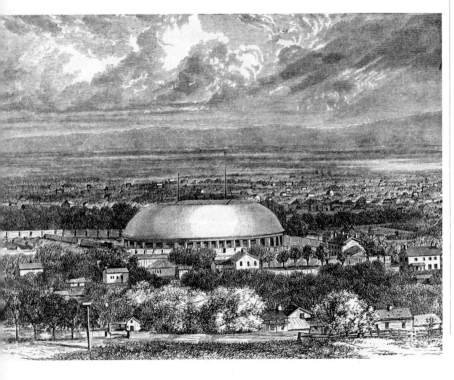

Salt Lake City in the year Utah was admitted to the Union

9. The Swift-Wagons of John Butterfield

'I was told that the Mormons would never permit any survey of their country to be made', said Captain Howard Stansbury when he was ordered into Utah in 1849 to find a more direct route to California. 'It was darkly hinted that if I persevered in attempting to carry it on, my life would scarce be safe.' Before beginning his surveys, Stansbury boldly called upon Brigham Young and told him what he had been ordered to do. To Stansbury's amazement, Young replied that he was highly in favor of better roads, that he and his church council had 'contemplated something of the kind, but did not yet feel able to incur the expense; but that any assistance they could render to facilitate our operations would be most cheerfully furnished to the extent of their ability'.

This attitude of a supposedly seclusionist people also surprised Sir Richard Burton in 1860. 'The Mormons, having lost all hopes of safety by isolation now seek it in the reverse: mail communication with the Eastern and Western States is their present hobby: they look forward to marketing for their produce, and to a greater facility and economy of importing.' Brigham Young and his followers were not ascetics, turning their backs on the world's material blessings. Men are that they might have joy, and prosperity is more joyous than adversity. They had caught the Western fever and as eagerly as the Gentiles, they sought California gold and what it would buy. To be safe, they reasoned, the Kingdom of the Saints must be strong, and wealth gained through communication and trade would make the Kingdom strong.

A month after they established their settlement in Salt Lake Valley, the Mormons pioneered the first mail service from the West, and kept irregular mails and baggage moving to Missouri and California until Deseret became the Territory of Utah. In 1850 the U.S. Post Office began providing regular service from the new territory, some of the carrier contracts going to bidding Mormons. Records for the winter of 1850–1 show that one mail from Salt Lake City to Independence 'passed through snow from one to three feet deep for seventeen days' and for another Brigham Young had to send out a road crew to clear the blizzard-blocked trail ahead of the mail wagon.

The Westerners

From late autumn to late spring, snows, rains, and floods plagued the carriers, the Wasatch Mountains being a most difficult barrier in bad weather. In 1854 the transcontinental contract went to a Gentile, W. M. F. Magraw, but two years later Hiram Kimball, a Mormon, won it back. Charging that Kimball's church had subsidized the low bid, the embittered Magraw hurried off to Washington to add his voice to the anti-Mormon uproar which finally induced President Buchanan to send an army against the 'despotic, dangerous and damnable' followers of Brigham Young. The Utah War virtually halted mail service just about the time that Californians were making their loudest outcry for faster and more regular overland transport. California's white population had jumped from 15,000 to 300,000 since the discovery of gold, and they were irked at being kept three to six months behind the rest of the country. Most of the mail, baggage, and travelers were carried by a high-priced steamship monopoly, and even with the completion of a forty-seven-mile railroad across the Panama isthmus in 1855, the time consumed in transfers and passage was intolerable to impatient go-ahead get-rich-quick Californians.

San Francisco's first post office building

POST OFFICE, SAN FRANCISCO, CALIFORNIA.

A FAITHFUL REPRESENTATION OF THE CROWDS DAILY APPLYING AT THAT OFFICE FOR LETTERS AND NEWSPAPERS.

In April 1856, 75,000 Californians in the San Francisco area signed a giant petition to Congress, demanding construction of a wagon road and daily overland mail service between East and West. This formidable list of angry voters was bound in leather and shipped off by slow steamship to Washington. A year later Congress responded by passing a bill authorizing the Postmaster General to contract for a semiweekly service from some point on the Mississippi River to San Francisco in 'good four-horse coaches or spring wagons, suitable for the conveyance of passengers as well as the safety and security of the mails . . . the said service shall be performed within twenty-five days for each trip'. Considerable political maneuvering preceded and followed passage of the bill. Every city along the Mississippi Valley from Chicago to New Orleans clamored for the privilege of being the Eastern terminus of the overland mail. The Postmaster General, Aaron V. Brown, was a Tennessean and he used his influence to favor Memphis. Brown also held out for a Southern route, a stand which aroused the ire of Northern anti-slavery forces who viewed it as a scheme to further the power of the South and extend slavery to the West. 'One of the greatest swindles ever perpetuated upon the country by the slave-holders', declared the Chicago *Tribune*, which had strongly advocated selection of Chicago for the Eastern terminus.

Actually the Post Office Department had lost faith in the ability of its carriers to move the mails with any regularity through the passes of the Rocky Mountains during winter months, and it was also uncertain of future conditions in Utah Territory which was in a state of armed turmoil when the overland mail contracts were being drawn up.

The route as finally approved by Postmaster General Brown had two Eastern originating points, one at Memphis, the other at St Louis. The routes converged at Fort Smith, Arkansas, and then proceeded in a southwesterly direction across Indian Territory and the Staked Plains of Texas to El Paso. From El Paso, the stagecoaches would move directly across three hundred miles of arid New Mexico Territory, through Apache Pass to Tucson, Maricopa Wells, and Yuma, where they would cross the Colorado River by ferry. From this southernmost point in California the route turned northward to Los Angeles and then up the central valley to San Francisco. The proud capital of Sacramento which previously had received Eastern mail and news by overland carriers before they reached San Francisco, was not on the route. 'A foul wrong,' a Sacramento newspaper editorialized, 'an outrage upon the majority of the people of the state!' Other critics of the route charged that it was excessively long, and they quickly named it the 'ox-bow route' because of its semi-circular shape on the maps.

Even the man who was awarded the overland mail contract, John Butterfield, believed he could have chosen a better route.

Butterfield, however, was not one to dodge difficult obstacles. Horatio Alger might have written his life into a novel without changing a line of it. Born in upper New York State the same year as Brigham Young, Butterfield received only a meager education before he had to begin earning his way as a boy stagecoach driver out of Utica, New York. By living frugally and hoarding his small wages, within a short time he was operating his own stage line and soon had most of the routes in western New York under his control. Branching out to packet boats on the Erie Canal, steamboats on Lake Ontario, and street railways in Utica, John Butterfield became a transportation tycoon. He also promoted railroads and telegraph lines, and when he discovered how much money two other New Yorkers, Henry Wells and William Fargo, were making in the express business, he established a competing company. In 1850 the three men merged their operations into the giant American Express Company, extending service to cities along the Western frontier and driving most of their rivals from the field. When Wells and Fargo formed a subsidiary bearing their names in 1852 to supply travel and transport demands to and from the California gold fields, John Butterfield was director of operations which guaranteed safe transportation of mail, passengers, and gold by way of the Panama isthmus. In 1857 when Butterfield went after the contract for an overland mail route to the West, one of his partners in the venture was William Fargo, and supporting them was the powerful financial structure of Wells, Fargo & Company. All three men were close associates of James Buchanan, bachelor President of the United States, who spent much of his time lavishly entertaining his friends in the White House while the nation was rocketing its way into a Civil War.

Butterfield's contract, signed on 16 September 1857, gave him a year to start the first mail coaches rolling from St Louis, Memphis, and San Francisco. One of his first tasks was to survey the route. When this work was completed, the distance from St Louis to San Francisco was charted at 2795 miles. Meanwhile orders went out to stagecoach manufacturers for 250 vehicles. Stations also had to be built, wells dug across the deserts, 1800 horses and mules purchased, hundreds of drivers and blacksmiths and local managers employed.

Personal overseer for this gigantic undertaking was John Butterfield himself, a physically imposing man with force in his eyes and voice. He might have been stamped out of the same material as his fellow New Yorker, Brigham Young – driven by tremendous energies in a never-ending search for power and wealth beyond the Western horizon.

Although he was in his late fifties when he won the overland mail contract, Butterfield devoted every moment of his time to preparations for its inauguration. He was convinced that the enterprise would make him into a much wealthier man than he already was. California was a treasure trove, and the men who linked it to the East could not help but share in its riches. He was certain that the ruts made by the rolling wheels of his stagecoaches soon enough would become steel rails for steam trains. Butterfield had seen it happening in the East; the controllers of railroads would control the wealth of America.

Even before his stations were built, John Butterfield was out on the roads making test runs. Dressed in high leather boots, a yellow linen duster, and a flat-crowned 'wide-awake' hat, he seemed to be everywhere at once. He cut such a dashing figure that general stores in all the towns along the route began displaying 'Butterfield' coats, hats, boots, shirts, and cravats.

'He is the most energetic president I ever saw', commented a newspaper reporter covering his activities. 'He appears to know every foot of the ground and to be known by everybody . . . Certainly if the overland mail does not succeed, it will not be for lack of his arduous exertions. He urged the men in changing horses at every station, often taking hold to help, and on one occasion driving for a short distance. He is, however, an old stager, and is in his element in carrying on this enterprise.'

Butterfield even found the time to draw up a list of special instructions for distribution to his conductors, drivers, and other employees. He stressed the importance of having all passengers' names entered on the waybill at point of departure, insisted that their fares be paid in advance, and that names on the waybill be checked off at time of stagecoach boarding. He set the price of through tickets to San Francisco from Memphis or St Louis at two hundred dollars, shorter distances ten cents per mile. 'The meals and provisions for passengers are at their own expense, over and above the regular fare. The Company intend, as soon as possible, to have suitable meals, at proper places, prepared for passengers at a moderate cost. Each passenger will be allowed baggage not exceeding 40 lbs. in any case.' Butterfield concluded by urging his employees to exert themselves in promoting the comfort and convenience of passengers and to treat both passengers and the public with civility.

Almost as an afterthought he then appended a note about Indians: 'A good look-out should be kept for Indians. No intercourse should be had with them, but let them alone; by no means annoy or wrong them. At all times an efficient guard should be kept, and such guard should always be *ready* for any emergency. JOHN BUTTERFIELD, President.'

By the time Butterfield was prepared to begin stagecoach service, a railroad had pushed out from St Louis to Tipton, Missouri, and he took advantage of its faster speed by establishing a transfer point at Tipton for mail and passengers, beginning his coach run to the West from there. On 16 September 1858 Butterfield in company with twenty-four-year-old Waterman L. Ormsby of the New York *Herald*, boarded the Pacific Railroad

The President and Secretary of the American Express Company: BELOW Henry Wells and BOTTOM William Fargo

Henry Wells

Wm. G. Fargo

in St Louis and rode 160 miles west to Tipton. He was carrying two sacks of mail. Waiting for them on the driver's seat of a shiny new stagecoach was Butterfield's son, John Jay, resplendently dressed in a 'Butterfield' costume which included an enormous checked bowtie. John Jay Butterfield had already posed for an artist from *Frank Leslie's Illustrated Newspaper* who also depicted 'the merry crack of young Butterfield's whip' as the coach rolled out of Tipton with its two sacks of mail and three passengers.

'We rode along at a somewhat rapid pace,' reported Ormsby of the *Herald*, 'because John Jr. was determined that the overland mail should go through his section on time, and though his father kept calling out, "Be careful, John," he assured him that it was "all right," and drove on.'

As the coach neared each station the conductor, who rode on the seat beside the driver, sounded a call on his bugle to alert station keepers to have fresh teams ready for exchange. Thanks to John Jay's lively driving and the promptness with which new relays of horses were harnessed to the coach, they established a new stage record to Springfield where the inhabitants greeted them with a salute of gunfire. Here they transferred to a Celerity wagon, a lighter and faster type of vehicle which Butterfield had developed for the rougher sections of the route.

The Celerity's body was similar to that of a regular coach, but rested on smaller wheels and was set closer to the road. Nine passengers could ride three abreast. The top and frame were covered with heavy canvas. 'Each one has three seats,' young Ormsby noted, 'which are arranged so that the backs let down and form one bed, capable of accommodating from four to ten persons, according to their size and how they lie.' As Butterfield's schedule called for night travel except when weather and road conditions made it impossible, this folding bed arrangement offered some relief, although the *Herald* reporter admitted that he was always happy to get out and walk when they came to steep hills because the exercise made him forget the terrible pain in his back brought on by the 'incessant riding without sleep'.

At Fort Smith, John Butterfield left the coach to await the arrival of the first overland mail from San Francisco. Ormsby was now the sole remaining passenger. On 28 September, twelve days after leaving St Louis, the reporter's coach met the east-bound mail. The meeting point was Guadalupe Pass, a hundred miles east of El Paso, and indicated that both coaches were maintaining schedules which should keep them within the twenty-five-day guarantee of the contract. 'After exchanging congratulations and telling bits of news, both parties passed on, I availing myself of the opportunity to send to the *Herald* a despatch which I had written for the occasion.'

According to Ormsby's calculations, the coach he was riding averaged about five-and-a half miles per hour from Tipton to

El Paso, but on the run from El Paso to Tucson the drivers almost doubled that speed. The Rio Grande was only an 'insignificant puddle' and Mesilla Valley was like a 'vast amphitheatre'. A few miles beyond Cooke's Spring they met the second mail coach from San Francisco maintaining the semi-weekly schedule of the Butterfield contract. On 1 October they rolled up to a tent with a crude sign beside it: SOLDIER'S FAREWELL. They were near the Continental Divide, and here was a spring where soldiers marching to California halted to fill their canteens and say a farewell to the East they were leaving.

The station workmen were beginning construction of a rock-walled structure to protect themselves from Apaches who were resentful of intrusions upon their land. By moonlight that evening the coach entered Apache Pass where three years later Cochise and Mangas Colorado would challenge the U.S. Army and halt the 'swift-wagons' of the Butterfield mail. 'We were entering the most dangerous portion of the Apache country', Ormsby recorded. 'I swallowed a hasty supper–beef, bacon, and shortcake–for the purpose of getting through the pass as soon as possible.'

Next evening they were in Tucson, 'a few adobe houses, the inhabitants mostly Mexicans, the first city in Arizona worthy of any note', with only 1163 miles yet to travel to San Francisco. At Fort Yuma they crossed the Colorado by ferry, and then for sixty miles traveled over heavy sands which dragged at the wheels of the coach. At intervals along the route, bleaching bones of animals had been piled up to serve as markers to keep drivers from losing their way during frequent sandstorms which stung the faces of the passengers and frightened the horses. On 7 October they were in Los Angeles, a 'thrifty and business-like' town of about six thousand inhabitants (in the decade since the Mormon Battalion had been there it had doubled in size). From Los Angeles to San Francisco the trails were good most of the way, the coach sometimes making twelve miles per hour. From Pacheco Pass to Gilroy, the eager driver let the coach fly down the steep hills at twenty miles an hour, and came near frightening Ormsby to death. 'I held on to the seat, and held my breath, hoping we might get through safe.'

At Gilroy most of the town's six hundred inhabitants gathered to greet this first overland mail from the East. 'How long have you been?' a man asked Ormsby.

'Left St. Louis on the 16th of September.'

'Well, that beats all stage ridin'. How's the line on the other end?'

Ormsby told him it was slow in comparison with travel over the California roads.

'Slow, eh. Of course, all the States people are slow. Let 'em come out here to California and see a little life. Here we do live–live fast, too.'

San Francisco and the end of the journey lay less than a

The War Path by J. A. Oertel. Butterfield instructed his drivers to watch out for hostile Indians, who no doubt also spied on the coaches.

hundred miles away now, and Ormsby had his first view of the magical city at sunrise of Sunday morning 10 October. 'Soon we struck the pavements, and with a whip, crack and bound, shot through the streets to our destination, to the great consternation of everything in the way, and the no little surprise of everybody. Swiftly we whirled up one street and down another, and round the corners, until finally we drew up at the stage office in front of the Plaza, our driver giving a shrill blast of his horn and a flourish of triumph for the arrival of the first overland mail in San Francisco from St. Louis.' The time of the run was 23 days, $23\frac{1}{2}$ hours. Ormsby who had been the only passenger to make the complete journey claimed that he was the first person to cross the Plains in less than fifty days. There was no disputing that John Butterfield now offered the fastest and longest stage ride in the world.

Because the overland mail had come in a day ahead of schedule, no welcoming committee was waiting for it. Next morning the San Francisco *Bulletin* hailed the arrival somewhat apologetically: 'Had it not been for the Sabbath, the extempore and spontaneous outburst of rejoicing would perhaps have even excelled the great announcement of the successful laying of the Atlantic cable . . . The importance of the enterprise cannot be too highly appreciated. California *is by it bound to the rest of the Union*.' Equally enthusiastic was the *Alta California* which said that the peal of the coachman's horn on the first overland mail from St Louis brought 'tidings of great joy' to San Francisco. 'The great truth flashed home at once to every heart, in all the multitude who have waited so long here upon the western shore of the continent, for the consummation of the opening of the great transcontinental highway.'

That evening San Francisco's Monumental Fire Company honored the occasion by firing off a salute of thirty-two guns, and next day the First California Guard fired two hundred guns. Citizens held a monster rally, and young Waterman Ormsby became the man of the hour. When the second Butterfield Mail arrived on Friday, the entire city turned out to cheer while bands played and cannon boomed.

John Butterfield kept improving his service, and by 1860 his 'swift-wagons' were carrying far more mail than the old steamship monopoly by way of Panama. Eventually he reduced his schedule time by two or three days. He cut passenger fares to $150 for through passage, and the demand for seats kept his Celerity wagons filled to capacity. A passenger attempting to buy a ticket at St Louis in December 1858 said there were so many applicants that they drew lots for the privilege of purchase. 'Upward of one hundred applications were made this trip and as high as one hundred dollars premium was offered for seats.'

William Tallack of London, England, who decided to make

the journey from San Francisco to St Louis in 1860, had to wait ten days for a through ticket, and then he was crowded in with so many other passengers that getting aboard was possible only 'by dint of close sitting and tightly dovetailed knees. Outside were the driver, the conductor, and an indefinite number of passengers, as, by popular permission, an American vehicle is never "full," there being always room for "one more" . . . What with mail-bags and passengers, we were so tightly squeezed that there was scarcely room for any jerking about separately in our places . . . Thus closely sleeping, we ascended fifteen miles of a mountain road.'

All the while, the energetic John Butterfield kept in close touch with his friends in government, maneuvering to gain as important a role in the planned transcontinental railroad as he was playing in the overland mail route. He also was determined to begin a tri-weekly mail service for his overland coaches. Driving himself as hard as his coachmen drove their teams, he collapsed one day early in 1860. He returned to Utica for what he expected would be a brief rest, but when his former energies failed to return he decided to give up the presidency of Butterfield's Overland Mail, at least for a time.

Meanwhile the first shadows of disunion had begun to fall over the nation. Butterfield's old friend, President James Buchanan, was beset by forces he did not understand and knew not how to control. John Brown raided Harper's Ferry and was hanged. Buchanan's efforts to conciliate North and South split his own Democratic party and paved the way for the election of Abraham Lincoln. South Carolina seceded, and other Southern states quickly followed, forming the Confederate States of America with Jefferson Davis as President. Buchanan forbade the secession but could think of no way to stop it. Texas left the Union on 1 February 1861, and a few days later Butterfield's coaches were stopped at Fort Smith and Tucson. On 9 March the last overland mail from the West passed through El Paso, reaching the end of the railroad in Missouri on the 21st only to discover that Confederate sympathizers had burned the station and were beginning to burn the railroad's bridges.

In a frantic effort to keep communication lines open to the wealth of California, the U.S. Congress ordered service discontinued on the Butterfield route and appropriated a million dollars to open a central route from some point on the Missouri River to San Francisco. As Butterfield still held the mail contract, his company transferred horses, mules, and stage-coaches from the southern route and joined in a contractual arrangement with the Central Overland California & Pike's Peak Express Company. This latter transportation system had been organized to serve the demands of thousands of wealth seekers who had descended upon Colorado after discoveries of gold and silver there in 1858–9 – the Pike's Peak or Bust emigrants. The C.O.C. & P.P.E.C. was owned by William H.

ABOVE Typical cancellations on a letter sent by stagecoach in 1860

BELOW Rough terrain in Utah, near Powell's Plateau

OPPOSITE Two extreme hazards of overland stagecoaches: desert and snowdrifts. TOP *The Mojave Desert* by George Brewerton (Butterfield's route skirted this region); BOTTOM *Why the Mail Was Late* by Oscar Berninghaus.

OVERLEAF Thomas P. Otter's *On the Road*. Very few operators realized that with the western extension of railroads, trains were quickly to supersede wagons and coaches.

Russell, Alexander Majors, and William B. Waddell, three gentleman entrepreneurs who had grown rich on government contracts and were beginning to overextend themselves with mail and passenger operations.

On 1 July 1861 daily mail service began between St Joseph, Missouri, and San Francisco, the running time averaging about eighteen days. For the next nine months from his sick bed in Utica, New York, old John Butterfield watched his golden dream of dominating Western transportation vanish in the smoke of the Civil War, in winter blizzards on the Plains, and through the financial maneuverings of a ruthless, domineering robber baron named Ben Holladay.

Six-foot-two, with powerful arms and legs, shaggy-haired and black-bearded, Holladay looked the pirate he was. He came out of the lawless Ohio River Valley of Kentucky to Weston, a brawling town on the Missouri River, and in 1839 at the age of twenty he was operating a saloon and taking easy money from fur trappers and Indians. He added a hotel to his saloon, started a packing business and a whisky distillery, and when General Kearny marched his Army of the West out of nearby Fort Leavenworth in 1846, Holladay grabbed for the supply contracts. He sold goods and livestock at high prices to the government and bought the same goods and livestock back from the government at low prices. When gold was found in California, he hauled merchandise out there and mined the miners.

Holladay saw that there was big money in wagon freighting, but the gentlemanly trio of Russell, Majors, and Waddell had beat him to a monopoly of that rich game. Like one of William Faulkner's fictitious Snopes clan, however, Holladay found his way into the firm. He began supplying draft animals to R.M.& W. on credit, and during the Utah War when William Russell was searching desperately for flour to fulfill a hauling contract with the Army, Holladay miraculously came up with barrels of flour. His price for the flour was a partnership in the venture. A few years later when Russell conceived the idea of a pony express to carry fast mail, again it was Holladay who loaned the hard cash to start that profitless mail service galloping back and forth across mountains and plains. By the time the Civil War began and Butterfield's Mail was combined with Russell, Majors & Waddell's express company, Holladay held a secret financial stranglehold on the new organization.

Unlike the men who preceded him in grasping for transportation power in the West, Ben Holladay kept his rapaciousness out in the open. 'Energetic, untiring, unconscionable, unscrupulous,' one of his rivals said of him, 'and wholly destitute of honesty, morality, or common decency.' On 7 March 1862 Holladay called in his mortgage and for about ten cents on the dollar took over the West's greatest transportation system. While John Butterfield was dying back in Utica, Ben Holladay became the Stagecoach King of the West.

10. The Napoleon of the Plains

'Russell, Majors and Waddell's transportation establishment is the great feature of Leavenworth', Horace Greeley noted on his tour through the West in 1859. 'Such acres of wagons! such pyramids of extra axletrees! such herds of oxen! such regiments of drivers and other employees! No one who does not see can realize how vast a business this is, nor how immense are its outlays as well as its income. I presume this great firm has at this hour two millions of dollars invested in stock, mainly oxen, mules and wagons.'

Of the three partners, Alexander Majors and William Waddell seemed content in 1859 to rest upon their millions, but to William Hepburn Russell, the West was ripe for endless exploitation. His mind never ceased devising schemes for pyramiding money and credit as high as his axletrees. All three men had similar backgrounds, coming young to the Missouri frontier when it was prospering from the fur trade, working as clerks in stores and banks, saving enough money to buy a few wagons and get into the Santa Fe trade. Merchandising was their game, and after they joined forces at Leavenworth they virtually monopolized wagon freighting across the West. Will Russell was the brains of the outfit, everyone said. They called him the Napoleon of the Plains.

When gold was discovered in Colorado in 1858, Russell thought he saw a chance to make a new fortune by opening a stagecoach line to Denver. His partners were dubious, and refused to put any of the company's money into the venture. Lack of cash never bothered William Russell. Using credit based largely upon his share of R.M. & W. holdings, he formed a separate partnership with John S. Jones, a former competitor, and together they purchased eight hundred mules and fifty Concord stagecoaches, the first of these luxurious vehicles to be used on the Kansas plains.

Russell's notes were payable in ninety days, and his expenses for drivers, livestock, and station-keepers rose to a thousand dollars a day before he ran the first Concord into Denver on 17 May 1859. 'It was looked upon as a great success,' Alexander Majors afterwards recalled, 'but when the ninety days expired and the notes fell due they [Russell and Jones] were unable to

Remington's *Coming and Going of the Pony Express*, showing the *mochila* saddle bag

157

A loaded Concord stagecoach

meet them. And in spite of my protests in the commencement of the organization as against having anything to do with it, it became necessary for Russell, Majors & Waddell to meet the obligation that Jones & Russell had entered into in organizing and putting the stock on the line. To save our partner we had to pay the debts of the concern and take the mules and coaches . . . to secure for us the money we had advanced.' This was done on 28 October 1859. R.M. & W. continued to operate the service, extending it to Salt Lake City in vain hopes of making it profitable. This was the line which eventually became the Central Overland California & Pike's Peak Express Company that was so eagerly coveted and finally taken by Ben Holladay.

Determined to recover the losses he had brought upon his partners, William Russell now journeyed to Washington and began lobbying to win the lucrative overland mail contract away from John Butterfield's southern route. He found an ally in Senator William Gwin of California, whose constituents were constantly demanding faster mail and passenger service to and from the East. During January 1860 Russell and Gwin made a mutual agreement: Russell pledged to organize a Pony Express mail service from the Missouri River to California, and Gwin promised to obtain a subsidy from Congress to insure its success. Thus by a practical demonstration of rapid mail service on a central route, they hoped to take over Butterfield's contract. On 27 January Russell telegraphed his partners from Washington that he was arranging to start the Pony Express on 3 April. Three days later, the Leavenworth *News* hailed Russell's glamorous project: GREAT EXPRESS ADVENTURE FROM LEAVENWORTH TO SACRAMENTO IN TEN DAYS. CLEAR THE TRACK AND LET THE PONY COME THROUGH.

When Russell returned to Leavenworth, he found his partners firmly opposed to the Pony Express. After all, they had already lost a great deal of money on the Napoleon of the Plains' stage line to Colorado, and his Pony Express appeared to be even more of a financial risk. Russell was baffled by his partners' lack of audacity. He had found no loss of confidence in R.M.&W. in Washington. The company's credit was so good that Russell had easily picked up cashable acceptances signed by the Secretary of War, John B. Floyd—promises to pay for past and future War Department contracts with R.M.&W. Ben Holladay, their sometime rival, was willing to buy these acceptances to put money into the venture. The Pony Express was a sure thing, Russell argued; he was positive he could move mail from Leavenworth to California in ten days, less than half the time of the Butterfield route. Such a demonstration was bound to win them millions of dollars in mail contracts.

'Mr. Russell strenuously insisted that we stand by him,' said Alexander Majors, 'as he had committed himself to Senator Gwin before leaving Washington, assuring him that he could get his partners to join him, and that he might rely on the project being carried through, and saying it would be very humiliating to his pride to return to Washington and be compelled to say the scheme had fallen through from lack of his partners' confidence.'

Majors and Waddell eventually agreed to go along with the undertaking, although reluctantly, and Russell was turned loose with his notes of credit to organize the Pony Express. In sixty days he expended hundreds of thousands of promissory dollars, acquiring fast and expensive horses, establishing stations, purchasing equipment and grain, and employing station-keepers and riders. To find the riders he wanted, Russell placed advertisements in newspapers along the frontier:

> WANTED–Young, skinny, wiry fellows not over 18. Must be expert riders willing to risk death daily. Orphans preferred.

From the numerous applicants he selected eighty, one of whom was a fifteen-year-old fatherless boy named William Frederick Cody, who a few years later would be known as Buffalo Bill. Contrary to legend, Cody's friend, James Butler (Wild Bill) Hickok, was not a fellow rider; Hickok was twenty-three and weighed more than the top limit of 125 pounds, but he found employment at one of the stations.

Wild Bill Hickok, a Pony Express station hand, and later a scout and deputy U.S. marshal

PONY EXPRESS.

Nine Days from San Francisco to New York

THE CENTRAL Overland Pony Express Company will start their LETTER EXPRESS from San Francisco to New York and intermediate points,

On Tuesday, the 3d day of April ne t,

And upon every Tuesday thereafter, at 4 o'clock P. M.

Letters will be received at San Francisco until 3¾ o'clock each day of departure.

OFFICE—

Alta Telegraph Office, Montgomery st.,

Telegraphic Dispatches will be received at Carson City until 6 o'clock P. M., every Wednesday.

SCHEDULE TIME FROM SAN FRANCISCO TO NEW YORK.

For Telegraphic Dispatches.............................Nine Days

For Letters...Thirteen Days

Letters will be charged, between San Francisco and Salt Lake City, $3 per half ounce and under, and at that rate according to weight.

To all points beyond Salt Lake City, $5 per half ounce and under, and at that rate according to weight.

Telegraphic Dispatches will be subject to the same charges as letters.

All letters must be inclosed in stamped envelopes.

WM. W. FINNEY,

m18   Agent C. O P. E. Co.

ABOVE An announcement of the start of the Pony Express

BELOW The arrival of the first Pony Express in Sacramento

Before each rider was hired he was required to take a solemn oath not to use profane language, nor get drunk, nor gamble, nor to treat his mounts with cruelty, nor interfere with the rights of citizens or Indians. He was then presented with a copy of the Holy Bible 'to defend himself against moral contaminations' and a pair of Colt's revolvers and a rifle 'to defend himself against warlike Indians'. The rifles were afterwards recalled, being too awkward to carry on swift-running ponies across the Plains.

Late in March, Russell announced through newspapers in California and the East the departure times for Pony Express mail from major cities to connect with either Sacramento or St Joseph, where on 3 April riders would be leaving on their first runs east and west. As a telegraph line had reached St Joseph, messages could be sent there from any city in the East for transfer to the Pony Express.

Right on schedule at five o'clock p.m., 3 April 1860, a cannon beside the R.M. & W. office in St Joseph boomed a salute, and a rider in a red shirt, blue trousers, and high boots, mounted upon a jet black pony, raced toward the river ferry with his bag of first-class mail. At about the same time in flag-decked Sacramento, a rider on a pure white pony galloped toward the East.

A Pony Express rider overtakes the telegraph line that was soon to outdate the venture

Seventy-five ponies were used in the first run west, and the time was ten and a half days. Only twenty-five letters were delivered, at a charge of five dollars per half ounce. As news spread of Pony Express speed and reliability, the number of letters began to grow. Correspondents learned to use tissue paper for their messages, and newspapers in New York, Chicago, and San Francisco printed special editions on thin paper for transmission by the 'pony'.

The saddle bag chosen by William Russell was the Mexican *mochila*, which had four separate pockets. An opening in its center allowed it to fit neatly over the saddle horn, so that when a rider was mounted he had a pocket in front of and behind each leg. Three of the pockets were locked at departure points and could be opened only at five points along the route for removal or addition of letters. The fourth pocket was used for local mail, and could be opened by any station-keeper.

About the time the Pony Express began attracting sizable amounts of mail—some business men and government officials expended as much as $135 per letter—the U.S. Congress took action to speed up construction of a telegraph line across the West. On 16 June 1860 funds were appropriated for completion of the line from Omaha to California. The contract, which was awarded on 22 September, called for work to be finished by 1 July 1862.

As in the building of the transcontinental railroad a decade later, construction of the transcontinental telegraph was organized as a race between competing companies, one moving eastward from California, the other westward from the Missouri River. The man responsible for the line moving west out of Omaha was Edward Creighton, an ambitious second-generation Irish Catholic. In 1840 at the age of twenty, Creighton won a contract for an Ohio section of the National Road – that highway which made west-bound emigrants less dependent upon rivers for travel, opened the land-locked Midwest for settlement, and doomed any hope the Indians of the Old Northwest Territory had for retaining their lands east of the Mississippi River.

When railroads began stringing wires along their right-of-ways to carry messages sent by Samuel Morse's amazing new invention, the telegraph, Creighton switched from road construction to the building of telegraph lines. In 1860 he built one from St Louis to Omaha, and that same year Western Union's Pacific Telegraph Company assigned him the task of building a line from Omaha to the West.

By November, Creighton had a wire strung to Fort Kearney, fulfilling the first stage of his contract before winter weather stopped the work. In a corner of a sod house used as the post office at Fort Kearney, the telegraph company installed instruments, batteries, and other equipment for use of their first operator, a recent graduate of Morse's school of telegraphy in Washington. His name was George Ellsworth, a jaunty practical joker who two years later joined General John Morgan's Confederate cavalry and became known as 'Lightning' Ellsworth, legendary bedeviler of Federal commanders until he was finally captured in one of Morgan's daring raids. During the winter of 1860–1, at Fort Kearney, Ellsworth was kept so busy that the company had to send him an assistant. Ellsworth's station was the end of the line and most of the messages that came clicking over the wire were transferred to the *mochilas* of west-bound riders of the Pony Express. The telegrams were primarily concerned with the newly elected President, Abraham Lincoln, and the approaching outbreak of the Civil War.

William Russell meanwhile was attempting to shore up the disintegrating financial structure of R.M. & W. He had sunk $700,000 in the Pony Express, and he knew very well that his expensive fast mail could never compete with the telegraph. The day that Edward Creighton completed construction of his line, the Pony Express would be finished. In the summer of 1860, Russell believed that he had about two years' grace in which to keep his ponies galloping while he worked toward winning the regular mail contract away from John Butterfield.

To keep R.M. & W. afloat, however, he had to go back East and try to borrow money to pay off notes against other borrowed money. Russell was dismayed by the reception given him in New York; the financial world was in turmoil over the situation in the South and was also aware of huge debts owed by R.M. & W. No money was available for William Russell.

Worried because a number of acceptance notes signed by his friend, Secretary of War Floyd, were falling due, Russell hurried on to Washington to find some way to keep the public from becoming aware of them and thus compromising Floyd's position in President Buchanan's cabinet. Through a grapevine of politicians and government officials, Russell found his way to Godard Bailey, a minor Interior Department official who had access to negotiable bonds held for the Indian Trust Fund. Being related to Floyd by marriage, Bailey was motivated to save the Secretary from disgrace. He handed over some Indian Trust Fund bonds to Russell, who took them to New York and borrowed enough money against them to pay off Floyd's overdue acceptance notes. Russell had promised Bailey that the hypothecated bonds would be back in his hands within ninety days and no one would be the wiser.

Instead of returning the Indian Trust Fund bonds, however, Russell was in Washington during September begging Bailey for more bonds to protect the ones he had already borrowed on. (The embezzled Indian Trust bonds which kept Russell's company from bankruptcy represented unpaid annuities to Indians who ironically were being driven from their lands by the stagecoaches and military supply trains of Russell, Majors & Waddell.) During the late summer Russell had issued another batch of acceptance notes bearing Secretary Floyd's signature to pay off debts of the Pony Express and R.M. & W. He had in fact during the ninety days spent seven dollars for every dollar the company had earned.

Godard Bailey knew he was in a trap, but he was still confident that Russell could extricate both of them. He turned over another batch of bonds, $387,000 worth. Unfortunately for the two embezzlers, the financial world was beginning to panic over the worsening situation between Northern and Southern states. Stock and bond values were collapsing, and bankers and private individuals, such as Ben Holladay, refused to extend any kind of loans, even those backed by Indian Trust bonds. Early in December, Russell was back in Washington, assuring Bailey that if he would only dig up another lot of bonds, about $350,000 worth, he could use them to recover the previous bonds and save both of them from being caught. Bailey reluctantly agreed, but a few days later when it became obvious that Russell was not going to be able to cover up the embezzlements, Bailey confessed to his superiors. On Christmas Eve, William Russell was arrested and jailed, his bond being set at half a million dollars.

Russell complained bitterly about the high bail, which he said exceeded 'anything ever before known in the annals of judicial proceedings in any part of the world'. That he had compromised a million dollars belonging to Indian tribes did not seem too important. He wrapped himself in the Stars and Stripes and said his actions were motivated purely by a patriotic desire to keep R.M. & W. wagon trains in operation so that supplies of the army would not be cut off.

The Civil War was almost at hand now. Secretary Floyd, caught in the scandal, resigned and went home to Virginia to become a general in the Confederate Army. In the springtime confusion of war, Godard Bailey vanished, probably also into the Confederacy. Russell was quizzed by a Congressional committee and was indicted for fraud, but in March 1861 was freed from prosecution on a legal technicality. He stayed in Washington for a while brazenly continuing to lobby for the Butterfield mail contract. Events of war as we have seen soon forced Butterfield to the central route, giving R.M. & W. only a sub-contract for their Central Overland California & Pike's Peak Express Company.

About the time that Fort Sumter was falling to the Confederates, Russell returned to the West to help his partners, Majors and Waddell, keep their once powerful organization from collapsing. In May 1861 he was in Denver, which had grown into a boom town of get-rich-quick boosters eager to be on the main line of all transportation systems—including the much talked about transcontinental railroad of the future. Russell, who was always looking for new and exciting projects, met with Jim Bridger to discuss the possibilities of a wagon route directly west from Denver over the Rockies to Salt Lake City. Such a road would cut two hundred miles off the old route through Wyoming, and Bridger thought it might be feasible. Russell now joined the Denver boosters in raising money to employ Bridger as a pathfinder and Captain E. L. Berthoud as engineer. That summer Bridger and Berthoud laid out a route through a pass which was named for Berthoud, but it was far from ready for use on 1 July, the date for the beginning of daily mail service over the newly combined Butterfield and R.M. & W. central route. Russell was so confident, however, in the future of the Bridger-Berthoud route that he drove up to Idaho Springs near the Pass and bought up city lots and mining claims with a fresh batch of promissory notes. He was sure the investments would make him very rich when the railroad came through.

Back East in Washington, President Lincoln was asking for 75,000 volunteer troops to put down the Southern rebellion, and maneuvers were beginning which would lead to the first battle of Bull Run. To the Westerners, the war seemed very far away, but Edward Creighton sensed the urgency of the government when he was given a monetary incentive to complete the telegraph line before the contracted date of 1 July 1862. A large bonus was offered the first company to reach Salt Lake City. Although the California company was only 450 miles from Salt Lake City, and Creighton had 1100 miles to cover, he readily accepted the challenge.

Surveyor's Wagon in the Rockies by Albert Bierstadt

Choosing eighty of his best men, Creighton divided them into three crews. He assigned one group to digging holes, another to cutting and setting poles, the third to stringing wire. A back-up force of about three hundred men was responsible for transporting materials and provisions, and included seventy-five ox-drawn wagons filled with insulators and wire and seven hundred cattle for beef.

Creighton's most difficult problem was securing suitable poles where the line crossed long stretches of treeless plains. Specifications called for poles twenty feet long to be sunk four feet in the ground, and sometimes they had to be hauled more than a hundred miles. Creighton had surveyed his route carefully, however, locating timber in advance, and he distributed his pole cutters and oxen so they were always in the right places at the right times. To keep his workmen satisfied, Creighton furnished them with good tents and large quantities of food cooked on portable stoves.

The race to Salt Lake began on 4 July 1861. The diggers averaged about twelve miles per day, sinking twenty-four holes per mile, but the pole crew gradually fell behind and was 150 miles from Salt Lake City when the last hole was dug. On 18 October Creighton strung the last roll of wire into the City of the Saints and won the bonus money. The California crew came in six days later, the wires were connected, and telegraphic communication established between the Atlantic and Pacific. The governor of California sent the first message,

President Lincoln responded, and Brigham Young dispatched greetings in both directions.

On 26 October brief notices appeared in newspapers in the East and West: PONY EXPRESS WILL BE DISCONTINUED FROM THIS DATE. On that same day the Sacramento *Bee* published a farewell salute:

> Our little friend, the Pony, is to run no more. 'Stop it,' is the order that has been issued by those in authority. Farewell and forever, thou staunch, wilderness-overcoming, swift-footed messenger. For the good thou hast done we praise thee; and, having run thy race, and accomplished all that was hoped for and expected, we can part with thy services without regret, because, and only because, in the progress of the age, in the advance of science and by the enterprise of capital, thou hast been superseded by a more subtle, active, but no more faithful public servant. Thou wert the pioneer of a continent in the rapid transmission of intelligence between its people, and have dragged in your train the lightning itself, which, in good time, will be followed by steam communication by rail. Rest upon your honors; be satisfied with them, your destiny has been fulfilled – a new and higher power has superseded you. Nothing that has blood and sinews was able to overcome your energy and ardor; but a senseless, soulless thing that eats not, sleeps not, tires not – a thing that cannot distinguish space – that knows not the difference between a rod of ground and the circumference of the globe itself, has encompassed, overthrown and routed you.

Ben Holladay, who was holding thousands of dollars in acceptance notes against R.M. & W. was not saddened by the 'Pony's' demise. In its eighteen months of existence, the fast mail service had returned less than a tenth of the money William Russell put into it. As the months passed with no improvement in the fortunes of R.M. & W., Holladay first asked for a bond to protect his loans, then a mortgage, and in March 1862 what had once been the largest and most powerful business enterprise in the West passed from the hands of the men it was named for to big, brash, poker-playing Ben Holladay. He soon had the name changed to Holladay's Overland Mail.

All three of the R.M. & W. partners passed rapidly into obscurity. Alexander Majors, who was forty-eight years old, moved to the Rockies and tried unsuccessfully to organize other wagon-freighting lines. He failed in prospecting for silver, took a job furnishing cross-ties for the new transcontinental railroad, and then virtually disappeared. In 1891 one of Majors' former employees, Buffalo Bill Cody, discovered him living alone and almost penniless in a shack near Denver. Cody loaned his ghost writer, Prentiss Ingraham, to Majors, and together they wrote *Seventy Years on the Frontier*, which brought the former transportation giant back into public notice. He lived to his eighty-sixth year, dying in Chicago, 14 January 1900.

William Waddell, deserted by many of his old friends, lost most of his personal fortune and saw his land sold off for taxes. He lived his last years on a daughter's farm near Lexington, Missouri, dying in 1872, at the age of sixty-five.

As for William Russell, whose frantic pursuit of wealth and power was largely responsible for the downfall of his partners and himself, he went off to the money founts of New York in hopes of restoring his lost fortune. Wall Street, however, rejected his overtures, and to support himself Russell became a salesman for a popular patent medicine. After that he moved on to Washington, seeking to renew old ties with politicians and bureaucrats, but with no better luck than he had with the financiers of New York. His spirit broken, his health failing, he sought shelter with a son in Palmyra, Missouri, and died there aged sixty only a few months after Waddell's passing.

Soon after Ben Holladay took over the R.M. & W. enterprises, he went to Colorado to look into the possibilities of the Berthoud Pass route which William Russell had been so enthusiastic about. Holladay was besieged by Denver boosters who urged him to open the new route so that Denver could become the 'great half-way station between New York and San Francisco'. Being shrewder than Russell, Holladay arranged for another engineer to survey Berthoud Pass. When the report came back that the grade was too steep for a railroad and that a tunnel would be needed most of the year because of heavy snowfalls, Holladay lost all interest in the route. In 1862 he was giving more thought to railroads than to shortcuts for stagecoaches.

Back in Washington, Congress had just passed an act 'to aid in the construction of a railroad from the Missouri River to the Pacific Ocean' and Abraham Lincoln signed it into law on 1 July. Among the partners listed in the act creating the 'Union Pacific Railroad Company' was Ben Holladay. He and his associates were authorized to construct a right of way two hundred feet wide across the West, taking whatever earth, stone, and timber was needed from lands adjacent to trackage. For each mile of track built they were to receive bonds worth from $16,000 to $48,000, depending upon difficulty of construction. As an added incentive, the government granted the railroad company ten alternate sections of land or 6400 acres for each mile of track constructed. To obtain this land for the railroad company, the Congress and President Lincoln promised to 'extinguish as rapidly as may be possible the Indian titles to all lands falling under the operation of this act and required for the said right of way and grants hereafter made'.

For forty-three-year-old Ben Holladay, the railroad was a long-term investment, something that he expected would keep him rich in his old age. Meanwhile he would build fortunes out of his monopoly of Western wagon freighting, passenger hauling, and mail contracting. During the latter half of 1862, the Plains Indians tried to block his vehicles along their Platte Valley hunting grounds. Holladay demanded soldiers from the government to protect his property, but the soldiers were busy fighting Rebels back East. He routed his traffic around the hunting areas, and the Indians left him alone.

In January 1863 the newly organized Central Pacific Railroad, which was to construct tracks eastward from California, held a ground-breaking ceremony at Sacramento. Eleven months later the Union Pacific Railroad, which was to build westward and join with the Central Pacific, broke ground at Omaha. Holladay took note of these occurrences, but they did not deter him from investing thousands of dollars in expensive new Concord coaches in 1864. One of his Concord drivers on the line west of Fort Kearney was eighteen-year-old Bill Cody of the defunct Pony Express. Holladay also had a coach especially designed for the exclusive use of the Stagecoach King himself. Painted in brilliant hues of yellow and red and pulled by teams of matching horses in silver-ornamented harness, and flying a red-and-white flag bearing his initials, the coach attracted attention wherever it appeared. Cushioned leather seats, kerosene reading lamps, a let-down table, and a built-in bar were among its interior features.

Wartime activities in the West only doubled and quadrupled Holladay's profits. To gain still more from military contracts, he traveled to the East, following the same paths as his luckless predecessor, William Russell. To impress government officials, Holladay bought a fine house in Washington and entertained extravagantly. Then he opened an office on Wall Street and bought a big New York brownstone to improve his connections with the financiers.

Back in Colorado, some of his Denver friends organized a volunteer regiment and slaughtered the Cheyennes at Sand Creek. The reaction from the infuriated Plains Indians brought Holladay's transportation empire to a standstill. Along a stretch of four hundred miles, they attacked wagon trains, stage-coaches, and stations. This time the government gave Holladay military escorts, and he rode out in his fancy coach to assess the damages. While he was doing this he kept in constant telegraphic communication with Wall Street, and during the inspection tour he made enough money gambling on the war-time gold market to pay for his losses.

In the peacetime spring of 1865, a Denverite dissatisfied with

The Attack on an Emigrant Train by Charles Wimar

Holladay's spur-line service to that city, opened a new overland route from Atchison, Kansas, direct to Denver, offering fast freight, express, and passenger schedules. He was David A. Butterfield (no relation to John). The new line was called Butterfield's Overland Despatch, but because it followed a straight-line route to Denver up the Smoky Hill fork of the Kansas River, everyone called it the Smoky Hill route. If Dave Butterfield did not know that the Smoky Hill fork watered a buffalo hunting area highly prized by Plains tribes, he soon learned that fact. In the autumn of 1865, Indians attacked his stagecoaches and burned his stations, often disrupting service. At the same time, Ben Holladay—who was jealous of all competition—reduced his rates and fares below any figure that Butterfield could match. By the spring of 1866, the Indians and Holladay bankrupted Dave Butterfield. Holladay added the Smoky Hill route to his expanding empire, demanding and obtaining military escorts. (Many of these soldiers were former Confederate prisoners of war known as Galvanized Yankees.)

About this time, Wells, Fargo & Company which had grown rich and powerful in California and had been eyeing the wealth that Holladay was taking out of the West, made an offer to buy his company. When Holladay refused to sell, Wells and Fargo threatened to organize competing systems to all his routes. Holladay was not a man to be intimidated, but through his connections with the Union Pacific he learned during the summer that the projected transcontinental railroad's difficult financing problems had at last been solved. The engineers were ready to begin building a mile of track a day toward the West.

Holladay estimated that in less than three years, wagon freight, stagecoach passengers, and mail contracts would go to the railroad. Late in 1866 he quietly let Wells and Fargo know that he was ready to sell out. The giant express company's directors met, weighed the prospects, and estimated that six years would surely pass before the transcontinental railroad could be completed. During that time their absolute monopoly should roll up tremendous profits with Holladay's equipment and contracts.

As usual, the uncouth Holladay was shrewder than the monied men who had tried to outbluff him. He exchanged his doomed empire for a fortune in cash, a large block of stock, and a directorship in Wells, Fargo & Company. Three years later, as he had foreseen, the railroad was completed, and the express company had to write off the Holladay venture at a huge loss. While Wells and Fargo desperately sought buyers for its superseded stagecoaches and freight wagons, the company's stock dropped from $100 to $13 a share, and the directors could find no money to issue dividends. Wells and Fargo, however, was too strong to go under, and with a new group of executives in command, soon became more powerful than ever by dominating express service on the railroads of the West.

11. The Grandest Enterprise Under God

In the decade following the great Civil War one event more than any other inspired the imaginations of Americans who believed in the Winning of the West. That was the building of the first transcontinental railroad, the tying together of East and West by thousands of miles of parallel steel rails into a glorious consummation of Manifest Destiny. Americans who had grown accustomed during the war to reading daily bulletins from battle fronts now picked up their newspapers each day to glance at progress accounts of Central Pacific crews building eastward from California and Union Pacific crews building westward.

It was such a grand and symbolic undertaking that few Americans paused to look beneath the surface of the spectacle to where a few dozen greedy men were boldly seizing the wealth of the West for later exploitation. Virtually no one seemed to care that the vast tracts of land being allotted to the railroad owners had been taken from Indian tribes in violation of treaties. As for the rich soils and forests, the fabulous deposits of coal and silver and iron and copper, were not these fair rewards for men who risked their fortunes to Win the West by building a railroad? Who would have dared spoil the illusion by pointing out that the fortunes being risked came from the pockets of the spectators themselves, the tax-paying citizens of the Republic, and that the actual builders of the tracks were not the smooth-talking gentlemen whose names appeared daily in the newspapers but were anonymous veterans of the Civil War, Irish and Swedish emigrants, former Negro slaves, and imported Chinese workers driven into a competitive madness by manipulators amassing millions from their labors?

No single human being could rightly assume credit for bringing the transcontinental railroad into being, although several men did boast so, and none with more flamboyance than George Francis Train. Perhaps no man deserves more of the hollow glory than Train, who has received precious little of it, although certainly it was he with his oratory and promotional genius who got the enterprise moving off dead center.

George Francis Train began his career as an accumulator of wealth, transportation magnate, promoter, communist, lecturer and author at the age of four. That was the year his father pinned a tag upon him and shipped him out of the New Orleans yellow fever epidemic of 1833 aboard a Boston-bound boat. On this voyage the four-year-old Train acquired a rich vocabulary of sailors' oaths and learned how to look out for himself. Until he was fifteen, the boy worked on his grandmother's farm near Waltham, and then he joined his Uncle Enoch's shipping business in Boston. By the time he was twenty, Train was earning ten thousand dollars a year, a magnificent income for 1849. The California gold strike inspired the young man to organize a fleet of sailing ships for the run around Cape Horn, and his uncle rewarded him by establishing him as manager of the firm's Liverpool office. Bored at twenty-four, Train journeyed to Australia, founded his own shipping firm, made an enormous fortune, toured the world, returned to the United States, and built a four-hundred-mile Eastern railroad which later became the Erie. At thirty he was back in England constructing horse-drawn street railways in Liverpool and London.

When the Civil War began, Train quarreled with his British associates, charging them with aiding the Confederate government. They in turn accused him of being a spy for the Union and he was held in jail for several days. After his release he returned to the United States and in 1862 became involved in spirited debates over the conduct of the war. In Boston he was arrested and jailed for interrupting a speech by Senator Charles Sumner. As soon as Train paid his fine, he was invited to go on a profitable lecture tour.

While in New York, Train became aware of discussions going around about a proposed transcontinental railroad. He afterward told of how he assembled a group of wealthy New Yorkers –including Commodore Cornelius Vanderbilt and William B. Astor–and tried to interest them in action rather than talk. He invited them to join him in financing the proposed railroad. From these men, he said, he received not a word of encouragement, not a cent of contributed funds, but only intimations that he must be a madman. 'Unaffected by this cold reception, I kept steadily on with my task, and proceeded to organize the great railway. Congress granted the necessary charter in '62.'

Other men than Train had preceded him, of course, in urging construction of the railroad, and had worked harder and longer than he to secure backing from the government. They included financiers Asa Whitney and Thomas Durant, Senators Thomas Hart Benton and William Gwin, engineer Theodore Judah, and four rich merchants of California–Huntington, Stanford, Hopkins, and Crocker–the Big Four of the Central Pacific Railroad. After President Lincoln signed the Pacific Railroad Act of 1862, the Big Four quickly organized the California end of the road and began construction eastward from Sacramento, although they were severely hampered by lack of rails and equipment which had to be shipped by sea from the East. In the East, the immediacy of the war's turmoil hindered efforts to

Timetable for the Central Pacific before it was extended to Promontory Point

CENTRAL PACIFIC RAILROAD.

NO. 1, TIME CARD NO. 1.

To take effect Monday June 6th, 1864, at 5 A. M.

TRAINS EASTWARD.			STATIONS.		TRAINS WESTWARD.	
Frt and Pass No 3	Frt and Pass No 2	Pass & Mail No 1.		Frt and Pass No 1	Pass & Mail No 2.	Frt and Pass No 3.
5 PM leave	1 PM leave	6.15 A M, L	Sacramento........	8.45 A M arr	12 M arr.	6.40 PM ar.
5.50 } mt frt 5.55 }	2.15	6.55........ 18	Junction............ 18	3........	11.20	5.55 } mt. Ft 5.50 }
6.09........	2.38........	7.05........ 22	Rocklin. 4	7.40........	11.07........	5.37........
6.22	2.55........	7.15 m;et F.. 25	Pino............ 3	7.15 mt pass	10.56	5.25........
6.40	3.30 PM arr	7.30 A M arr 31	Newcastle........ 6	3.45 A M, L	10.30 A M, L	b P M, L. ......

Trains No. 2 and 3 east, and 1 and 3 west, daily, except Sunday.

Trains No. 1 east and 2 west, daily.

LELAND STANFORD, President.

organize the Union Pacific, and not until October 1863 did U.P. stockholders gather in Wall Street to elect a board of directors.

Among those present was George Francis Train, who later claimed that he held the balance of power and used it to keep the New York Central and other Eastern roads from gaining control of the fledgling Union Pacific. The record indicates, however, that it was Thomas Durant who manipulated the choice of directors, arranging matters so that General John Adams Dix was named president, Durant himself becoming vice-president and general manager. An aging veteran of the War of 1812, Dix was a perfect figurehead for Durant because the old soldier had a reputation for honesty in a time when that quality was scarce in business and politics. In 1860 the Wall Street financiers had sent Dix to Washington to save Buchanan's treasury from collapse after exposure of William H. Russell's government bond deals with Secretary Floyd in the Pony Express fiasco.

As for forty-three-year-old Thomas Clark Durant, he was interested only in generating wealth for himself. He had a mania for money equal to that of Coronado's goldseekers, and to him the West offered a golden opportunity to extract vast amounts of money by spinning webs of mortgage bonds and high-interest loans around the building of a railroad to the Pacific. Durant saw no romance in the railroad itself; what appealed to him was the fortune which could be amassed from its construction. Although he had graduated with honors from an Albany medical college, he became bored with medicine and turned to making fortunes by speculating in grain futures and railroad stocks. Piling money upon money was Durant's reason for existence; any method that worked, regardless of how it affected other human beings, was acceptable in Durant's money game.

George Train, who was Durant's junior by a decade, had already lost interest in money for money's sake but he enjoyed the excitement of grand undertakings. For this reason he attached himself to the frenzied juggler of paper wealth, and assisted him in extracting venture capital from clever hoarders of it such as August Belmont, William H. Macy, Cyrus McCormick, Ben Holladay, Samuel J. Tilden, Thurlow Weed, and Brigham Young.

Even so, demand for Union Pacific stock continued slow, and in hopes of generating nationwide interest in the railroad, Train journeyed to Omaha for a ceremonial ground-breaking. 'None of the directors was with me', he said. 'I was entirely alone.' When it came to beating promotional drums, however, Train needed no help. He rounded up the governor of Nebraska, the mayor of Omaha, two companies of artillery, and after the firing of cannon had attracted a large crowd on the west bank of the Missouri, he read telegrams from President Lincoln and other notables, turned a few shovelfuls of muddy clay for the ground-breaking, and made a stirring speech.

'The great Pacific Railway is commenced', he cried, 'at the entrance of a garden seven hundred miles in length and twenty broad. This is the grandest enterprise under God!... Immigration will soon pour into these valleys. Ten millions of emigrants will settle in this golden land in twenty years.' Train then appealed to the 'average man' who might hear or read his speech: 'My idea is that the shares, $1,000, are too high. They should be reduced to $100, and subscriptions should be opened in every town of 500 inhabitants. Let the laboring man have one share; make it the people's road in reality.' The day ended with a grand banquet in the Herndon House and an expensive display of fireworks.

Although newspapers in the West carried Train's ground-breaking ceremonies in detail, back East where most of the investment capital was, the papers buried the story under reports of bloody Civil War battles, long casualty lists, and the prison escape of Confederate General John Morgan. The monied men preferred to place their cash in the hands of war manufacturers who paid interest as high as thirty per cent, and no laboring man had a thousand dollars to buy a share in a paper railroad to be built across a country inhabited by Indians whom they believed to be dangerous savages.

Undaunted, Train and Durant shifted their energies toward Washington and began lobbying for a more generous Pacific Railway bill—one which would grant twice as much land per mile (12,800 acres), the right to sell first-mortgage bonds equal to those of the promised government subsidy, and a change in capital stock from 100,000 thousand-dollar bonds to one million hundred-dollar bonds.

About this same time Train conceived the idea of establishing a holding company to be controlled by the directors of the railroad. Train and Durant both had learned from previous experience in railroad building that the big money was made in construction contracts rather than by waiting for long-delayed earnings from operation of completed roads. Through a closely held company they could make contracts with themselves for road construction, funneling all subsidies guaranteed them by the government into road building and thus evading any division of these funds with the ordinary stockholders.

During his experience in Europe, Train had observed the operations of a similar company which was organized with the blessings of the French government 'to facilitate the construction of public works and develop internal industry'. It was known as the Crédit Mobilier of France. Train borrowed the name, and he and Durant called their company the Crédit Mobilier of America.

In its original organization, Durant held the controlling interest, Train taking shares in his own and his wife's name. Among trusted friends allowed to purchase shares of Crédit Mobilier were Cyrus McCormick, Ben Holladay, and William H. Macy. To assure plentiful cash in its first year of operation, Durant also decided to admit Oakes Ames, a Congressman from Massachusetts. Ames with his brother Oliver had built a considerable fortune from war contracts for shovels and other hand tools. With the war coming to an end, the Ames brothers were seeking new markets for their tools, and railroad construction was an excellent prospect. The brothers eagerly bought into Crédit Mobilier. Durant shrewdly accepted their participation as an opening to Congress, and the Congressional bribery which followed would be exposed ten years later as a major government scandal of the Gilded Age.

One of the first actions taken by Durant as vice-president and general manager of Union Pacific was to receive a proposal from one H. M. Hoxie for construction of the first hundred miles of railroad track. One week later Hoxie, who was a dummy contractor, transferred the contract back to Durant as head of Crédit Mobilier. A few weeks after that, Durant accepted the resignation of the U.P.'s chief engineer, Peter Dey, who had turned in a cost estimate of thirty thousand dollars per mile of construction. Durant then appointed a new engineer who obligingly raised the estimate to fifty thousand dollars, or twenty thousand dollars more per mile for Crédit Mobilier stockholders who soon would be receiving a hundred per cent annual dividends on their investments while the Union Pacific stockholders received nothing.

Not until 10 July 1865 was the first rail laid at Omaha, and a month later in a publicity move designed to sell more U.P. stock, arrangements were made to display the great war hero, General William Tecumseh Sherman. Very likely it was George Francis Train who ordered the railroad's Locomotive No. 1 to be emblazoned with gold letters: 'Major General Sherman'. When Sherman arrived at Omaha, Durant rode with the general behind the locomotive named for him over the fifteen miles of

Union Pacific graders at work

track which had been completed. With the press in attendance, Durant entertained Sherman with a picnic of roast duck and wine, and converted the war hero into an enthusiastic booster for the railroad's builders.

Durant undoubtedly brought up the matter of Indian hostilities which were expected to intensify as the rails moved deeper into Sioux and Cheyenne country, and Sherman certainly assured him that the Army would offer full protection. As Durant was searching for an engineer with military connections to continue unfinished surveys through the hostile areas of Wyoming, the name of General Grenville Dodge must have been mentioned. Dodge had soldiered with Sherman in Georgia, keeping the railroads running for him. In that summer of 1865, Dodge was out on the high Plains in pursuit of Indians who were desperately attempting to halt the massive post-war invasion of their lands.

A few months later, Durant met Dodge at St Joseph, Missouri, and in the spring of 1866 Sherman's former military engineer became chief engineer for the Union Pacific. In addition to a salary which was more than double that which he had received in the Army, Dodge received a block of Crédit Mobilier stock which was cautiously registered under the name of his wife. Not long after this, the company quietly offered Sherman an

Although the railroads trespassed on Indian lands, the constructors were outraged by Indian attacks.

The mansions of the railroad barons, Hopkins and Stanford, in San Francisco

entire section of its Nebraska land grant at thirty per cent of the appraised value. Sherman bought the land, thus solidifying the military-industrial complex which would dominate the Winning of the West for the next generation.

Out in California in the meantime, the Big Four of the Central Pacific had created their own holding company, the Credit and Finance Corporation, which purchased all materials and contracted all construction. Collis P. Huntington, a former watch

peddler, was now in charge of peddling stock in the East and lobbying in Congress. As governor of California, former groceryman Leland Stanford kept the state legislature in line. Mark Hopkins and Charles Crocker, former operators of hardware and drygoods stores, handled the business and construction work of the Central Pacific. None of these men knew anything about railroads except that enormous profits were to be got out of the government and from stockholders for building a roadbed through the Sierras. Being even greedier than Thomas Durant, they kept all the stock of the Credit and Finance Corporation for themselves. To break a strike they imported several thousand Chinese laborers, paid them one dollar per day, or about half what the white laborers had received, and drove them hard so as to build tracks over as many government-subsidized miles as possible before they met the rails of the Union Pacific. Like Durant, they spent excessive amounts (the profits from waste all went to their Credit and Finance Corporation), and years afterward experts estimated that half of the many millions of dollars received from government and stockholders for the building of the Central Pacific went into the pockets of the Big Four—Huntington, Stanford, Hopkins, and Crocker. (During the Congressional investigation of the 1870s, the Credit and Finance Corporation's records were conveniently destroyed in a fire, so that no exact estimate ever was possible.)

In the summer of 1866 Crocker and Hopkins were blasting tunnels through the high Sierras (their mileage subsidy in the mountains was triple that of Durant's on the level plains). In August the Union Pacific announced that west-bound travelers could now ride on their passenger trains to Fort Kearney where they could transfer to one of Ben Holladay's stagecoaches for California. To drum up interest in stock-buying in the East, George Francis Train organized a Grand Excursion from New York to the 100th meridian in Nebraska. Ironically the 100th meridian was 250 miles west of the 95th meridian which in the lifetimes of most of these railroad promoters had been solemnly established by the United States government as a 'permanent Indian frontier'. The railroad was rapidly encroaching upon the most highly prized hunting reserves of the Plains Indians.

Among the rich and notable who came aboard the palace cars for the Grand Excursion to the 100th meridian were Rutherford B. Hayes, who ten years later would euchre Samuel Tilden out of the Presidency, Robert T. Lincoln, son of the martyred President, George M. Pullman, whose railroad sleeping cars would soon earn him a fortune, John Crerar and Joseph Medill of the Chicago financial community, several U.S. senators and congressmen, the Earl of Airlie and the Marquis Chambrun from abroad. General Sherman was unable to be there, but he sent his commander for the Department of the Platte, General Philip St George Cooke who twenty years earlier as a young captain of dragoons had assisted James Magoffin in 'capturing'

219.—*The Directors of the U. P. R. R. at the 100th Mer.*

Santa Fe and the Southwest from Mexico. George Francis Train was aboard, of course, with his wife Wilhelmina and her French maid. Accompanying the party was the Great Western Light Guard Band of Chicago which played appropriate patriotic airs, and there was also a photographer, John Carbutt, to record the events for posterity. Seated on buffalo grass at the end of track, Train posed for one view at the feet of his wife and Thomas Durant.

To entertain the wealthy Easterners, Train and Durant staged a grass fire at night on the prairies and a sham Indian

The Union Pacific's directors pose for John Carbutt.

fight. The Indians were all Pawnees, about half of them playing the roles of their enemies the Sioux. All were mounted, racing toward each other to do mock battle.

Horses reared and plunged against each other, Indian grappled Indian, and both fell to the ground in deadly embrace. Rifles, revolvers and arrows were discharged apparently with deadly effect. Riderless horses, and horseless riders were to be seen roaming wildly over the plain. And all was confusion and intense excitement, until at length the victorious Pawnees brought their vanquished enemies into camp, amid the most tempestous shouts of triumph and exaltation.

After the battle had ended, Mr. Durant distributed several hundred dollars' worth of presents among the Indians and their squaws . . . Perhaps no better illustration could have been given of the extremes of civilized and savage life, standing face to face with each other, than the one now before us. On the one side was the track of the Union Pacific Railroad, upon which stood that great civilizer, the locomotive and the train, looking westward over the Loup-Fork bridge, fifteen hundred feet in length; and in the foreground stood the group of excursionists, composed of beauty, intelligence and refinement; while, on the other hand, were grouped these uncouth savages, many of them almost in their normal state, except for the profuse display of feathers and trinkets which bedecked their persons; low and brutal in their habits, and mentally elevated but slightly, if at all, above the level of the beasts that inhabit this vast and beautiful country with them.

Some of the excursionists: George Francis Train, seated, with his wife and Thomas Durant standing behind him

But the laws of civilization are such that it must press forward; and it is in vain that these poor ignorant creatures attempt to stay its progress by resisting inch by inch, and foot by foot, its onward march over these lovely plains, where but a few years since, they were 'monarchs of all they surveyed.'

The locomotive must go forward until it reaches the Rocky Mountains, the Laramie Plains, the great Salt Lake, the Sierra Nevada, and the Pacific Ocean. Lateral roads must also be built, extending in all directions from the main line, as veins from an artery, and penetrating the hunting-grounds of these worse than useless Indian tribes, until they are either driven from the face of the earth; or forced to look for safety in the adoption of that very civilization and humanity, which they now so savagely ignore and despise.

Such was the view of Silas Seymour, consulting engineer of New York, who was among those present on that fine autumn afternoon in western Nebraska. He and the other beautiful, intelligent and refined excursionists had scarcely returned to their elegant homes in the East when a well-organized war party of *real* Sioux and other 'worse than useless Indian tribes' entrapped an invading force of eighty-one U.S. soldiers and killed all of them. The Army called it the Fetterman Massacre; to the Sioux and Cheyennes it was the Battle of the Hundred Slain.

The event sent a tremor of fear through the stockholders of Crédit Mobilier and Union Pacific. Durant demanded more protection from the Army. General Sherman replied that he would do his best to protect the graders and track layers, promising that as soon as the trains could take his soldiers closer to the hostiles 'we can act so energetically that both Sioux and Cheyennes must die or submit to our dictation'.

In March 1867 Sherman authorized organization of some of the sham-battle Pawnees into a mercenary force of scouts divided into four companies of fifty men each, with two white men, a captain and a first lieutenant to each company, and Major Frank North commanding. The principal duty of the Pawnee Scouts was to fend off raids by Sioux and Cheyennes against the track builders and their livestock.

To the resisting Plains Indians, the mercenaries offered a challenge, and on 12 August, six miles west of Plum Creek, a party of Cheyennes responded by wrecking a train. They accomplished this by piling loose ties across the rails. When the locomotive crashed into the barrier, it left the track, killing the engineer and fireman. The crew in the caboose escaped, however, and sent the Pawnee Scouts in pursuit. Union Pacific officials pleaded for more military protection, and Sherman himself came out in September to deal with the Red menace. To Sherman, completion of the railroad 'in its effect upon Indian affairs was equivalent to a successful campaign'. He ordered new forts built along the right of way and reinforced the old ones, thus expending more of the taxpayers' money to

Soldiers discover the skeletons of comrades killed by Indians in 1867, as depicted by an over-imaginative contemporary artist.

OPPOSITE General William Tecumseh Sherman, painted in 1866 by George Healy

keep dividends churning out to the seventy-five lucky stock-holders of Crédit Mobilier. (Three of them, Thomas Durant and Oakes and Oliver Ames, owned one-third of this stock.)

In September 1867 George Francis Train took on the task of escorting two hundred newspaper editors to the end of the Union Pacific track. He called this excursion the Great Rocky Mountain Editorial Buffalo Hunt, but his heart was not in it. During the summer he had met and been charmed by four ardent young women who were members of the much maligned Woman's Suffrage Movement. Because he loved desperate causes more than he loved money, Train promised to aid them in Kansas, which they hoped would be the first state to give women the right to vote. Several national leaders of the suffrage movement would be campaigning there.

On 2 October Train received a telegram signed by Susan B. Anthony, Elizabeth Cady Stanton and several others: 'Come to Kansas and stump the State for equal rights and female suffrage. The people want you. The women want you.'

He wired back: 'Shall be with you as soon as our Editorial Party have shot their buffalo and seen the Rocky Mountains. If women can rule monarchies they should vote in republics. The wedge once inserted in Kansas, we will populate the nation with three millions voting women.'

Train could hardly wait to join the suffragists, and in two whirlwind weeks in late October and early November he toured most of populated Kansas, delivering thirty speeches. Judging from the newspaper headlines, Train created a considerable stir on the golden Plains where three centuries earlier Coronado had sought riches in vain: TRAIN FIRES A BOMBSHELL INTO OLD FOGEYISM. THE PRAIRIES ABLAZE WITH EXCITEMENT. FEMALE SUFFRAGE PROUDLY IN THE ASCENDANT. TRAIN CARRIES KANSAS BY STORM. WOMAN SUFFRAGE FOREVER. TRAIN AT FORT SCOTT. LOOK OUT FOR THE ENGINE WHEN THE BELL RINGS.

Before the cheering stopped, his enthusiastic supporters nominated him to run for President of the United States in 1868 'on a platform of ideas – Woman Suffrage and eight hour labor'. Although he demurred, and Woman Suffrage in Kansas was voted down by the exclusively male electorate, the intoxication of politics had entered his blood. After that autumn, George Francis Train had little time to give the Union Pacific Railroad.

Thomas Durant, however, carried on, quarreling with General Dodge over route surveys, and also with the Ames brothers who were steadily gaining control of finances through their connections in Congress. While the financiers argued, the graders swung their picks and shovels, moving mountains of earth and rock with wheelbarrows and wagons. Behind the graders came the tracklayers, the muscular rail gangs lifting

OPPOSITE The safety of the railroad stations was not extended to the open spaces where trains were sometimes vulnerable to attack. TOP *Western Railway Station* by Oscar Berninghaus; BOTTOM *Railway Train Attacked by Indians* by Theodor Kaufmann

and dropping the lengths of heavy metal into place, the gaugers, spikers, and bolters following close behind. 'It is a grand "anvil chorus" . . . three strokes to the spike', said one observer. 'There are ten spikes to a rail, 400 rails to a mile, 1,800 miles to San Francisco—21,000,000 times are those sledges to be swung; 21,000,000 times are they to come down with their sharp punctuation before the great work of modern America is complete.'

Occasionally there would be a random Indian raid, but never any organized massed assault. The thousands of shouting, cursing workers, the ringing of metal against metal, the noisy puffing Iron Horses on their lengthening rails—it was all happening too fast for the awestruck Plains Indians to deal with. The Indians stabbed instinctively at the intruders, but far more workers suffered casualties from accidents, from venereal and other communicable diseases contracted in the hell-on-wheels tent camps which followed construction, and from overwork and exposure during the maddening race to cross the Wasatch Mountains in the winter of 1868–9. They laid tracks on beds of snow, were buried in avalanches, blew themselves up in tunnels, and were dashed into icy streams.

Few workmen complained. Their race with the Chinese laborers on the Central Pacific had become an obsession carefully orchestrated by Durant, Dodge, and the Ames brothers, and fanned into patriotic fervor by newspapers. The Central Pacific track was out of the Sierras now and moving swiftly across the Nevada and Utah deserts which only a few years earlier had come near defeating Jedediah Smith and numerous California-bound goldseekers.

So eager were both railroads to claim as many subsidized miles and mineral-rich landgrant acres as possible, they sent

ABOVE Once the railways were built the vast distances between East and West rapidly diminished.

RIGHT The Central Pacific employed underpaid Chinese to replace strikers.

After a desperate race which did not balk even at murder the two teams joined the rails at Promontory.

grading crews far out in front of the tracklayers. In the spring of 1869, U.P. and C.P. graders met and passed each other, running parallel grades across northern Utah, the opposing workmen engaging in daily brawls. On one occasion a group of U.P. graders placed blasting powder beneath a crew of C.P. graders and blew them up. President Grant and Congress finally had to settle the rivalry, choosing Promontory Point just north of Great Salt Lake as the place where the tracks of the two railroads must join.

On 7 May, Leland Stanford and a number of Central Pacific directors and public officials from California and Nevada arrived at Promontory on a special train. They brought along with them four golden and silver spikes, a silver-plated sledge hammer, and a polished laurel railroad tie, to be used in the planned ceremonies for the joining of the rails. These ceremonies were delayed for three days while Union Pacific contractors deliberately slowed completion of the final stretch of track. The contractors were waiting for Thomas Durant to bring his special train out of Bear River City, where several hundred angry workmen were holding him under siege until he paid them their overdue wages. The workmen chained the wheels of Durant's ornate parlor car to the rails until he arranged for a paymaster to bring up their money.

Durant, suffering with an acute headache, arrived at

Promontory on 10 May, and the speechmaking and drinking of toasts began to the accompaniment of music from two brass bands. A young man named Alexander Borthwick, who was a wood hauler for the Central Pacific, was there. An older man named Alexander Majors, once wealthy partner of Russell and Waddell but now a hauler of railroad ties for the Union Pacific, was also there. Borthwick received twenty-five cents per cord for his wood; Majors' pay must have been equally low. Had it not been for the disaster brought upon him in 1861 by his avaricious partner William H. Russell, Alexander Majors most likely would have been among the frock-coated, speech-making, champagne-drinking dignitaries that day, instead of merely a forgotten spectator.

'There was a great crowd of people and many big railroad men there', Borthwick recorded.

> A gap of only one rail remained to complete the work, and the bedding and laying of that was done with much ceremony. The last tie was of Laurel handsomely ornamented, was laid & 2 gold & 2 silver spikes were driven . . . Gov. Stanford performed the last act, driving them with a silver hammer. [The soused and boisterous crowd roared with laughter when he missed the first stroke.] To the last spike was attached a telegraph wire and news sent to California after which photographs of Gov. Stanford and group were taken, also of many other high officials. [The photographers had great difficulty persuading their inebriated subjects to stand still long enough to have their pictures made.] General Stoneman was there with a corps of Infantry en rout to California from Washington. After the work was completed many of the chiefs had a jolly time in which whiskey flowed abundantly and seemed to be the chief attraction.

George Francis Train, whose oratory had launched this Grandest Enterprise under God six years earlier at Omaha, was so busy with a new cause–the Irish Fenians–that he was a few days late in reaching Promontory Point. On 16 May, Alexander Borthwick noted in his diary that he went up in the evening to hear speeches by Isaac Morris and George Francis Train.

Morris was a government commissioner appointed by President Grant to inspect the condition of the completed transcontinental railroad, but Borthwick made no comment about Morris' remarks. Three days later Morris reported to Grant that the western portion of the road was very dangerous, the worst he had ever traveled over. 'The road, by the charter, was to be completed by the first day of July, 1876,' he said, 'but its completion is announced in May, 1869! This may be American enterprise, or, it may be American recklessness . . . The whole road was pushed forward in too much of a hurry both in regard to economy and durability. There was a temptation to do this offered by subsidies and lands too great for poor, avaricious human nature to resist, and it was done in direct violation of the standard of construction agreed upon by the board.' All that the people of the United States were getting for the enormous amount they had contributed for the railroad's construction, Morris concluded soberly, was the right to pass over the road by paying for it, 'and they are certainly entitled to have a "first-class road in all respects," that they may be assured of life and limb'.

Borthwick did not comment upon Train's speech, either, but the orator's subjects must have included the Grandest Enterprise under God, Women's Rights, the downtrodden Irish, the ineptitude of the Democratic and Republican parties, and the hypocrisy of professional churchmen. A few days later, he traveled on to the Pacific coast, and found himself to be in such demand as a speechmaker that he acquired ten thousand dollars which he did not need by delivering lectures on a tour through the Far West. He spent most of the money on a challenge that he could not travel around the world in eighty days. After he accomplished this feat, Jules Verne wrote a book about it, transforming Train into Phileas Fogg.

Happening to be in Marseilles in 1870 during an uprising of the French Commune, Train declared himself to be a communist devoted to the liberation of France. The French government deported him. In 1872 he ran for President of the United States against Greeley and Grant, charging an admission fee for the privilege of hearing his political speeches and thus earning ninety thousand dollars which he did not need. He spent most of it aiding Victoria Woodhull in her campaign for the Presidency. When Victoria charged Henry Ward Beecher with adultery and was arrested for obscenity, Train joined the battle in her defense. To confound Anthony Comstock, protector of the people's morals, he published excerpts from the Bible which he claimed were more obscene than the language in Victoria's newspaper; he then walked naked on the streets of New York and was jailed. After the courts declared him to be 'of unsound mind, though harmless', they took away a considerable amount of his property.

In his later years Train adopted the 'strenuous life' advocated by Theodore Roosevelt, engaging in boxing matches at the age of seventy; he went on a diet of peanuts, and occasionally ran for President of the United States. At the turn of the century he was living quietly in a New York hotel. Most of his fortune was gone now, given away for lost causes or to aid needy children. He had grown so disillusioned with the perfidy of adult human beings that for days at a time he would speak only to children. When he died in 1904 at the age of seventy-four, no representative of the Union Pacific came to honor his memory, but a school named for him in Omaha, Nebraska, near where he had broken ground for the first transcontinental railroad, lowered its flag to half-mast. In New York, fifty children brought flowers–single roses, single carnations–to place upon his coffin.

12. The Indian Slayers

On 10 May 1869, the day the rails were joined at Promontory Point, William T. Sherman, newly appointed General of the Army, received the news by telegraph in his War Office in Washington. A few minutes later the Union Pacific's chief engineer, General Dodge, sent Sherman a personal message: 'As a steadfast earnest friend of the Pacific Rail Road, I send you greetings the fact at twelve (12) M. today the last connection was made, and you can visit your old friends in California overland, all the way by rail.' Sherman replied: 'I heard the mystic taps of the telegraph battery announce the nailing of the last spike in the great Pacific road. Indeed, am I its friend? Yea.'

Shortly afterward Sherman urged General Philip H. Sheridan, his successor as commander in the West, to protect the new railroad 'as it will help bring the Indian problem to a final solution'. Over the next decade, these two men would direct military operations against American Indians west of the Mississippi, killing thousands of them and crushing the spirits of the survivors so thoroughly that even after three generations few tribes have yet recovered from the desolation inflicted upon them. In their own words Sherman and Sheridan viewed their native opponents as inferior beings, as beasts like the buffalo who stood in the way of a superior civilization.

Ironically, Sherman's father had named him after the great Shawnee leader, Tecumseh ('Will we let ourselves be destroyed without a struggle, give up our homes, our country bequeathed to us by the Great Spirit, the graves of our dead and everything that is dear and sacred to us?'). Some members of the Sherman family protested christening the boy after a savage Indian, and he was soon being called 'Cump' instead of Tecumseh. After he learned to write his name, he always signed himself William T. Sherman. He took no pride in his Indian name.

When the Civil War began, Sherman was superintendent of a Louisiana military academy. He resigned immediately and offered his services to the Union. He was a graduate of West Point, but his only real military experience had been scouting in Florida against the elusive Seminoles. He spent most of his time there collecting sea shells and rattlesnake skins, and he

The first Battle of Bull Run was fought on a Sunday, 21 July 1861; there were great losses on both sides.

reached the conclusion that the only way to defeat the Seminoles was through a 'war of extermination'.

To Sherman the first months of the Civil War were a period of intense anguish. As a colonel he survived four hours of bloody combat at Bull Run, and he was more sickened by the dead and the dying than by the rout of the Union Army. Promoted to brigadier-general he was ordered to Kentucky where his strange behavior attracted the attention of newspaper reporters. 'Dirty newspaper scribblers', Sherman called them. 'They are a pest . . . and I'll treat them as spies which in truth they are.' For the remainder of his life he warred with the press, swearing 'to get even with the miserable class of editors'. Some papers bluntly described him as being insane, and his military associates remarked on 'a wild expression about his eyes' which they attributed to 'emotional imbalance' or 'morbid melancholy', although one officer described him as 'gone in the head'. Evidently he was suffering a nervous breakdown.

He resigned his Kentucky command and went home to Ohio to recuperate. His wife nursed him back to physical health, but being aware of the strain of madness in his family background she tried to persuade him to remain permanently out of the Army. In December 1861, however, he went to St Louis for a non-combat assignment. He could not immediately shake off the spells of depression which besieged him, and in a frank letter to his brother he confessed that he 'should have committed suicide were it not for my children'.

During that winter Sherman underwent a startling change. He was invited to participate in the strategic planning for General Grant's 1862 campaign in the West and then was given command of a combat division. At Pittsburg Landing in the Battle of Shiloh, he fought like a man in deep fear of failure. From that time, he learned to view with equanimity 'the piles of dead and wounded and maimed'. He became the scourge of the South, intent upon killing until there were no more opponents to be killed, rejoicing in the exhilaration of conquest. At the beginning of the war in Kentucky he had forbidden his men to 'take a green apple, or a fence rail to make a cup of coffee'. At the end of the war he was plundering through Georgia, destroying homes, courthouses, libraries, barns, crops, and livestock, and he looked upon war as a 'grand and beautiful game'.

After it was all over and he took command of military forces in the West, one of Sherman's first decisions was to build a line of forts six hundred miles long across the frontier, not to protect the Indians from the flood of white settlers invading their treaty lands but to aid the settlers in their Western advance. For Sherman, the Indians of the West had conveniently replaced the white Rebels of the South as enemies to be destroyed in a grand and beautiful game. Determined to improve his expertness as an authority upon Indian matters, he toured much of the West, reporting that nomadic and predatory bands infested the whole area.

'These Indians are universally, by the people of our frontier and of our isolated Territories, regarded as hostile, and we, the military, charged with a general protection of the infant settlements and long routes of travel, have to dispose our troops and act as though they were hostile; while by the laws of Congress, and the acts of our executive authorities, these Indians are construed as under the guardianship and protection of the general government, through civilian agents.' It rankled Sherman that civilians should have any authority over Indians, and he demanded that the military establishment be given 'the entire management'. His plan for managing them was to push the tribes north of the Platte and south of the Arkansas, leaving a wide belt between for travel routes and settlement. In addition he wanted to build forts and place troops along a road which ran from Fort Laramie northward to Montana, where gold had been discovered. It did not occur to him that the wide belt across the Plains and the road to Montana amounted to intrusions upon, or elimination of, the richest hunting grounds of the Indians of those regions. Any interference with the hunting of buffalo and antelope threatened the food, shelter, and clothing of Plains Indians, forcing even the most peaceable tribes to fight for their existence.

The Indian Slayers

In 1864, while the gold rush in Montana was at its height, old Jim Bridger marked out a trail from Fort Laramie to Virginia City. Being aware of the Indians' determination to keep white men out of their prized Powder River country, Bridger routed his trail west of the Big Horn Mountains. Trader John Bozeman, however, mapped a road east of the mountains directly through the hunting country, mainly because of the excellent grazing available for wagon teams and the ready accessibility of wild game for meat. Travelers preferred the Bozeman Trail, but some were fearful of Indians and demanded military protection.

Although the Sioux, Cheyenne, and Arapaho tribes, which were sustained by the Powder River country, fought back in 1865 when General Patrick Connor invaded with three columns of soldiers and attacked their villages, they offered little interference to civilians who wished only to pass through their country. In June 1866 a civilian train of twenty-five wagons traveled over the Bozeman route from Fort Laramie to Virginia City, on some nights not even bothering to corral the vehicles. Along the way they met Cheyennes and Arapahos who wanted to trade Indian goods for sugar and flour. On 20 June 'the Indians led the way around for us to cross another bad stream, and rode along with us nearly all the forenoon trying to "swap". More came up near the river and one old chief made the captain of the train a present of a nice buffalo robe.' The young white women of the train mingled freely with the so-called 'hostiles', trading cups of sugar for moccasins.

That same week back at Fort Laramie a column of infantry and cavalry under command of Colonel Henry B. Carrington started northward under orders from General Sherman to establish three forts along the Bozeman Trail and 'complete the wagon road from Fort Laramie to Virginia City, which the Indians give notice they will resist. They represent it as passing through the only remaining hunting grounds they have; but this road is necessary to Montana, and must be finished and made safe.'

Jim Bridger, a scout with a rare consideration for the Indians

Although Red Cloud and other Indian leaders from the Powder River country warned that they would not tolerate this military occupation of their treaty lands, Sherman apparently was surprised when the first attacks began against the soldiers of Fort Phil Kearny. At Crazy Woman's Creek on 22 June, *before the soldiers came there*, a passing civilian train camped with 'wagons and tents scattered here and there ... the blazing fires shining through the trees ... and the quiet moon looking down on all'. At Crazy Woman's Creek one month later, the Indians attacked a well-armed vanguard of invading soldiers, inflicting several casualties. 'These deaths must be avenged', Sherman declared. Six months later he was dumbfounded when he received the report of the ambush of Captain William J. Fetterman's party of eighty-one men near Fort Phil Kearny.

Indian leaders, including Red Cloud, would suffer transitory emigrants but not a permanent military force on their land.

'I do not understand how the massacre of Fetterman's party could have been so complete', he telegraphed General Grant from St Louis. 'We must act with vindictive earnestness against the Sioux, even to their extermination, men, women and children. Nothing less will reach the root of this case.'

For weeks he fretted over how he was going to get at Red Cloud's warriors and begin the extermination. 'These roving bands have no real chiefs,' he wrote General Grant in July 1867, 'but are a pure democracy; each man does as he pleases regardless of his so-called chief.' He went on to recommend that all past treaties be abrogated, and Indians not on fixed reservations be considered as enemies at war with the United States. The U.S. Congress, however, reflecting the will of a nation seeking a peaceful solution rather than more bloody warfare, appointed a peace commission to deal with the Indians. To Sherman's disgust, he was placed on the commission along with Generals Alfred Terry and W. S. Harney, and four civilians.

In September, Sherman and his fellow commissioners boarded a Union Pacific train at Omaha and rode out to North Platte, where several Sioux and Cheyenne leaders had agreed to meet them for a peace council. Spotted Tail, Pawnee Killer, Standing Elk, and several others were there, but Red Cloud refused to come, sending as his emissary a warrior who twenty years earlier had been much admired by Francis Parkman. He was Man-Afraid-of-His-Horses, and he had taken as his wife the half-blood daughter of Parkman's guide, Henry Chatillon.

Although Sherman attempted to ban newspaper reporters from the Indian parleys, a young Welshman representing

Treaty commissioners—from the left, Terry, Harney, Sherman, Taylor, Tappan and Auger—pose awkwardly round a young Sioux woman at Fort Laramie during the talks of 1868.

Signing the treaty—the commissioners and the Indians they had cajoled and threatened, including Spotted Tail, Man-Afraid-of-His-Horses, Big Mouth and Pawnee Killer

papers in St Louis and New York was there. He was Henry M. Stanley, who later achieved fame during his search for David Livingstone in Africa. 'General Sherman', he wrote, 'inhaled with befitting gravity three distinct whiffs' from each of the peace pipes handed around by the visiting chiefs. Sherman then sat listening to the Indians' speeches.

Spotted Tail was the first to protest the building of forts and roads through the Powder River country. 'I want these roads stopped,' he said, 'or turned in some other direction. We will then live peacefully together.' Pawnee Killer said virtually the same thing: 'The cause of our troubles is the Powder River road. In that country there is game. That is what we have to live upon.' Most of the chiefs offered no objection to the building of the railroad; the iron track was already there and they could do nothing about it.

Through the warm September afternoon the speeches con-

tinued, and then, according to Stanley, Sherman replied 'in his own peculiar manner'. He said he thought the Indians had given permission for the Bozeman road to run through the Powder River country, but whether they had agreed to this or not, the road would not be given up 'while the Indians continue to make war'. With bizarre military logic he explained: 'The Powder River road was built to furnish our men with provisions.' He promised, however, to look into any damages which might be caused the Indians by the presence of the road and forts. 'If we find that the road hurts you, we will give it up or pay for it.' Money and presents, Sherman believed, would buy anything. 'You must submit and do the best you can', he warned. 'If you continue fighting you will all be killed . . . live like white men, and we will help you all you want.'

Most of the Indian leaders, however, knew there was no way they and their people could live like white men even if they wished to do so. With Red Cloud and warriors such as young Crazy Horse leading them, they were determined to keep their last hunting reserve inviolate. When the commissioners arranged a second meeting with the chiefs at Fort Laramie in the autumn of 1867, none of the resistance leaders came in for the council.

In the spring of 1868, the commissioners tried once more to persuade the Indians to cease their opposition to military occupation of the Powder River country, proposing in fact that they give it up entirely and move to a reservation somewhere along the Missouri River–where they could more easily be controlled. Red Cloud and his followers would have none of it, refusing to come in to Fort Laramie until all soldiers were withdrawn from their country. Red Cloud did send the commissioners a message: 'We are on the mountains looking down on the soldiers and the forts. When we see the soldiers moving away and the forts abandoned, then I will come down and talk.'

Sherman departed Fort Laramie in exasperation, but a few weeks later he approved orders for all soldiers to abandon the forts along the Bozeman road and leave the Powder River country. Red Cloud and the resistance leaders had won, temporarily. 'In time we must take these wild Indians in hand,' Sherman wrote Grant, 'and give them a devil of a thrashing. They deserve it now, but they are so scattered and so mixed up that even if we were prepared we would hardly know which way to strike.'

After Grant was elected President a few months later, he appointed Sherman General of the Army with headquarters in Washington. Sherman's replacement as commander in the West was Lieutenant-General Philip Henry Sheridan. Although ten years younger than his commanding general, Sheridan knew considerably more than he about Indian fighting. Upon graduation from West Point in 1853 he had been assigned to the Far West, and spent several years there pursuing and killing

Yakimas and other native Americans in California and Oregon. A half century earlier these same tribes had aided Lewis and Clark in their journey to the Pacific, but in the 1850s white invaders were taking their lands and when they objected to this, soldiers were summoned to drive away the original inhabitants. Sheridan evidently enjoyed the work.

During the Civil War, Sheridan devastated the Shenandoah Valley somewhat in the same way that Sherman plundered Georgia. In temperament, however, the two men were opposites. Sheridan had fought his way up from Irish poverty to become a pugnacious posturer. His dark leathery face and grotesque figure made him the butt of jokes at West Point, and even President Lincoln laughed at his appearance–'long body, short legs, not enough neck to hang him, and such long arms that if his ankles itch he can scratch them without stooping'. On horseback Sheridan was transformed into a centaur, and his supreme joy was to ride at a mad gallop with banners flying and sabers rattling. George Armstrong Custer admired and emulated him.

'The Indian is a lazy, idle vagabond', Sheridan declared at the end of his first year of command in the West. 'He never labors, and has no profession except that of arms, to which he is raised from a child; a scalp is constantly dangled before his eyes, and the highest honor he can aspire to is to possess one taken by himself. It is not to be wondered at, therefore, if he aims for this honor when he grows up, especially if there is no punishment to follow the barbarous act. The government has always been very liberal to Indians, especially whenever they have settled on reservations; the lands alloted to them have been of the best character, making them, perhaps, by far the richest communities in the country.' It is possible that Sheridan believed that what he said was true; if so, he certainly must have spent no time observing the customs of Plains Indians or visiting their reservations.

In 1868, after Red Cloud had won his temporary peace in the North, Sheridan proposed to Sherman that the Army turn its attention upon the tribes along the Arkansas, the river which Sherman had chosen as the southern limit of his 'wide belt' across the Plains which was to be cleared of Indians. For the Southern Cheyennes and Arapahos, the Kiowas and Comanches, the Plains of western Kansas enclosed a wild game reserve as important to them as the Powder River country was to the Northern tribes. Red Cloud's success in driving the white invaders from his country was not lost upon the Southern leaders, although the wisest of them realized that stagecoach lines, railroads, and white settlement had doomed their old hunting grounds between the Republican and Smoky Hill rivers. Black Kettle, an aging chief of the Southern Cheyennes, wanted no part of defending the Kansas buffalo range. In 1864 he had barely survived the horrors of Sand Creek where his people had lost many women and children to the soldiers of Colonel John M. Chivington. Most of the warriors were away at the time, hunting buffalo in Kansas, and some of them had been engaged since that time in a revenge war against the bluecoated soldiers. In the summer of 1868, Black Kettle had obeyed the advice of soldiers and agents and drifted south of the Arkansas with a few hundred followers, to hunt buffalo where they told him it would be safe. In the autumn he established a winter camp along the Washita River.

During that summer, however, a number of Cheyenne warriors went north of the Arkansas where the hunting was better. A band of about two hundred young Indians, including Cheyennes, Arapahos, and Sioux, went on a rampage, striking at settlements and stagecoach stations. They chased stagecoaches, ambushed wagon trains, and on two occasions raped white women.

These depredations infuriated Sheridan, but his cavalrymen had no luck in overtaking the outlaws: 'The Indian mounted on his hardy pony and familiar with the country', he complained, 'was about as hard to find, so long as the grass lasted, as the *Alabama* [an elusive cruiser of the Confederate Navy] on the ocean.' In his frustration, Sheridan placed responsibility for the offenses upon tribal leaders, although most of them were hundreds of miles away from the scenes of action. When these leaders heard that Sheridan was at Fort Dodge, a number of Cheyenne, Arapaho, Kiowa, and Comanche chiefs went there to discuss with him means of keeping the peace. Sheridan refused to meet with them. 'They asked me to have an interview with them, which I declined', he said afterward. 'The manner of the Indians, so far as I saw, was insolent and overbearing.'

Sheridan had already made up his mind to wait until the tribes formed their winter villages so that his soldiers could surround them and attack without warning. General Sherman approved this plan for a winter campaign, but being fearful of

Land ceded by the Indians

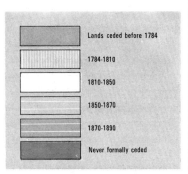

Lands ceded before 1784

1784-1810

1810-1850

1850-1870

1870-1890

Never formally ceded

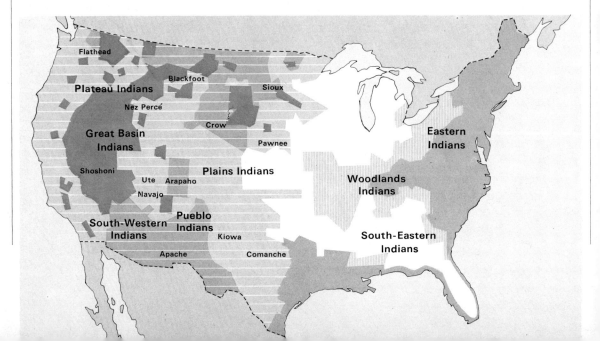

criticism from the press he went through the motions of establishing a sanctuary at Fort Cobb where peaceable Indians were promised safety from Sheridan's search and destroy missions. Indians who did not report to General William B. Hazen at Fort Cobb in Indian Territory, Sherman announced, would be considered outlaws. 'I propose', he said, 'that Sheridan shall prosecute the war with vindictive earnestness against all hostile Indians, till they are obliterated or beg for mercy; and therefore all who want peace must get out of the theatre of war.' Sherman did not explain exactly where the 'theatre of war' was to be, nor how General Hazen was to provision the thousands of Indians who would surely seek shelter around Fort Cobb. On 17 September 1868 he wrote to the Commissioner of Indian Affairs informing him of the Fort Cobb refuge, and recommending that Indians be forbidden to hunt buffalo (the source of their food, shelter, and clothing) unless they first secured a permit from the commanding officer of the nearest military post.

'The more we can kill this year,' he said on 23 September, 'the less will have to be killed the next war, for the more I see of these Indians the more convinced I am that they all have to be killed or be maintained as a species of paupers. Their attempts at civilization are simply ridiculous.' The next day he informed General Dodge of the Union Pacific that the Army was not going to let up all winter. 'Before spring comes I hope not an Indian will be left in that belt of country through which the two railroads pass.'

General Sheridan meanwhile was energetically organizing the winter campaign. He established headquarters at Fort Hays, wheedled added reinforcements out of Sherman, employed dozens of famous civilian scouts—including the former Pony Express rider and stagecoach driver, Buffalo Bill Cody. In the midst of these preparations, old Jim Bridger showed up unexpectedly at Sheridan's headquarters.

The previous year Bridger had resigned his job at Fort Laramie as civilian scout for the Army. After visiting the riproaring new town of Cheyenne and taking a brief look at the Union Pacific railroad pushing across Wyoming, he knew that the West of his day was gone forever. Ailing from arthritis, his eyesight fading, he had retired to Westport, Missouri, to live with his two half-blood Indian daughters. Yet when he heard of the Army's plans for a winter campaign, he traveled all the way to Fort Hays to warn Sheridan not to go through with it. Here was a man who knew more about the West and its native inhabitants than any other living member of the white race, but Sheridan scorned his advice.

'I am of the belief that these Indians require to be soundly whipped,' Sheridan said on 26 September, 'and the ringleaders in the present trouble hung, their ponies killed, and such destruction of their property as will make them very poor.'

After an exchange of opinions, Sheridan and Sherman agreed

that the best choice for a field commander to lead the strike against the Indians was the golden-haired George Armstrong Custer. Only the previous year the Army had courtmartialed Custer and suspended him from command after a series of wild actions in which he had executed enlisted deserters without trials and then had deserted his post himself in order to visit his wife. On 9 October Sheridan received formal orders to set the winter campaign in motion. On 23 November Custer marched his Seventh Cavalry out of Camp Supply, heading straight for the peaceful Indians' camps on the Washita.

In the meanwhile, leaders of the Southern tribes had learned of the Army's planned winter campaign against the 'hostiles' and of the refuge at Fort Cobb for the 'friendlies'. Late in November, Black Kettle with several other Cheyenne and Arapaho leaders made a hurried journey to Fort Cobb and asked General Hazen for protection. Hazen afterwards tried to explain why he turned them away. He said that he had just received information that Sheridan's forces in the field were under orders

> to pursue and punish the Indians that had depredated in Kansas, *even into the reservation under my charge and to Fort Cobb should it become necessary* . . . When Black Kettle, with a delegation of his people and the Arapahos came to Cobb to make peace . . . I advised all who really wanted peace to return without any delay to their camps, to call their people in from the warpath, and to avoid the threatening war by watchfulness, but not to come to Cobb until they should hear from me . . . They returned to their camps then on the Washita . . . and the next morning the battle under General Custer occurred, in which Black Kettle was killed.

Hazen knew that in turning Black Kettle and his friends away from Fort Cobb, he was sending them to almost certain death at the hands of Custer's cavalrymen, and he also must have known that Black Kettle was high on the list of the Army's most wanted Indian leaders. Since Sand Creek, Black Kettle had become a symbol who represented all the wrongs which had been done by the military to Indians during the Winning of the West. Black Kettle had to be eliminated, and it had to be done in such a way that he and his people would appear to be the wrongdoers.

Sheridan used the big lie in damning the reputation of Black Kettle, claiming that before the winter campaign he had offered the chief sanctuary in a fort. 'He refused, and was killed in the fight.' He then declared that Custer's men had found photographs and daguerreotypes, clothing and bedding, from the houses of persons massacred on the Solomon and Saline in Kansas. He did not explain that neither Black Kettle nor the great majority of his people had been anywhere near the scenes of the summer depredations. To punish the few outlaws in camp, Custer's cavalrymen killed indiscriminately 103 Cheyennes, only eleven of whom were warriors; they

Philip Henry Sheridan in the portrait by Thomas Buchanan Read celebrating his famous ride to rally his troops after a setback at Cedar Creek during the Civil War

burned the tipis, slew 875 horses, and marched 53 women and children in triumph back to Camp Supply.

'Although Custer had struck a hard blow, and wiped out old Black Kettle and his murderers and rapers of helpless women,' Sheridan said, 'I did not feel that our work was done yet.' With the Cheyennes and Arapahos beaten into the snow, Sheridan and Custer now went after the Kiowas and Comanches. They arranged the capture of Satanta and Lone Wolf by inviting them to a council under a flag of truce, and then in violation of the truce they arrested the Kiowa chiefs and put them in irons. To force the tribe to surrender, Sheridan sent messages out to the fleeing Kiowas, informing them that unless they all came into Fort Cobb and gave up their arms, their chiefs would be hanged. It was during this mass surrender of the Kiowas that Sheridan uttered his famous phrase: *The only good Indian is a dead Indian.*

After the Kiowas surrendered, Sheridan kept his word and freed Satanta and Lone Wolf. 'I shall always regret, however, that I did not hang these Indians; they had deserved it many times; and I shall also regret that I did not punish the whole tribe when I first met them . . . but a person sometimes gets confounded as to what is his duty.'

For the next five years Sheridan, with occasional assists from Sherman, carried on a blood feud with the obstreperous Kiowas and their allies the Comanches. Both of these horse tribes detested being confined to reservations, and several of their leaders died violently in struggles to keep their people free.

By the summer of 1874 the Army had whipped most of the Kiowas and Comanches into confinement in Indian Territory. A few bands, however, managed to elude the soldiers and found a place of refuge in that remarkable oasis on the Staked Plains of Texas where Coronado and his men had saved themselves in May of the year 1541. This was Palo Duro Canyon, invisible from the plain, a thousand feet deep in some places, with perpetual water and grass, an Eden where lived the last buffalo herds on the Southern Plains. Coronado's Spaniards had also found mulberry and nut trees, wild plums and grapes and turkeys, and these food sources were still there for the growing bands of Kiowas, Comanches, and Cheyennes. They set up their tipi villages along the floor of the canyon in 1874 and tried to live as free peoples in the way they had always lived.

Such a paradise could not be kept a secret; their friends and relatives on the reservations learned of the Palo Duro and tried to join them. The Army heard rumors of free Indians on the Plains, but patrols could find no trace of them. In September, Sherman interrupted the writing of his memoirs long enough to issue orders sending five columns to criss-cross the Staked Plains; he sent thousands of soldiers marching out to find those few hundred free Indians.

On 26 September Colonel Ranald Mackenzie's cavalrymen

ABOVE Guipa'go or Lone Wolf, *c.* 1870

LEFT The fugitive Indians and buffaloes sheltering in the Palo Duro Canyon were soon to be displaced by cowboys and Longhorns. TOP Charles Russell's *Broken Rope*; and BOTTOM *The Herd* by Frank Reaugh

found a narrow trail descending into the Palo Duro. At sight of the first tipi village, they opened fire. The warriors held a defense line long enough for their women and children to escape, and then all fled before the superior fire power of the soldiers. Mackenzie's men then burned the tipis, blankets, and pemmican; they rounded up two thousand ponies which the Indians had abandoned in their flight up the bluffs to the open plain, and then shot every captured animal to death. During the next few days the mounted soldiers overtook the scattered bands of unhorsed Indians and forced them to walk more than two hundred miles back to Fort Sill.

In less than ten years, Sherman and Sheridan had destroyed the tribes of the Southern Plains. Now they could turn the full power of the Army upon the proud Sioux and their allies in the North. They were confident that these unyielding Indians also could be crushed by ambitious and aggressive young field commanders such as Ranald Mackenzie and George Armstrong Custer.

LEFT The forced camp of Mow-way or Swinging Hand of the Comanches outside Fort Sill. BELOW, a bleak contrast to the Palo Duro Canyon

13. The Father of the Cowboys

Not quite two years after Colonel Mackenzie's soldiers left the Palo Duro to the buzzards–which quickly converted the dead horses of the Indians into a bone pile–a slow-moving herd of 1800 Longhorn cattle appeared on the northern horizon of the Staked Plains. They were being driven down from Colorado by a forty-year-old man as tough as the rawhide boots he was wearing. His name was Charles Goodnight, and he meant to inherit the vast plain where Coronado had found Indians whom he called Teyas and herds of buffalo numerous as fish in the sea. Now the Indians were locked on reservations and the buffalo were gone from the Southern Plains. To replace them, Goodnight came with the cowboys and Longhorns.

The maps showed the Staked Plains to be a pitiless desert, and travelers for three centuries had turned far out of their way to avoid crossing that dry country of burning winds and tree-less expanses broken by dull-hued escarpments. 'The country is like a bowl,' Pedro de Castaneda had said, 'so that when a man sits down, the horizon surrounds him all around at the distance of a musket shot.' Charles Goodnight had been a Texan long enough, however, to remember the endless herds of buffalo that drifted down from the Red River country to feed on the Plains' rich grama grasses and drink from its hidden springs and streams.

Charles Goodnight

Goodnight had never seen the Palo Duro, but he had heard of a deep canyon somewhere on the Plains, a place said to be always green. In the spring of 1876, Goodnight found it, a deep gash in the arid land, a buffalo trail leading down into a green oasis of cottonwood, chinaberry and cedar trees, and a carpet of grass.

When Charles Goodnight was a boy growing up north of St Louis in Macoupin County, Illinois, his father died. His mother married again, to a man spell-struck by the expansionist fever of the 1840s. In 1846, the Year of Decision, young Goodnight's stepfather felt compelled to migrate to Texas. He put Charles on a mare, but could not afford a saddle, and the eleven-year-old boy rode bareback for seven hundred miles, his crotch and buttocks rubbing raw, then healing and callousing. Two miles west of a Texas trading post called Dallas–a pair of log cabins and a ferryboat landing–young Goodnight saw his first buffalo.

A decade later, in 1857, the year that John Butterfield began preparing the route for his Overland Mail, Goodnight was twenty-one, and he was herding Longhorns near Fort Belknap, one of Butterfield's stagecoach stops. Goodnight and his stepbrother had contracted to keep four hundred skittish cows from straying and to brand the calves. Their pay for this work was one-fourth of the calves born during the year. 'As the end of the first year's branding resulted in only 32 calves for our share,' he said, 'and as the value was about three dollars per head, we figured out that we had made between us, not counting expenses, 96 dollars.'

In the 1850s Longhorns had to be driven hundreds of miles, to New Orleans or Galveston, and if the drover was lucky enough to find a buyer, he *might* receive as much as three dollars per head. For Charles Goodnight, however, there was nothing else to do, and so he persevered. After four years of hard work, he and his partner assembled a herd of four thousand. And then the Civil War began.

Out in the thinly populated Cross Timbers country, Negro slaves were rare, and the war was so far away it seemed of little importance, attitudes being based upon one's emotional ties with the region of his origin. Goodnight vaguely remembered Illinois, but he had little feeling for the war one way or the other. When a company of Confederate mounted riflemen was organized to patrol Red River, a hundred miles north of Goodnight's ranging Longhorns, he joined on as a scout.

One of his first duties was to guide a cavalry detail across Red River for a council with the Comanches. The Texas Confederates hoped to persuade the tribe to join their cause. Considering the fact that Texans for years had been using force to drive the Comanches out of Texas into Indian Territory, this mission must have required a considerable amount of gall. 'The Comanches flatly refused to join the Confederacy,' Goodnight recalled, 'saying we Texans were heap rich in cattle and horses and that they preferred to fight us and steal from us and trade to Mexico–which they did. We were at the Indian camp only a day and night–there was no use staying with the buggers.'

For the remainder of the Civil War, Goodnight's company of Texans spent most of their time disputing control of the upper Brazos and the Red River country with Comanches and Kiowas. They never saw a blue Yankee uniform, and most of their casualties were from rattlesnake bites. When the war ended, their makeshift uniforms were worn out; their Confederate money was worthless. All that they owned were scattered herds of Longhorns, and there was no market for them in the bankrupt South. 'I suffered great losses', Goodnight said. 'The Confederate authorities had taken many of them without paying a cent. Indians had raided our herds and cattle thieves were branding them, to their own benefit without regard to our rights.' He was thirty years old and financially destitute.

By early spring of 1866, rumors reached the Texas cattle country that meat was in short supply in the North, and that a Longhorn steer would bring as high as forty dollars delivered in Chicago. The nearest railhead was in Missouri, and during the first warm days of spring, Texans began driving Longhorns up the trails across Indian Territory. Goodnight watched the herds move out and guessed there was going to be a glut of cattle in Missouri. (He was right; 100,000 Longhorns went unsold for lack of buyers and rail transport facilities.) Instead of joining the drives to Missouri, Goodnight and a fifty-four-year-old neighbor, Oliver Loving, decided to combine their herds and drive west into New Mexico. Cattle were reported to be in demand there by miners and by government agents who bought them for Apaches and Navahos whom General James Carleton and Kit Carson had penned on reservations. The pay was in gold and silver rather than in paper money which Goodnight and Loving had grown to distrust after the collapse of the Confederacy.

To reach New Mexico, they could follow John Butterfield's abandoned Overland Mail route. Most of the stations, water-holes and wells which had sustained Butterfield's employees and passengers were still there. On 6 June Goodnight and Loving started a herd of two thousand Longhorns moving westward from Fort Belknap. For this hazardous journey, Goodnight constructed what was probably the first chuck-wagon. He bought the gear of a government wagon, and rebuilt it with the toughest wood he knew, a wood used by Indians for

ABOVE Camp cook in his kitchen

RIGHT Lead steers crossing a stream that will settle the dust kicked up by the following herd

fashioning their bows – Osage Orange or *bois d'arc*. He replaced the wooden axles with iron, and for lubrication carried a can of tallow rather than the usual Army tar bucket. Instead of horses he chose alternating teams of six sturdy oxen to draw the wagon. At the rear he built a chuckbox with a hinged lid which dropped to form a cook's work table. A generation of trail drivers would adopt Goodnight's invention for long drives to markets, and variations of it are still in use today on larger cattle ranches.

The drive was uneventful until they began the last eighty miles of the Butterfield route to the Pecos River. On this lower edge of the Staked Plains, the water holes were all dry. They crossed the barren land in three days, moving slowly by darkness and daylight. On the third day the rangy Longhorns became unmanageable because of their craze for water. When the thirsty herd scented the Pecos, they stampeded, piling into the river, some drowning under the onrush of those in the rear.

For three days the drivers rested, letting the herd recuperate, and then moved upriver to Fort Sumner where eight thousand Navahos confined to the Bosque Redondo were near starvation. A government contractor offered the cattlemen the fabulous price of eight cents per pound on the hoof for more than half the animals and paid them off with twelve thousand dollars in gold. By the standards of that day, Goodnight and Loving suddenly became wealthy men, and they still had Longhorns to spare.

While Loving drove the remainder of the herd north into Colorado, Goodnight and three of his drivers started back to Texas with the gold. Quite aware that Comanches were opposed to invasions of their Plains, and would be likely to challenge a small party of four men, Goodnight chose four mules for riding and four fast led horses for emergency use in the event of an attack. A fifth mule was used to pack their food and the fortune in gold. Late one evening just before they reached the Pecos, a

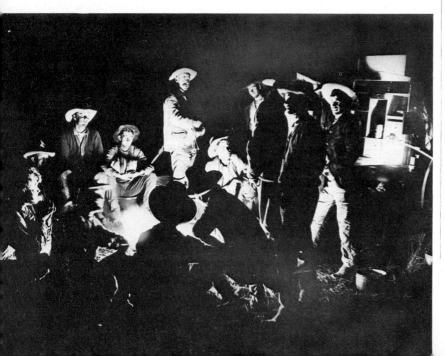

A yarnspinner was a good companion for long evenings on the range with no town in reach.

sudden thunderstorm frightened the pack mule into a frenzy. The animal broke its tie rope and dashed away, carrying off the provisions and gold. Goodnight pursued in the gathering darkness and finally managed to overtake the mule. 'I grabbed a rope that was dangling from the pack and checked the frantic animal after being dragged quite a distance down a rocky slope at the risk of a brbken neck. The gold was saved, but our provisions were entirely lost, and there was no way to get them renewed.'

Next morning they searched the rugged Guadalupe country for the lost food, but could find only one six-inch square of bacon. 'I learned a lesson that I never forgot as I looked at the boys and thought to myself: "Here you are with more gold than you ever had in your life, and it won't buy you a drink of water, and it won't get you food. For this gold you may have led three men to their death—for a thing that is utterly useless to you."'

Goodnight was luckier than Jedediah Smith had been forty years earlier on the Colorado and the Klamath. He did not lose his 'boys', but they had to travel for three days across eighty-six miles of wasteland with nothing to eat until they reached the Pecos where they 'accidentally ran across a man who divided his meager stock of food with us'. After that experience, Goodnight might have understood Smith's preoccupation with the terrors of life and death, his fear of entanglement in 'the things of time'. But he would have better perceived the Mountain Man's fascination for ordeals deliberately sought, for challenges flung into the face of violent natural forces.

Without waiting for Loving to return from Colorado, Goodnight and his 'boys' gathered another herd of Longhorns and again dared the fierceness of the Staked Plains. It was late in the year, and when he met Loving in New Mexico, they established a winter ranch at Bosque Grande, selling off their beef in small lots each month to government contractors at Fort Sumner and Santa Fe. Theirs was the first cattle ranch in southern New Mexico, but whether it was established for gold or the challenge of adventure, Goodnight did not say.

By the next year, several other Texas cattlemen were driving their stock over what was coming to be known as the Goodnight-Loving Trail. The presence of so many men and animals on the Plains soon attracted the attention of Comanches, Kiowas, and Apaches, who were still convinced that the Plains country was Indian country and that whoever or whatever intruded upon it was for the Indians to control. The Indians had little interest in the Longhorns; what they wanted were the accompanying *remudas*, the horse herds.

Not long after Goodnight and Loving returned to Texas and started another herd toward New Mexico, they began sighting Comanches on the flanks of the drive. Thunderstorms, stampedes, and darting forays by the Indians delayed their progress, and Oliver Loving volunteered to ride ahead to Fort Sumner and contract for beef deliveries before competitors arrived there ahead of them. He took one companion, Bill Wilson, a one-armed trail driver.

Near the Pecos, Comanches challenged their presence, and the two men took cover in a brush-bordered gully beside the river. The Indians tracked them down, surrounded them, and began firing arrows at angles which would bring them point down upon Loving and Wilson. The Indians also hurled rocks upon the besieged cattlemen. During the ordeal, Loving was wounded in the wrist. By nightfall he was too weakened from loss of blood to try for escape in the darkness. He ordered Wilson to make the attempt, and then lay down expecting to die–from his wound or by a bullet from his own sixshooter if the Comanches closed in on him.

One-armed Bill Wilson's escape is one of the classics of Western legend. He crawled down the gully to the river, floated submerged past dozens of watchful Comanches, and then walked for three days and nights over rocks and cactus. When he reached Goodnight and the herd Wilson was almost blind, his face swollen, his feet cracked and bleeding. Only by his missing arm was Goodnight able to recognize him.

Disregarding the safety of the herd, Goodnight called for volunteers and led a relief party in a fast ride to save Loving. They could find no trace of him, only the piles of hurled stones in the gully and dents in the earth left by arrows which had been retrieved by the Indians. After a thorough search of the area, Goodnight gave his partner up for dead. When the herd reached the Pecos, he took the Longhorns on to Fort Sumner, mourning for Oliver Loving. As Goodnight entered the fort, however, he found Loving standing there with his arm in a sling. Loving's escape from the Comanches had been even more miraculous than One-armed Bill Wilson's, yet in the end fate was against him. His wounded arm became affected by gangrene, and although Goodnight sent men on relays of horses to Las Vegas for a surgeon, Oliver Loving died. His last request was for Goodnight to take his body back to Texas. To keep the promise, Goodnight and his drivers collected discarded cans from the Fort Sumner dump, flattened and soldered them into a tin coffin, packed Oliver Loving's body in charcoal, and then took him and his saddle home to Texas over the Goodnight-Loving Trail.

Not long after this, Goodnight decided he had made enough crossings of the Staked Plains. Perhaps the continuous challenges of Comanches and Kiowas convinced him that the Indians meant to keep their Plains and buffalo. In Colorado the tribes had been driven out by the Indian-hating miners and settlers, and good grazing land was plentiful and cheap. 'I purchased in 1868 a large tract of land in Colorado near Pueblo,' he said, 'and in 1871 I bought forty miles from Trinidad a large ranch.'

Drag riders under a trail herd's dust

During the Civil War, while he was scouting for the Texas Confederates, he had met Mary Ann Dyer, and every time he returned to the Cross Timbers country he made a courting call. In 1869, he asked Mary Ann to marry him. 'After I married I thought I would no longer follow my wild trail life. I concluded to settle down and take up ranching instead.' And so while thousands of other Texans were driving their Longhorns north over the Chisholm Trail to Abilene, Newton, Ellsworth, Wichita, and all the other booming railheads of Kansas, Goodnight became a Colorado rancher, a cattleman who made money so fast he had to turn banker to take care of it all.

He missed the excitement of life on the trail, the early morning coffee and sourdough biscuits at the chuckwagon, the routine of drives which he had perfected—trail boss out in front, horse herd and chuckwagon following, then the point riders directing the lead steers, and strung along the widening flow of the herd the swing and flank riders, until at the end came the drag riders in clouds of dust, keeping the weaker cattle moving. Most of all, he missed being with the 'boys'.

In Colorado he experimented with irrigation and corn raising. He built an opera house in the boisterous town of Pueblo, and tried to fathom the mysteries of banking. He knew the Colorado range was being overstocked and grazed out by greedy newcomers to the cattle business, but he never understood how the thousands of dollars which passed through his hands all vanished suddenly in the Panic of 1873. One day in 1875 he discovered that the only thing he had left on earth was a herd of 1800 unmarketable Longhorns, about the same number he had owned when the Civil War ended. He was nine years older, and as financially destitute as he had been in 1866.

He remembered the immense buffalo herds on the Staked Plains. Most of them were gone now, killed off by hide hunters. The fiercely competitive Comanches and Kiowas were no longer there, either, to contest an intruder's presence. He decided to take his Longhorns to the dry Plains and find the water and grass that had drawn the buffalo there.

In 1876 Goodnight assembled a group of dependable 'boys' for a drive from Colorado back to Texas. Among them were a Scotsman and an Englishman. (Wealthy Britons were venturing into the Western cattle trade in the 1870s, and would soon make their presence felt from Texas to Montana.) James T. Hughes was the Englishman, and he had come to Colorado to learn the cattle business. 'In this life,' he said, 'there is a very happy combination of business and pleasure . . . I have hired with a cattle king, Goodnight by name, to go to Texas to drive a herd.' Young Hughes wrote enthusiastic letters home to his father, Thomas Hughes, author of *Tom Brown's School Days*, who used the earnings from that popular book to found the experimental cooperative colony of Rugby, Tennessee.

'On the 22nd I washed all my clothes, a very great undertaking,' James Hughes wrote with the earnest zeal of his father's fictitious hero, 'not having washed my clothes since we left the Canadian River. On the 23rd and 24th it snowed. We all shaved and "greased up" with bear oil for Christmas–the only thing we could think of doing, as we had run out of all grub except flour; but then flour, bear, buffalo and turkey is pretty good living.'

When Goodnight and his 'boys' trailed the Longhorns down from Colorado, he had no exact place in mind where he would stop, but he knew that water and grass were to be found somewhere in that long shunned part of Texas. Along the way he encountered occasional sheep herds that had been brought over from New Mexico, and their presence confirmed his belief that the Panhandle could become a 'fair and productive part of Texas'. One evening an old Mexican trader drifted off the Plains into Goodnight's camp and gave him the clue he was seeking. The Comanchero told of having seen a deep canyon in the Llano Estacado, a hidden valley of trees and grass and water where buffalo still lived, and whitening under the sun was a great pile of horse bones left after the soldiers drove away the Indians.

Goodnight asked the Comanchero to take him there, but the place was not easy to find. They wandered for several days, following arroyos that led nowhere, and then finally one day they came to the edge of a deep canyon. The old Mexican raised his hands. 'At last', he cried. 'At last!' They had found the Palo Duro.

They discovered a narrow buffalo trail down which the cattle could enter single file. At the bottom was a plenitude of grass and a creek filled with clear water. Buffalo herds, the last remaining from the hunter-ravaged Plains were also there in large numbers, competing for the forage. Goodnight took young Hughes and some of the other 'boys' and chased the buffalo away by firing off their pistols and rifles until the startled animals stampeded through the cedar brakes and disappeared down the canyon in a cloud of red dust.

The most difficult task was getting Goodnight's cherished chuckwagon and the supply wagons down into the Palo Duro. James Hughes told of how they accomplished this: 'We were able to make a "kinder" road for the first third and the last third of the hill, but the middle was too steep, and we had to unload the wagons and carry the things down on our backs. We then let the wagons down, hind end first, with a rope attached to the pole and turned once around a tree, and a man at each wheel. We got everything down safely and broke nothing, which was lucky. Almost the first thing done in the canyon was the slaying of two wild turkeys, which were very good eating.' (When Coronado's men entered the canyon in 1541, one of the first things noted by Pedro de Castaneda were 'turkeys of the variety found in New Spain'.)

As soon as his Longhorns and his wagons were safely in the Palo Duro, Goodnight hurried back through a snowstorm to Pueblo for his wife. He also needed money badly. He had to buy corn for his horses and equipment for the new ranch, and he wanted some Durham bulls to upgrade his Longhorn stock. He went to see John G. Adair, one of the wealthy Britons recently arrived in Colorado. Adair had been piling up money by borrowing at low rates in England and lending at high rates in the United States. In 1875 he had established a brokerage office in Denver, and when Goodnight proposed a partnership for a ranch in the Palo Duro, Adair offered to furnish the money.

This was the beginning of the famed JA Ranch, the brand representing Adair's initials, the first of many great ranches in the buffalo land of the Comanches and Kiowas. If Goodnight resented not having his name on the ranch or the brand, he never mentioned it. When their partnership ended eleven years later, the Palo Duro was filled with 100,000 cattle. 'To care for them over such an extensive range,' Goodnight said, 'we employed a little army of men called "cowboys".' In his early years, he had always called them 'boys', the word 'cowboys' not being easily accepted in the West. Since the time of the American Revolution, there had been a taint of disrepute about the word 'cowboys', it being an appellation used by revolutionaries to describe supporters of King George III: 'The cowboys were the

Remington's *Arizona Cowboy*

worst kind of Tories; they went around in the bushes armed with guns and tinkling a cowbell so as to beguile the patriots into the brush hunting for cows.' The first hostelry for trail drivers in Kansas was called the *Drover's* Cottage, and the drovers were called *Texans* (or *Rebels* if they were confronted by their recent enemies, the Yankees). By the late 1870s 'cowboys' was coming into general use, however, and Goodnight like everyone else began to use the word.

Soon after starting operations on the JA Ranch, Goodnight began replacing the Longhorns with Herefords, although he always kept a few of the rangy, tough-fibered animals around to remind him of the old days. There was symbolism in the fact that he placed the expensive Herefords on the ranch's finest grass, along Tule Creek where Mackenzie's bleaching horse bones still lay. The cowboys who worked this area claimed that on moonlight nights near Bone Ford, they could see ghostly files of riderless mustangs galloping along the rim of the canyon.

Late in 1878, a large band of Comanches and Kiowas, starving for meat on their reservation in Indian Territory, crossed Red River and headed for the Palo Duro, hoping to find buffalo there. Goodnight's cowboys had driven most of the animals out upon the Plains where white hunters were rapidly gunning them down. Although the hungry Indians would have preferred buffalo meat, they took several of the JA Ranch cattle instead and slaughtered them for beef.

As soon as Goodnight heard of this, he arranged a meeting with the Indian leaders, one of whom was Quanah Parker, a half-blood Comanche. Goodnight told the Indians that he wanted a private treaty with them.

'Don't you know this country is ours?', one of the Comanches asked him.

Goodnight replied that he had heard such was the case, but that the great Captain of Texas also claimed the land and was making him pay for it. (Goodnight and Adair were then buying

365 square miles for twenty cents an acre.) The palavering continued for some time until Quanah Parker and some of the others promised to allow Goodnight to stay on their land provided he paid them two beef cattle each day. Goodnight agreed, of course; he knew that soldiers would be coming soon to force the Indians back to their reservation.

After eleven years of managing the JA, Goodnight decided the time had come to establish his own ranch. He acquired a ranging area along the new Fort Worth & Denver City Railroad; the town which developed near his headquarters was given his name.

In 1877 when Goodnight's partnership began with Adair, he was broke; in 1888 when he ended the partnership, he was worth more than half a million dollars. As Goodnight grew older, he also grew cranky in his ways, treating his cowboys like children. He forbade them to gamble, to drink liquor, to use profanity, or even to play cards in the bunkhouses. He particularly disliked mumbletypeg, a game played by flipping a knife into the ground, and in his efforts to stop it, he asked the Cattlemen's Association to ban mumbletypeg completely in the Panhandle. This restrictive regimen imposed by Goodnight may explain why his cowboys had such a reputation for wildness when they reached Dodge City after a long trail drive. On a diet of beef and black coffee and sometimes a full box of Cuban cigars a day, Charles Goodnight lived until 1929 when he died at ninety-three, the first and last of the pioneer cattlemen, the father of the Western cowboys.

Relief from the rigors of the trail gave cowboys a bad name off the range.

14.The Petticoated Rebels

During the period of intensive exploitation of the American West in the second half of the nineteenth century, women were in short supply in most regions. While armies of males were frantically digging for gold, rounding up Longhorns, seizing land, and killing Indians, small groups of Western women were quietly casting off shackles which the males had devised for them throughout past centuries.

In the beginning only a few women who came to the West realized that they held strategic advantages not available to their sisters left behind in the East. First, the extreme shortage of women on the frontier elevated their status; they were a rare commodity and thus became highly valued by the males. Second, the males were so busy trying to accumulate riches that they had no time to enforce the old laws which kept women subservient and under the same civil codes as infants, idiots, and criminals. A few of the more astute women quickly saw that, temporarily at least, nothing barred them from doing as they pleased. Exigencies of Western life, in fact, often forced women to work alongside men at tasks which formerly had been accepted as being exclusively the prerogatives of males.

Women found that they could equal men in most endeavors, and during physical ordeals which were common frontier experiences they often bested them in techniques of survival. For instance, at the end of the terrible winter endured by the Donner party trapped in the Sierra snows and feeding upon each other's flesh, all the women survived while eight of ten men perished.

In the quarter century after 1850, Western women burst loose from centuries of restrictive laws and customs, flaunting their new-found freedoms and accelerating a movement which is still spreading around the world. They invaded domains long held sacred by males–politics, business, the professions, even outlawry–and did it with such gentle deftness that the kingpins who held these bastions were barely aware of what was happening. It was typical that Charles Goodnight on his millionaire's ranch in Texas should design a new sidesaddle especially for Western women precisely at the time when they were beginning to ride astraddle–and doing so in hard rodeo competitions.

A standard image of the frontier
mother courageously defending
home and family against savage
attack

Women riders were weary of pleasing their masters by riding
across the Plains and the Rockies in modest sidesaddle positions
which twisted their spines askew.

It was not random selection that brought the Women's
Suffrage movement into Kansas in 1867 when, with George
Francis Train's oratorial assistance, they made a strong attempt
at winning the vote for their disenfranchised sex. Leaders of the
Eastern suffragists such as Susan Anthony and Lucretia Mott
were well aware that women in the West were loosening their
shackles. They tried again two years later farther west, in
Wyoming, and they won–thanks to the ingenuity of Esther
McQuigg Morris of South Pass City. Mrs Morris adroitly

At the polls in Cheyenne; these Wyoming voters were pioneers on the frontier of woman suffrage.

persuaded candidates of opposing political parties to support women's suffrage in Wyoming. After the elections, the Democrats controlled the legislature, the Republicans the governor's office. To embarrass their opponents, the Democrats passed a women's suffrage bill, fully expecting the Republican governor to veto it. The governor, however, surprised his political enemies and signed the bill. To the astonishment of the entire United States, women had the right to vote in Wyoming Territory–fifty years before the constitutional amendment of 1920 brought the same right to other American women.

Although the women's suffrage leaders turned their attention to other Western states, the frightened males fought them off everywhere until Colorado finally capitulated in 1893. During that long period, a considerable array of fighters for women's rights arose in the West. Some fought for the vote, some for property rights, others for social equality and sexual freedom. Many have been forgotten, a few remembered– Esther Morris, Calamity Jane, Laura Fair, Belle Starr, Cattle Kate, Carry Nation, Mary Ellen Lease, Lola Montez, Julia Bulette, Clarissa Nichols, Jeanette Rankin, and others. The one who created the greatest stir was Ann Eliza Young, rebellious wife of Brigham Young, who lived in the only part of the West where there was a surplus of females.

She was born Ann Eliza Webb on 13 September 1844, next

Ann Eliza Webb LEFT, *n*th wife of
Brigham Young (seen BELOW at his
unending dining table) loathed the
atmosphere of Young's harem.

door to Brigham Young in Nauvoo, Illinois. When she was two years old, Young convinced her father, Chauncey Webb, that he should begin to take additional wives. By the time Ann Eliza was twelve, there were five wives in the Webb household and more than a dozen children to share the affections of a busy father who was often away on extended missionary journeys. A sensitive child in a crowded household of bickering women, she acquired an early hatred of polygyny and no doubt a hostility toward all males.

Her family was among the first to reach the Salt Lake basin in 1848. 'I suppose the journey must have been a tiresome one to the older members of the party,' she remembered, 'but I enjoyed it extremely. I ran along, during a portion of the day, by the side of the wagons, picking flowers by the way, and talking to the different members of the train.' By all accounts she was a pretty child, and in her early teens was attracting the roving eyes of elderly polygamists who preferred nymphets for their additional wives. Her father discouraged approaches from these suitors, and encouraged her to attend social events with young boys of her own age.

When Ann Eliza was seventeen she fancied herself to be in love with the younger brother of Emmeline Free–Brigham Young's Wife No. 12, sometimes called 'the Light of the Harem'. Finley Free often escorted Ann Eliza to the splendid theater which the Lion of the Lord had ordered built in Salt Lake City so that his people might have joy. One evening Brigham chanced to see them together at the theater; the next day he visited the Webb's house and warned Ann Eliza's mother to break up the match. 'She ought not to have anything to do with those Frees', Brigham said. 'They are a low set anyway and don't amount to anything.'

Years later Ann Eliza recalled her anger at the Prophet of the Lord, and of how she had gone to her teen-age companions for sympathy. 'Perhaps Brother Brigham means to marry you himself', one of the girls said. 'But he won't', Ann Eliza replied furiously. 'I wouldn't have him if he asked me a thousand times–hateful old thing.'

A day or so after that she was out for a walk when Young came riding by in his carriage; he stopped the horses and ordered her to get in. As they rode along toward her home, he remarked: 'I heard you said you wouldn't marry me if I wanted you to ever so much.' Ann Eliza was so embarrassed she became incoherent, the Lion of the Lord obviously enjoying her discomfiture.

'I think Brigham's mind was made up from that time', she said afterward, 'that I should one day be his wife, not from any particular affection, but to punish me for my foolish speech, and to show me that his will was stronger than mine.'

As soon as she was eighteen, Young ordered her to join the dramatic company at his theater, and to move her home to the

Lion House—where he kept his wives and children. She was to live with his older daughters, who were also learning to be actresses. 'It was while I was acting', she said, 'that I met my first husband, Mr. James L. Dee. He was an Englishman, a very handsome fellow, and a very great favorite with all the girls. It was one of those romantic affairs called "love at first sight".' They were married 4 April 1863. 'I gave him the truest love a woman can give a man . . . and he repaid it as men of his class, selfish, overbearing, and domineering, usually repay it—in neglect and abuse when once I was in his power.'

Ann Eliza testified that James Dee frightened her with his furious fits of anger, insulting her and threatening her person. Soon after the honeymoon he was out looking for an additional wife. In their two years of stormy relationships, she bore him two sons, but after Dee began beating and choking her, she decided divorce was the only solution. Her parents suggested that she seek advice from Brigham Young, who as head of the church claimed the power to grant divorce to members. 'He it was who counseled me to go to the regular courts, rather than to depend on his divorcement, which he knew would not stand out of Mormondom.'

A happy divorcée, Ann Eliza took her two sons to live on the Webbs' farm at South Cottonwood. One Sunday in the summer of 1867, Brigham Young arrived at South Cottonwood to preach in the town's brush-arbor church. Ann Eliza was in the congregation and she soon became uneasy under the steady stare of the preaching Prophet, who was denouncing alcoholism among the men and immodest attire among the women. 'I thought that possibly there was something about my appearance that displeased him. Possibly he did not approve of my dress . . . That he was not looking at me indifferently or carelessly I knew very well, from the bent brows and keen gaze that I felt was making the most complete scrutiny, and I wished he would look somewhere else . . . I did everything but jump up and run away, and I even wanted to do that, to get out of the reach of those sharp eyes, and that steady unflinching gaze. I am sure he saw my discomfort; but he was pitiless, and all the while the speaking was going on he scarcely turned his eyes from me a moment . . . I felt his power then as I never had felt it before, and I began to understand a little how it was that he compelled so many people to do his will, against their own inclinations. I learned the lesson better still subsequently.'

At the end of the services, according to Ann Eliza, Young sought her out and complimented her on her appearance. 'You are a very pretty woman. I suppose you have had offers of marriage since your separation from Mr Dee.'

'Yes, many', she replied.

'Do you feel inclined to accept any of them?'

'No, not in the slightest degree; none of them move me in the least.'

That afternoon, Young visited the Webbs' house and had a long private meeting with Ann Eliza's father. After the Prophet departed South Cottonwood, Chauncey Webb informed his daughter that Brigham Young wanted her for his wife.

Ann Eliza always maintained that she–who was then only twenty-three–could not endure the thought of marrying the sixty-six-year-old Prophet who already possessed two dozen or more wives. She said that she finally persuaded her reluctant father to inform Young that she did not wish to marry him, and that Young then tried to bribe her with gifts. When this failed, she said, Young arranged to entrap her brother Gilbert in a financial scheme, drove him into bankruptcy, and threatened to excommunicate him from the church. To save her brother, she finally agreed to become the nineteenth (some records indicate twenty-seventh or possibly the fifty-first) wife of Brigham Young. For a time the Prophet kept the marriage a secret from his other wives, assigning her a separate house in Salt Lake City.

(A few years later while being interviewed by a New York *Times* reporter, Young told a different version. 'My marriage to Ann Eliza was a foolish thing', he said, 'that I allowed her parents to persuade me into. I did it for her good . . . Ann Eliza was a pretty widow–silly and vain. She was born close to my door. Her father was Chauncey Webb. I baptized her when she was 16 years old. She married a man by the name of D-D-D—'. Young could not recall the name, but added that 'he had sense enough to run away from Ann Eliza and leave her and her two boys to shift for themselves'. He declared that her parents had importuned him to marry Ann Eliza because she 'must have a solid man to lean on or she would go to ruin, and then, like a fool, I married her. Why, I, an old man, didn't want anything of Ann Eliza, anymore than I did from the Sultan of Turkey. She was an elephant, silly, vain, and unfaithful . . . She even drove her own mother away, so as to keep the company of different men. One man later baptized into our church made oath that he'd done wrong with Ann Eliza many times.')

In the spring of 1870, Young transferred her from Salt Lake City to a place he called The Farm, four miles out of town, and gave her the responsibility of supervising the production of milk, butter and cheese to supply the needs of his many wives and children. According to Ann Eliza, she lived a life of drudgery at The Farm for three years, and then Young ordered her to move back to Salt Lake City. 'It was out of no feeling of regard for me, or care for my comfort', she said. 'He simply wished to put some one else in the farmhouse.'

(When the New York *Times* reporter asked Young about Ann Eliza's complaint of hard work for him at The Farm, he replied: 'Work for me! Why the little fraud never did a thing for me in her life but cheat me and make a fool of me. The very day she ran away with a Boston fellow who was traveling for a furniture

Young's farmhouse

house, she went and traded out over a hundred dollars at the cooperative store.')

Ann Eliza's flight from Brigham Young's domination took place on 15 July 1873, a few months after he placed her in a Salt Lake City cottage and virtually cut off 'the commonest necessaries of life'. Soon after she moved to the cottage, she realized that to provide herself and her children with food and clothing she would have to take in boarders.

Completion of the transcontinental railroad in 1869 had brought many non-Mormons to Salt Lake City where they were establishing businesses, churches, and even newspapers. Young evidently considered these Gentiles to be prime candidates for conversion to his church; after all, he had once been a Methodist himself. When Ann Eliza asked his permission to take in boarders, he must have known that most of them would be non-Mormons, yet he offered no objections to her earning her living in this manner.

Among her boarders were Judge Albert Hagan, a mining attorney, and his wife, and James Burton Pond, a reporter for the non-Mormon Salt Lake *Tribune*. From one of them she evidently obtained a copy of *Exposé of Polygamy in Utah*, by Fanny Stenhouse, an Englishwoman who had lived for twenty years as a Mormon and then rebelled against the church because of its endorsement of plural wives. Ann Eliza, who felt 'neglected, insulted, humiliated . . . and tied to an old man', saw parallels with her own situation, in fact, found her own name in the book as one of Brigham Young's wives.

She was receptive, therefore, when she met the Reverend C. C. Stratton, pastor of the new Methodist Church in Salt Lake City. For a young woman born into the Mormon Church, it was not easy to make the final break. She knew that if she did so, she also would have to divorce Brigham Young and abandon the cottage he had provided for her. In a final effort to regain her faith, she arranged to be re-baptized, but the ceremony seemed only a farce to her. During the next few days she consulted with her non-Mormon friends, and made plans for her 'flight' from the power of Brigham Young.

To obtain funds, she secretly arranged to have all her household goods auctioned off, realizing $380 from the sale. With only that small fortune to sustain her, she and her sympathetic boarders moved quietly to the Walker House, a hotel owned by non-Mormons and used as headquarters by the Governor of Utah and other territorial officials appointed by the United States government. These included Chief Justice James B. McKean, a crusader against polygamy.

'I had abandoned my religion, left father, mother, home, and friends,' Ann Eliza said, 'knowing that the step I was taking could never be retraced . . . I was among people who I had been taught were my bitterest enemies, I was overwhelmed by a sense of desolate helplessness.'

Reporter James Pond, however, helped take her mind off these troubles by urging her to tell her story for the press. Pond knew what he had. He could visualize the headlines across the country, and instead of confining news of Ann Eliza's actions to his local paper, he telegraphed it to the Associated Press. Newspapers everywhere turned the story into A MORMON SENSATION! WIFE OF BRIGHAM YOUNG FLEES TO FREEDOM. POLYGAMY HAS RECEIVED A HEAVY BLOW.

Pond was not in the least surprised when messengers began bringing basketsful of telegrams to the Walker House for Ann Eliza. They came from 'theatrical managers, showmen, and speculators from all parts of the country', Pond said. 'One was from P. T. Barnum and another from James Redpath, owner of the Lyceum Bureau in Boston. It asked her to lecture.'

Ann Eliza was overwhelmed by the storm which broke around her, the shouts of newsboys calling her name in the streets, the besieging army of reporters from newspapers East and West demanding interviews with Brigham Young's 'rebellious wife'. Her new friends, eager to strike at polygamy, urged her on to further actions. Judge Hagan offered to handle her divorce suit; the Reverend Stratton invited her to join the Methodist Church; James Pond insisted that she journey to Washington and tell her story to the U.S. Congress. Pond certainly viewed her as a lucrative source of income if he could only persuade her to take to the lecture circuit with himself as manager.

After convincing her that it was her duty to go to Washington and expose the evils of polygamy, Pond helped her prepare a lecture and arranged for her to deliver it before a friendly audience in the Walker House. 'I was startled to see the number of persons who had assembled to listen to me', she said. 'My first impulse was to run away and hide myself in my own room. But the applause which greeted me, the smiling, reassuring faces . . . and the sympathy which I read in them all, gave me courage.'

(Of these developments, Brigham Young said: 'Judge Hagan and some of the Methodist people here filled her head full of lectures and the little silly woman has been traveling around ever since, reading her school-girl compositions about Mormons when her whole stock in trade is the fact that she was Brigham Young's 19th wife, or as the courts have decided, Brigham Young's 19th mistress.')

For Ann Eliza's departure from Salt Lake City, Pond arranged a melodramatic 'escape' which later on would make good material for her lectures. She had told newspaper reporters that she feared she would be kidnapped and murdered if she left the safety of the Walker House. On the night of 27 November, with a small group of friends which included an elderly chaperone, she left the back door of the hotel, entered a waiting carriage, and traveled forty miles through the darkness to Uintah, a station on the Union Pacific Railroad, and there she boarded a passenger train for the long journey to Washington.

Instead of taking her directly to Washington, however, Pond decided to stop in Laramie, Wyoming, so that he could test her abilities before a crowd of strangers. He set the admission price high for those days, $1.50, but the lecture was a sell-out, and even the cynical Pond was surprised at how well his protégé performed and by the enthusiasm of an audience eager for revelations concerning the 'inner domestic life of the Prophet' in their neighboring Kingdom of the Saints.

From Laramie they went on to Denver, where not even a blizzard could stop a standing-room crowd from filling the lecture hall. Pond immediately scheduled a second appearance for the following evening. Quotations from Ann Eliza's lectures were quickly spread across the nation by note-taking journalists, and every hour brought more telegraphed demands for her to speak in numerous cities and towns. The Redpath agency offered a substantial guarantee for a series of fifty lectures, and Pond persuaded her to accept, with himself as her manager.

The duty mission to Washington had to be postponed for five months while Brigham Young's rebellious wife traveled across the land, titillating audiences with her stories of Brigham's harem. When she finally reached Washington in the spring of 1874, Congress received her as if she had been a visiting princess. James G. Blaine, the Speaker of the House, escorted her upon the floor where she was given an ovation. President Grant attended her first lecture, applauded her remarks, and at the end strode forward to shake her hand.

The Washington publicity only increased demands for her appearance in other places. Throughout the spring and into the summer of 1874 she journeyed from lecture hall to lecture hall, her lithe figure, flashing blue eyes, and pretty face with its Mona Lisa smile becoming familiar to thousands of curious Americans.

By August 1874 she had grown self-assured enough to return to Utah for six lectures scheduled by the Redpath agency. Crowds filled the streets of Salt Lake City, and a band serenaded her. Because she had become such a national celebrity, both Mormons and non-Mormons came to hear her speak at the Salt Lake City Methodist Church. Brigham Young sent a corps of his daughters to sit in the front seats and make faces at Ann Eliza. 'Instead of annoying me, and causing me to break down completely, as the Prophet hoped, it only lent new strength to my purpose, new fire to my words.'

She continued her Western tour into the winter, and after a short rest, started out upon another round of jolting trains, uncomfortable hotels, and demanding audiences. In 1876 she published a book – *Wife No. 19, or The Story of a Life in Bondage*. Although it was more of a diatribe against Mormonism than an autobiography, it was a financial success and renewed public interest in her as a lecturer.

Until well into the 1880s Ann Eliza was still making her annual tours, eight months out of every twelve; but the lecture bureau eventually had to lower admission prices to fill the auditoriums. On one of her last tours she met Moses Denning, who invited her to be his house guest in Manistee, Michigan. Denning was so smitten by the thirty-eight-year-old ex-wife of Brigham Young that he soon afterward divorced his own wife, and proposed marriage. On 24 April 1883 Ann Eliza gave her farewell lecture in Napoleon, Ohio, and a month later was wed to Moses Denning. Her third marriage lasted for ten years, most of them unhappy ones to judge from the divorce proceedings.

Once again she was a free woman, but from that time Ann Eliza lived a life of such obscurity that it is difficult to trace her activities. Brigham Young was long dead; his church had abolished polygamy; and Utah was a state like any other. In 1903 she was living in El Paso, Texas, on a street named for a man who had been instrumental in the seizure of the South-west from Mexico – James Magoffin. In 1907 she returned to the East to re-write her book, calling it *Life in Mormon Bondage*. It was published in 1908, but the public was no longer interested in Ann Eliza Young. After that, she vanished at the age of sixty-four, and no one knows when she died or where.

OPPOSITE Traditional values, attached to passive women keeping house and caring for children while their husbands provided, are reflected in Jewett's painting *The Promised Land* (detail); Western women, however, were greatly to expand their role to fill their new life.

15. Libbie and Autie

One of Ann Eliza Young's rivals on the lecture platforms of America during the final quarter of the nineteenth century was a small, delicate-featured woman with dark wavy hair who devoted the last fifty-seven years of her life to creating a myth about a golden-haired young man who died foolishly and violently on 25 June 1876, beside the Little Big Horn River in Montana. She was Elizabeth Bacon Custer, and she and George Armstrong Custer first saw the West in 1865. During the decade in which they lived there, they viewed the raw land and its Indian inhabitants as the key to their most passionate desire – to secure for Lieutenant-Colonel Custer the permanent rank of General. During the Civil War, Custer at twenty-three became the youngest brigadier-general, and a year later he was a major-general, but these were brevet or temporary ranks that vanished with the smoke of the last battle.

'Libbie' Bacon and 'Autie' Custer were not childhood sweethearts as some legends have it, although they lived near each other in Monroe, Michigan, during the 1850s. When Autie was about fifteen, Judge Daniel Bacon sometimes hired him to do odd jobs, and after these tasks were done the boy would linger around the backyard hoping for glimpses of beautiful twelve-year-old Libbie, who probably never even glanced in his direction or had a word to say to him. Autie was the rough son of a blacksmith, Libbie the valedictorian of her seminary's graduating class and daughter of the town's most distinguished lawyer.

Autie decided that he too could become a lawyer like Judge Bacon, but his family had no funds to support him in this endeavor. Following the example of other ambitious but poor boys of his time, he turned to West Point. He had no desire for a military career, but he knew that after West Point he would have the education to become a lawyer. When he was seventeen the Secretary of War, who happened to be Jefferson Davis, approved his appointment to West Point. His record there indicates that he was a poor student and a slovenly cadet. He graduated under a disciplinary cloud, thirty-fourth in a class of thirty-four, and probably would not have been commissioned at all had the year not been 1861 – the beginning of the Civil War. Between the Battle of Bull Run and Lee's surrender at

PREVIOUS SPREAD A pictograph by Red Horse, a Minneconjou chief who took part in the Battle of the Little Big Horn. The drawings show Indian warriors leaving the battle ground with horses of the dead fighters (the cavalry horses have long tails; the Indians' have theirs bound).

OPPOSITE An assortment of frontier weapons: STANDING percussion Plains rifle, c. 1840; TOP (lying on the holster) ·36 calibre Navy Colt, c. 1851; MIDDLE ·44 calibre Remington percussion revolver (cylinder removed) with staghorn grips, c. 1861; BOTTOM ·44 calibre percussion Army Colt, c. 1860. The Bowie knife has a staghorn handle and is lying on a buckskin sheath studded with *conchas*.

229

Appomattox, Custer learned that it was not high marks but showmanship that won military promotions, and he was a born actor.

In the fall of 1863 when Custer returned to Monroe on furlough he was wearing a brigadier's star, a flashily modified uniform with a crimson necktie, and golden curls which hung to his shoulders. All the best families invited the Boy General to their hops and balls, and Libbie Bacon thought he was beautiful. Her father disapproved of their close friendship, but when Judge Bacon finally understood that his Little Girl wanted the Boy General and no one else, he withdrew objections to an engagement.

Libbie and Autie were married 9 February 1864. They went East for their honeymoon, carrying an immense lot of baggage to contain his uniforms and Libbie's nine hoopskirted dresses and white merino silk-lined, hooded and tasseled opera cloak which she had seen actresses wear on the stage. Autie arranged their itinerary so they could spend part of the honeymoon at West Point, but he became jealous of the attention she received there, and swept her off to New York City. When they were not in bed in the Metropolitan Hotel, they shopped for more clothes for Libbie. They also went to the theaters and wept together at the sad scenes in *Uncle Tom's Cabin* and *Rip Van Winkle*.

As the time neared for him to report back for duty in Virginia, they moved on to Washington where he found a place for Libbie to live, but she refused to stay there. She insisted on going to the battle front so that she might sleep each night beside the Boy General with the Golden Locks. His uxoriousness had already become so pronounced that he helped pack her wardrobe and then took her to his Michigan Cavalry Brigade's headquarters near Brandy Station, Virginia, where he kept her in a farmhouse.

They had barely settled down when Custer received a query from Army headquarters concerning one Annie Jones, who was under military arrest in Washington. She was suspected of being a spy for the Confederacy. Annie Jones was a randy teen-age camp follower who made no secret of the fact that she had been a tent-mate of Franz Sigel and other Union generals on their campaigns. Now she was trying to secure her release from jail by offering the name of Brigadier-General Custer as a former 'friend and companion' who should be willing to swear that she was not a spy but a loyal Massachusetts Yankee who loved handsome generals. Among other statements, Annie claimed that General Judson Kilpatrick of the New York Cavalry had quarreled with Custer because Kilpatrick wanted Annie to be his exclusive tent-mate, but Annie preferred to share her favors.

In his reply to Army authorities, Custer admitted that Annie Jones had visited his headquarters twice, but declared that he had promptly sent her away. To have his name bandied about

Elizabeth Bacon Custer

by the raunchy Miss Jones so soon after being married evidently made him nervous about Libbie's proximity to brigade headquarters where military communications could not be kept secret. He convinced his wife that the Rebels were readying a spring campaign, and that she would be in danger at Brandy Station. Finagling several days of sick leave, Autie took Libbie back to Washington and found lodgings for her. His fame and her beauty brought them immediately into the capital's social whirl, and Libbie promised to endure his absence for a little while if he would write her a letter every day. Autie did his best, addressing letters to 'Dear Little Durl', 'My Rosebud', and 'Little Army Crow'. She responded in kind: 'Beloved Star', or 'My Darling Boy'.

Custer had now become Phil Sheridan's fair-haired trooper, and they spent the summer together bleeding Virginia to death. Between cavalry charges upon decimated ranks of Confederates in the Shenandoah, Autie hastened often to Washington where he and Libbie, always gay and irrepressible, moved like actors on a stage. They met General Grant who had come from the West to finish the war; they went to the White House where President Lincoln took Libbie's hand and said: 'So this is the young woman whose husband goes into a charge with a whoop and a shout.' In the autumn of 1864, they made Autie a major-general. He was not yet twenty-five.

George Armstrong Custer

With his skill for showmanship, Major-General Custer arranged to be at center stage when General Lee surrendered; it was Custer who took into his own hands the white linen towel used by Lee's emissary for the surrender meeting. He was disappointed that Sheridan could not get him into Wilmer McLean's farmhouse with Lee and Grant for the signing at Appomattox, but after the two leaders departed and the farm-house was looted for souvenirs, Custer went in and found an oval-topped table for Libbie.

It was all over now except the big parade up Pennsylvania Avenue in Washington. Custer led the procession, of course, the Boy General with the Flowing Yellow Curls, his name in all the newspapers, his picture on the covers of *Harper's* and other illustrated weeklies. The music publishers were issuing galops and marches with his name in the titles and his portrait on the sheet covers. For his last big scene he wore a broad-brimmed hat and a bright red scarf. As he trotted his mount toward the Presidential reviewing stand, a group of girls dressed in white showered him with bouquets of flowers. His horse bolted, and seemed to fly through the air in front of the President while Autie expertly brought the animal under control. It was a splendid exit.

Phil Sheridan, his old patron of the Shenandoah, already had another assignment for him down on the Texas border. A few stubborn Confederate officers had joined up with Maximilian in Mexico, and there was talk of Union forces allying themselves with Juarez to drive out the French tyrants. Libbie and Autie packed up for the long journey and their first experience in the West. 'We were like children let out of school,' she said, 'and everything interested us.' For the crossing of Texas, Autie had an army ambulance fitted out as elaborately as Susan Magoffin's carriage for her journey to Santa Fe twenty years earlier. The seats of Libbie's ambulance were arranged so that the leather backs could be unstrapped and let down to form a bed. 'There was a pocket for my needlework and book, and a box for luncheon, while my traveling bag and shawl were strapped at the side, convenient, but out of the way. It was quite a complete little house of itself.' One of the soldiers who rebuilt the vehicle presented her with a leather canteen cover, her name stitched in yellow cavalry silk: Lady Custer.

Headquartered at Austin with practically nothing to do, the Custers attended horse races, visited San Antonio, enjoyed a warm sunny Christmas, and awaited orders to invade Mexico. The civilians whose taxes supported them, however, were weary of bloodshed and wanted no Mexican adventure; their responsive Congress ordered a drastic reduction of the expensive U.S. Army, the men to be sent home. Autie received the bad news on 31 January 1866. He was no longer a brevet major-general, but only a captain of cavalry, his pay cut by three-fourths, with no prospect of an assignment.

On the way home they stopped in New Orleans long enough to spend most of Autie's last pay dining in expensive French restaurants and refurbishing Libbie's outdated wardrobe. When they reached Monroe, they had to move in with Judge Bacon while Autie looked for employment. Finding nothing in civilian life that appealed to him, he boarded a train for Washington; there was not enough money left to take Libbie along. He found Washington filled with unassigned officers like himself, all pleading for commands in the shrinking Army. Disgusted, he went on to New York, hoping the glory that still surrounded him would bring something remunerative. On a visit to Wall Street, he was pleased when the brokers stopped their trading long enough to give him three rousing cheers, but no one offered him a salaried position.

At this desperate moment, Judge Bacon providentially died, leaving Libbie enough cash for them to return to Washington for a long siege of the War Department. The irrepressible Custers, with their gay and swaggering style, were not to be denied. A new cavalry regiment was being formed to drive the Indians from the Plains. On 28 July 1866 George Armstrong Custer was commissioned lieutenant-colonel and assigned to the Seventh Cavalry.

Three months later he and Libbie reported for duty at Fort Riley, a post on the high Plains of Kansas strategically located for striking at Indians in the buffalo country along the Smoky Hill and Republican forks. It was irksome for Lieutenant-Colonel Custer to be second in command of a single regiment when only a short time before as a major-general he had commanded several regiments. Fate was kind, however, and in the spring of 1867 Autie was given command of the Seventh and ordered to join Major-General Winfield Scott Hancock's expedition against the Cheyennes, Sioux, and Arapahos.

All that Hancock or Custer knew about Plains Indians was what they had read in the newspapers, but both men were hunting for glory. Hancock had political ambitions, and Custer wanted to be a general like Hancock. For three hundred miles across Kansas and Nebraska they chased small bands of Indians, killing indiscriminately and burning tipis, robes, and pemmican. To survive, the Indians had to rob the settlers, who in turn attacked the Indians until the Great Plains was ablaze with conflict.

In May, while the Seventh Cavalry was bivouacked at Fort Hays, Custer received orders to make a sweep against the Cheyennes and Sioux by way of Forts McPherson, Sedgwick, and Wallace. From Fort McPherson he wrote Libbie, asking her to join him at Fort Wallace before the end of June. While the column was en route to Wallace, about fifteen men deserted. As soon as their absence was discovered, Custer sent out a pursuit party with orders 'to follow those men and shoot them and bring none in alive'. The deserters were soon overtaken and

fired upon, three being seriously wounded, the others sur-
rendering. When they were brought back to the column, Custer
forbade a surgeon to dress the deserters' wounds. One of the
men died.

On 13 July the Seventh Cavalry reached Fort Wallace, but
Libbie was not there, and he ached for her presence. He was
supposed to await further orders from General Hancock;
instead, he decided to march to Fort Harker which was two
hundred miles closer to Libbie. On this march he became so
eager to see her that he drove the column until men and horses
were strung out over several miles, many falling down from
exhaustion and summer heat. One group of these stragglers
was attacked by Indians; the casualties included at least one
killed and one wounded, but when Custer was informed of the
action he made no effort to aid the men or recover the dead.
Instead, he ordered the column to move on.

When they reached Fort Hays, Custer commandeered an
ambulance for his personal use, and with a small escort pushed
on toward Fort Harker. Along the way he met a courier who was
carrying orders meant to be delivered to him at Fort Wallace.
The orders instructed him to remain at Wallace, using it as a
base for operations against Indians. He ignored the orders and
continued to Fort Harker, reporting on 19 July to Colonel
A. J. Smith, the district commander. Custer did not explain to
Smith why he was at Harker, merely informing the colonel that
he was boarding the train at the end of the new Kansas Pacific
Railroad track to go to Fort Riley.

Next morning Colonel Smith discovered that Custer was
acting contrary to orders, had in fact abandoned his command.
The colonel telegraphed Custer at Fort Riley, ordering him to
report to headquarters immediately. Autie and Libbie meanwhile had enjoyed, as she said, 'one long, perfect day' before
the telegram reached them. Neither could bear separation
again so soon; when Autie boarded the Kansas Pacific train for
Harker, Libbie was at his side.

At Fort Harker, Colonel Smith had bad news for them.
Lieutenant-Colonel Custer was under arrest to await a court-
martial. According to Libbie, the action was not unexpected.
'Autie took a leave himself, knowing none would be granted
him, and General Hancock ordered his arrest ... When he ran
the risk of a court-martial in leaving Wallace he did it expecting
the consequences ... and we are quite determined not to live
apart again, even if he leaves the army otherwise so delightful
to us.'

The charges and specifications against Custer included
absence without leave from his command, ordering deserters
to be shot dead without trial, forbidding treatment of wounded
deserters and probably causing the death of one, overmarching
and damaging horses of the Seventh Cavalry, unauthorized use
of military ambulances for private use, failure to relieve a

detachment of his command attacked by Indians or to recover casualties. To Libbie and Autie the entire affair was 'nothing but a plan of persecution' to cover up Hancock's military failures against the Indians, but to their dismay the court found the golden-haired cavalryman guilty. He was 'to be suspended from rank and command for one year, and to forfeit his pay proper for the same time'.

They waited hopefully for General Grant to overrule the court's findings, but instead Grant remarked on the 'lenity of the sentence considering the nature of the offenses', and ordered the verdict carried out effective 20 November 1867. Forever after, Custer was Grant's implacable enemy.

In the meantime Phil Sheridan had replaced Hancock as commander on the Plains, and in Sheridan's eyes the Boy General could do no wrong. Sheridan invited Libbie and Autie to occupy his luxurious quarters at Fort Leavenworth, and they spent a jolly winter there play-acting as if nothing had happened, Libbie almost gloating in a letter to a friend: 'Now we can be together for a year and a half . . . Autie and I are the wonder of the garrison, we are in such spirits.'

In June (1868) they abandoned the charade and returned to Monroe where they lived apparently on their mutual admiration for one another. Autie was twenty-eight now, and he and Libbie were sure that he was old enough to begin work on his memoirs. This would fill in the time until the year of penance ended and Phil Sheridan called him back to the West to resume his efforts to win the rank of general. Sheridan did not disappoint them. Two months before the court-martial sentence expired, Custer received a telegram from Fort Hays: 'Can you come at once? Eleven companies of your regiment will move about the first of October against hostile Indians.' It was signed P. H. Sheridan. Six days later Autie was at Fort Hays, booted and spurred and ready for duty.

For the winter campaign, he created a dashing uniform of warm furs. At dawn on 27 November, with his new regimental

Captives of the 1868 Indian Campaign

band blaring 'Garry Owen', he led the Seventh Cavalry into Black Kettle's peaceful village for a smashing blow that he was sure would win him promotion to a full colonelcy.

Even with the bountiful accolades of Phil Sheridan to back him, however, the promotion did not come. Perhaps there were too many whispered remarks among regimental officers concerning Custer's abandonment of Major Joel Elliott's detachment during the assault on Black Kettle's Cheyenne village, the 'Battle of the Washita'. While Elliott and sixteen men were out on a reconnaissance scout, they had been cut off by a force of Arapahos coming upriver to aid Black Kettle. When Custer discovered that he was in danger of attack by warriors from nearby villages of Arapahos, Kiowas, and Comanches, he withdrew hurriedly in a forced march back to his base at Camp Supply, without waiting for Elliott to rejoin him. Several days later when Custer returned to the burned village with General Sheridan and heavy reinforcements, they searched for Elliott and his men and found all of them dead. From that time, several officers in the Seventh Cavalry began to distrust Custer's leadership abilities; they also remembered that Major Elliott had not been an especially friendly witness during Custer's courtmartial, that Elliott had acted for a time during Custer's enforced absence as commander of the regiment, and might well have become its permanent commander had Custer not been permitted to return.

Five years later, when the regiment was ordered to Fort Abraham Lincoln in Dakota Territory, Autie was still a lieutenant-colonel. To Libbie, however, he was always 'the General', and with her inexhaustible energy and ebullience to support him, he entered upon the Dakota assignment as though he had been given a new chance for glory in the glamorous world of clanking sabers and jingling spurs. The Black Hills, sacred center of the Plains tribes' world, were only two hundred miles to the west, and rumors came constantly to the fort of immense gold deposits hidden in the rocks and streams. While it was true that the Treaty of 1868 had given that territory in perpetuity to Northern Plains tribes, forbidding white men 'to pass over, settle, or reside' upon the land, there was a loophole which permitted representatives of the government to go there 'in discharge of duties'. To Custer, exploring the Black Hills was a duty to be discharged; if he found gold, the discovery would bring him fame and perhaps the long-delayed promotion.

In the spring of 1874, Phil Sheridan came out from his Chicago headquarters to visit the Custers and inspect Fort Abraham Lincoln. During this visit, the two men developed a scheme for invading the Black Hills. In May, after Sheridan had returned to Chicago and obtained General Sherman's enthusiastic backing, he dispatched orders to Custer's department commander, General Alfred Terry, instructing him to send the Seventh Cavalry into the Black Hills. The purpose of the expedition, according to Sheridan, was to obtain 'information in regard to the character of the country' and to investigate the practicalities of establishing a military post in the Black Hills 'in order to better control the Indians'. Gold was not mentioned, but Sheridan quietly arranged for geologists to accompany the column.

The geologists found gold in the Black Hills, and the newspaper headlines called it Custer's Gold: RICH MINES OF GOLD AND SILVER REPORTED FOUND BY CUSTER. The Boy General was back on the front pages, and within a matter of weeks thousands of gold-crazy prospectors were violating the sanctity of the Indians' *Paha Sapa*, the Black Hills. When Sioux leaders such as Red Cloud protested violation of the treaty, the government made a pretense of enforcement by sending in soldiers to drive out the miners. But the miners stayed, and the soldiers stayed, and the sacred land was daily violated. In an effort to stave off an Indian war, the government offered to buy the Black Hills, but they were not for sale.

Through a series of carefully contrived moves, the government now prepared to seize the Black Hills by first ordering all Indians to report to their agency headquarters before 31 January 1876, or be considered 'hostiles'. The timing of the order – in the midst of winter – made it impossible for messengers to reach many tribes, or for them to comply if they did receive the order. On 7 February 1876 General Sherman notified General Sheridan to begin preparation for military operations against Indians in the area of the Black Hills. The War Department's excuse for its violation of the Treaty of 1868 was that these Indians were hostiles because they had refused to report to their agencies by 31 January, and therefore it was the Indians who had violated the treaty.

Libbie and Autie were on leave in New York when they heard the exciting news that the Seventh Regiment was to begin preparations for a spring campaign in the direction of the Rosebud and Big Horn rivers 'where Sitting Bull, Crazy Horse and their allies frequented'. Although Custer, by finding gold in the Black Hills, had precipitated this onrushing collision between cavalrymen and Indian warriors, he almost missed being present for the final showdown on the Little Big Horn. In March he was summoned to Washington to testify in a Congressional investigation of the so-called Indian Ring which involved President Grant's Secretary of War, William W. Belknap, in the sale of post traderships and in other forms of graft on Indian reservations. Custer had long suspected that Belknap or Grant or perhaps both were blocking his military promotion. He traveled eagerly to Washington and gave the committee a considerable amount of hearsay evidence, some of which implicated the President's brother, Orville Grant, in the sale of corn stolen from the Indian Bureau.

When Custer prepared to leave Washington, President

Custer with Indian scouts during an expedition to the Yellowstone in 1873

The Westerners

Grant refused to give him the required permission to rejoin his regiment. Custer, fuming at the President, left without permission, but found himself under military arrest when he reached Chicago. Again it was Phil Sheridan who interceded for him, and after a lengthy exchange of telegrams with the President, Custer was permitted to resume command of the Seventh Cavalry. There were two conditions: General Terry instead of Custer would be in command of the expedition, and no newspapermen were to accompany the regiment to glorify the exploits of the Boy General.

These restrictions did not bother Autie. He arranged for an unknown reporter, Mark Kellogg, who worked for the Bismarck (Dakota Territory) *Tribune*, to accompany him as a special guest. And he was confident that once in the field and away from General Terry, he could take the Seventh Regiment into glorious battle whenever and wherever he chose. He meant to come back from this campaign with an eagle or perhaps a general's star.

On 17 May, with Autie at its head and the band playing 'The Girl I Left Behind me', the Seventh Cavalry marched out of Fort Abraham Lincoln. 'From the hour of breaking camp, before the sun was up,' Libbie said afterward, 'a mist had enveloped everything.' As the sun broke through the mist, the light formed a mirage so that the line of horsemen seemed lifted into the heavens. 'For a little distance it marched, equally plain to the

Plan of the Battle of the Little Big Horn

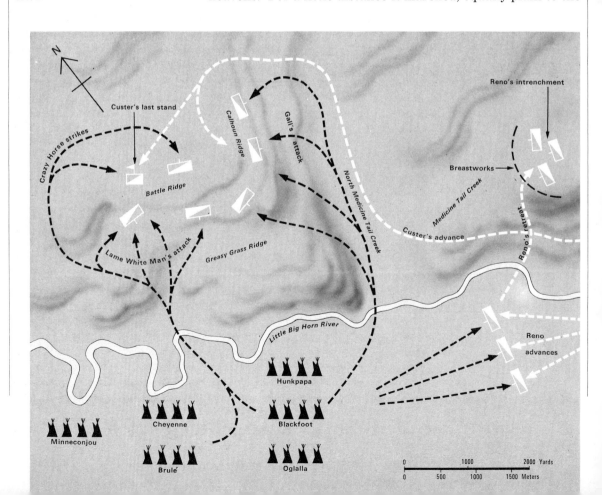

sight on the earth and in the sky.' To Libbie the mirage was a portent of danger. Her anxiety would have turned to terror had she known that in the Indian camps along the Little Big Horn, Sitting Bull was telling his people of his Sun Dance vision: 'I looked into the sky and saw soldiers on horseback coming down like grasshoppers, with their heads down and their hats falling off. They were falling right into our camp.'

On the first day's march Libbie rode beside Autie to spend one final night with him in his tent. Next morning at dawn, they told each other goodbye. He was dressed in the costume he had designed for the West–broad-brimmed white hat, fringed buckskin shirt, scarlet necktie.

This was the way she saw him for the remaining fifty-seven years of her life–a gallant, golden-haired young man of thirty-six who waved his big hat to her in farewell and then rode away on his steed across the Dakota plain to challenge the Red Menace. For her he never really died; he never grew older.

Soon after the startling news came to Fort Abraham Lincoln that Custer and more than two hundred of his men had been killed, General Terry sent a confidential report to the War Department placing the blame for the disaster upon Custer because he had disobeyed orders in the movement of his troops. An enterprising journalist obtained a copy of the confidential report and it was spread across the front pages of the newspapers. In her anger over this charge, Libbie forgot her grief and began a long campaign to keep the name of the Boy General bright and shining in history. For more than half a century whenever the slightest criticism of Autie appeared in print, Libbie pounced upon it, demanding retractions.

She enlisted the support of chivalrous generals in the War Department; she conspired in forged affidavits to prove Autie's innocence of disobedience; she constantly maneuvered to place the blame upon her villains–Terry, Benteen, and Reno. She moved her one-woman headquarters to New York so that she could keep a close watch over editors and publishers who might betray her. She became the terror of authors who dared to seek out the truth.

At every opportunity she lectured to American audiences, furthering the legend. She wrote three books, shaping and perfecting the image of her Beau Sabreur, referring always to Autie as 'the General'. Those who hoped to explode her folk-myth bided their time, expecting to outlive this determined little woman so that they might tell the whole story of Lieutenant-Colonel George Armstrong Custer, the incorrigible, impulsive adolescent who hated authority yet was a fanatical disciplinarian of men under his command. One by one, however, the men who knew the truth passed from the scene. Libbie outlived them all, keeping Autie's knighthood unstained until she died at the age of ninety-one on 6 April 1933, almost unnoticed during the first hectic days of Franklin Roosevelt's New Deal.

The remains of the Seventh Cavalry

16. The Dispossessed

'Let us alone', Sitting Bull said whenever the white men sent emissaries demanding the Black Hills or some other piece of coveted land. These white men came again and again, inviting him to bring his people to the agencies so that the Indians might learn to live like white men. 'Let us alone', he told them repeatedly. 'We want only to be left alone.'

By 1876, the year that Lieutenant-Colonel Custer marched his Seventh Cavalry to the Little Big Horn, Sitting Bull had accepted the fact that the white intruders were not going to leave him and his people alone. Peace with the white men was impossible; they wanted everything in the West. The only peace obtainable was agency imprisonment, and to a free Indian of the Plains such a peace was nothing but a long dying.

And so the blue-coated soldiers came to the Little Big Horn just as Sitting Bull had seen them falling from the sky in his Sun Dance vision. One bunch of them came charging into the south end of the tipi villages; another bunch came from the east. The Sioux and their Cheyenne allies fought hard that day, and all the soldiers on the hills east of the Little Big Horn died under the onrush of warriors. After it was over and Sitting Bull led his victorious followers away from the field of death, he hoped that now the white men would respect his power and leave him alone to live in peace.

He did not know then that Custer, the golden-haired Boy General, had died on one of the Greasy Grass hills; probably none of Sitting Bull's followers knew until afterward – when the myths began of the Long Hair and his valiant Last Stand. The warriors remembered one brave man who fought like a buffalo bull, his body bloody with wounds, a circle of spent cartridges around him. The soldier wore three stripes on his sleeve, and they learned afterward that he was called Sergeant James Butler. But the brave sergeant was soon forgotten; the Boy General was the hero who must be avenged, and Sitting Bull was the monster who had killed him.

Tatanka Iyotake, Sitting Bull, was born and grew up in the Dakota country along Grand River. This was in the 1830s when fur traders were pushing up the Missouri, but Sitting Bull's Teton Sioux people, the Hunkpapas, preferred to hunt toward the west around the sacred Black Hills where few white men ventured. When George Catlin traveled up to Fort Pierre in 1832, he described the Hunkpapas as 'those who camp by themselves', and he had difficulty persuading them to pose for his paint brush. In the late 1830s Sitting Bull was learning how to hunt buffalo, and after he reached his teens in the 1840s he was invited to join a horse-raiding expedition against the Crows.

Like most of his tribesmen, he avoided the white men who kept coming from the East, giving little thought to them until he was in his early thirties. This was in 1863, during the time of the white men's Civil War, a year of little rain on the Northern Plains. In that summer the Hunkpapas followed the buffalo herds eastward off the parched grass and across the Missouri River, only to be attacked by General H. H. Sibley's soldiers for no reason other than that they were Indians. Although the hunters that Sitting Bull was traveling with missed the brief skirmish, they did catch up with Sibley's supply train and Sitting Bull captured a mule from the teamsters. Sibley was finishing up his war with Little Crow's Santee Sioux in Minnesota, and had marched his troops out on the Dakota plains to kill the Santees who were fleeing for their lives.

Later that same year Sibley shipped hundreds of captured Santees up the Missouri to Crow Creek, where the soil was barren, the wild game scarce, the alkali water unfit for drinking. More than half of them died during the first winter. Sitting Bull visited his woodland cousins there on the reservation; he looked upon them with pity and listened to their stories of the Americans who had taken their land and driven them from their homes. He guessed that these greedy white men already had their eyes fixed on the buffalo country of the Tetons, but he resolved that he would never submit to imprisonment upon a reservation.

The next summer, 1864, the Hunkpapas were camped along the Little Missouri near Killdeer Mountain enjoying a fine season of hunting. Many of their Teton relatives joined them there–Oglallas, Sans Arcs, Minneconjous and others. Every tipi had its curtains of pemmican drying for the cold months ahead, and the ponies were growing sleek and strong on rich prairie grass. There was time to lie in the sun, play with children, study clouds against a pure blue sky, or listen to bird songs. Sitting Bull had a special feeling for birds–eagles, falcons, magpies, and meadow larks. He believed he could exchange words with meadow larks, and that when danger threatened they gave him warnings.

This tranquil interval was broken later in the summer with the arrival of some Santees who told of how General Alfred Sully was bringing hundreds of soldiers west from the Missouri River forts. These soldiers not only killed Indians wherever they could find them, they cut off their heads and mounted them upon poles. When the Teton chiefs heard of these barbaric

A signed photograph of Tatanka Iyotake

Crow Indians pitching tipis in an encampment in Montana

acts, they knew that their people were doomed unless they could make their hearts strong enough to save themselves from the blue-coated killers. Some chiefs called for war; others said they should turn their backs to the soldiers and travel westward to sanctuary in the Bad Lands and the Black Hills. Before a decision could be reached, the soldiers found them near Killdeer Mountain.

This was the first time that Sitting Bull had fought with blue-coated pony soldiers. They swept toward the tipi camp in skirmish lines a mile long, their carbines chattering. Behind them was the roar and echo and smoke of big cannons that hurled whistling bits of metal into the women and children trying to escape. The bows and arrows and old muskets of the Tetons were no match for the bluecoats' deadly firepower, but the warriors fought like surrounded buffaloes, shielding the flight of their women and children until they could all scatter to the hills.

That winter the soldier chief at Fort Rice on the Missouri sent out messengers to all the Sioux camps inviting the Indians to come to the fort in the spring for a peace council. Sitting Bull would listen to none of this. Alarming news had come from the

242

south of a massacre of Cheyennes at Sand Creek; it seemed the white men who talked so much of peace had made up their minds to rub out all Indians everywhere. Although some Teton leaders decided to go to Fort Rice, only a few Hunkpapas joined them. These Hunkpapas were so suspicious that they would not go into the fort but remained camped out on the plain waiting to see how the soldier chief would treat the Tetons who had gone inside the stockade. While the Hunkpapas were waiting, the fort's big cannons began to boom. It was only a salute, but the Hunkpapas had felt the effects of those guns at Killdeer Mountain, and they were sure that the soldiers were killing their Teton relatives in the fort just as Chivington had killed the Cheyennes at Sand Creek. The Hunkpapas mounted their horses and raced back to their main camp to tell of how the soldier chief had trapped the Indians in his fort and was massacring them with his big-talking guns.

Sitting Bull became so furious when he heard of this that he gashed his flesh with a knife and rode through the camp assembling warriors for a vengeance raid upon Fort Rice. With five hundred braves following, he led the way down through the hills, placed his men in an arc around the west side of the fort, and challenged the soldiers to battle. The bluecoats poured out of the gates, rolling their big cannons into position, and for three hours Sitting Bull's inspired horsemen made darting raids against the defenders. 'When the Indian ponies ran,' one soldier said afterward, 'they went so fast they seemed to lie out entirely straight.'

As at Killdeer Mountain, the soldiers' superior firepower was

Three Sioux chiefs in war bonnets. The feathers signified various exploits.

too much for the Sioux. They withdrew, and soon afterward learned that their friends who had gone into the fort had not been massacred after all. This bold attack upon Fort Rice did not go unnoticed by the soldier chief, Alfred Sully. For the first time the name of 'a chief called Sitting Bull' was entered into the official records of the United States.

After that summer a few Hunkpapas and other Tetons, who had acquired a taste for crackers and molasses and the white man's whisky, continued to camp around Fort Rice. But most of the Sioux viewed the Missouri River as a despoiled road through their country, the trees along its banks all cut down to fuel steamboats, the wild game all killed or frightened away. Sitting Bull's people stayed as far from the river as possible, making their camps west of the Black Hills along streams that ran into the Yellowstone–the Powder, Tongue, Rosebud, and Big Horn. The Powder River country was a paradise of wild game, but the Sioux had to fight Crows and Shoshones to keep it, and then white men invaded from the south, opening forts along the Bozeman Trail. Red Cloud of the Oglallas was the heroic defender, rallying not only the Tetons but Cheyennes and Arapahos into uncompromising resistance to invasion of the Powder River country.

Recognizing in Red Cloud a fellow stalwart, Sitting Bull encouraged the Hunkpapas to give the Oglalla chief their allegiance. If the Plains Indians were to survive, they must unite and refuse to surrender any more land. Sitting Bull's Hunkpapas raided Army wagon trains along the Bozeman Trail, and they fought General Patrick Connor's invading soldiers who had orders to 'kill every male Indian over twelve years of age' in the Powder River country. Sitting Bull and his people, however, were in winter camps far up on the Yellowstone when Red Cloud's warriors won their great victory at Fort Phil Kearny.

The news of that Battle of the Hundred Slain and the exploits of a young Oglalla named Crazy Horse spread quickly throughout the Northern Plains, and as the moons passed, Sitting Bull was not surprised to hear rumors that the white men were eager for a treaty of peace. He was ready for peace also; he wanted only to be left alone so that his people could live as they had always lived, free to go where they pleased when they pleased, living in harmony with the natural world of birds and plants and animals. But he wanted no peace if it meant surrender of more land and imprisonment upon reservations.

In the spring of 1868, Sitting Bull and his growing number of followers were camped near the mouth of Powder River when agents of the Great Father in Washington invited him to sign a peace treaty at Fort Rice. After he learned that the treaty fixed boundaries within which the Indians must live, and named agencies to which they must report as if they were prisoners, he refused to attend. He was bitterly disappointed to hear that

Red Cloud had promised to sign such a treaty as soon as soldiers were withdrawn and forts abandoned on the Bozeman Trail.

In June of that year a message came to Sitting Bull's camp from Running Antelope, a Hunkpapa chief who had chosen to live near Fort Rice. The message said that a trusted white friend of the Indians, the Black Robe (Father Pierre-Jean De Smet), was coming to see Sitting Bull. Sitting Bull had heard much of this sixty-eight-year-old priest who communed regularly with the Great Spirit and was said to have powers of divination. With Gall, Black Moon, Four Horns and other camp leaders, Sitting Bull went to meet the Black Robe and make him welcome. When the Tetons saw a banner unfurled above Father De Smet's approaching caravan, they drew back, preparing to alarm their camp and flee out of fear that the banner was a soldier flag signaling an attack. The banner was not a flag of war, however, but a flag of peace bearing an image of the Holy Virgin Mary.

After exchanging pledges of friendship, the Black Robe and the Indian leaders assembled for a council. The Black Robe said that he had come to help them stop the fighting that was killing too many good red men and white men. Sitting Bull replied that he was as strong in his heart for peace as was the Black Robe. Peace, he said, meant being left alone, and he did not know how there could be peace if the white men kept cutting the country up with roads, building forts, shooting all the buffalo, and chopping down all the trees. 'I am and always have been a fool and a warrior', he said. 'My people caused me to be so. They have been troubled and confused by the past, they look upon their troubles as coming from the Whites and become crazy, and pushed me forward . . . I will now say this in their presence, welcome father–the messenger of peace. I hope quiet will again be restored to our country.' Sitting Bull paused to shake hands with the Black Robe, and then added firmly: 'I wish all to know that I do not propose to sell any land to the Whites, nor do I wish them to cut timber.'

At the end of the council, however, not even the Black Robe's warmest persuasion could win Sitting Bull's consent to return with him to Fort Rice and sign the peace treaty. The Hunkpapa leader had never been inside a white man's fort, and he feared the corruptive force they represented. Instead, Sitting Bull sent his protégé, Gall, as a representative. Gall was covered with scars, the result of being kicked and trampled and bayoneted by bluecoat soldiers, and he knew the ways of white men. Gall signed the treaty.

That autumn when the Great Father ordered the Hunkpapas to report to their new agency on Grand River to begin life as farmers on a reservation, Sitting Bull ignored the summons. But he told Gall that since he had made his mark on the treaty, then Gall was honor bound to go. Gall went, but not even his acquired relish for crackers and molasses could keep him there long. He was soon back in Sitting Bull's camp. And after Red Cloud obeyed the Great Father's command to take the Oglallas to an agency and keep them within the confines of a reservation, young Crazy Horse broke away with his people to join the camps of Sitting Bull and give allegiance to the mystic leader who wanted only to be left alone to live in freedom.

In 1872 the government made another strong effort to persuade Sitting Bull to abandon freedom and bring his followers to the Grand River reservation. That year his camp consisted of seven hundred tipis. More Oglallas came to join Crazy Horse's people. Many Brulés from Spotted Tail's reservation also came, and there were growing numbers of Cheyennes and Arapahos. These breakaway Indians were a threat to the entire reservation system, and the alarmed Indian Bureau sent an investigating commission from Washington to Fort Peck in Montana Territory to deal with Sitting Bull. After Sitting Bull ignored their blandishments sent by messengers, the commissioners offered to visit him in his camp if he would only let them know where he was.

Sitting Bull's answer was to send his brother-in-law, Techanke (Gray Eagle), to Fort Peck. 'Go there,' Sitting Bull told Techanke, 'and when you find a white man who tells the truth, return and I will go see him.' Techanke evidently failed to find a commissioner he could trust. At any rate Sitting Bull did not visit the fort to pay his respects. Later that summer he went on a horse-raiding expedition against the Crows, and after returning to camp he started work on his pictographic autobiography. In the autumn, the discouraged Indian Bureau officials made one more attempt to win him over. They persuaded Red Cloud to send Sitting Bull a message:

> Listen to me and save your country. Make no trouble for our Great Father. His heart is good. Be friends to him and he will provide for you . . . Take his hand and hold it fast . . . Open your ears and listen to him. His words are good – remember them.

Sitting Bull did not bother to reply. The white men had taken his old friend Red Cloud to Washington and thrown dust in his eyes; he had been bought by them.

The next year Sitting Bull heard that the Great Father had moved the reservation Hunkpapas up the Missouri to Standing Rock and was trying to get them to dig in the ground with hoes and cut down what trees were left along the river to make log-houses for them to live in. He declined another summons to join the endeavor. During the spring many hungry people came to his camp from nearby reservations, telling of rotten beef and weevily grain which had been doled out to them by their white agents. Because of all these new people, the camp's food supplies ran short and they had to start the summer hunts earlier than usual. With so many families camping together, the village sites had to be moved frequently to find enough buffalo and antelope to feed them.

It was the same during the next year, 1874, the summer that Custer chose to violate the Treaty of 1868 by invading *Paha Sapa*, the Black Hills. Sitting Bull was busy hunting up buffalo herds along the Yellowstone to keep his people in food, shelter and clothing, but when he heard of the invasion he wondered how the Great Father could expect the Indians to observe their treaty obligations when he permitted his soldiers to break them by marching into the most sacred country of the Plains tribes. The soldiers, however, left Sitting Bull's people alone that summer and the next.

By the end of 1875, Sitting Bull realized that the soldiers were drawing a noose tighter and tighter around the last of the great hunting grounds. In all the four directions they were building more forts and opening more roads. The Black Hills were overrun with digging white men, and on the buffalo grasslands to the south white ranchers were bringing cattle herds to graze. In the Moon When the Deer Shed Their Horns (22 December 1875) the agent at Standing Rock received orders to notify all Hunkpapa Sioux to move within the bounds of that reservation before 31 January 1876, or 'be deemed hostile and treated accordingly by the military force'.

On that day Sitting Bull and his people were in winter camp on Powder River, 250 miles to the west. The Plains were deep in snow. It was mid-January before the courier from Standing Rock found them. Sitting Bull sent the messenger back to the agent, informing him that he would consider the order to come

The buffalo was central to the life of the Plains Indians. BELOW This 'winter count' drawn on a buffalo robe has a symbol for each year from 1800 to 1871. The blotched man in the center represents the smallpox epidemic of 1801–2, the arrow-pierced tipi marks a massacre by the Dakotas in 1839–40, and so on.

in, but could not do so until the Moon When the Green Grass is Up so that there would be enough forage to feed the ponies on the long journey by travois across Dakota.

Sitting Bull had no white man's calendar, but in June when the green grass was up he was camped on the Little Big Horn, his allied villages enlarged by hundreds more refugees from reservations. It was there that Lieutenant-Colonel Custer found him. 'We were camped there awaiting the will of the Great Spirit,' Sitting Bull afterward told Father Jean Genin, 'at the same time praying to the Great Spirit to save us from the hands of our enemies, now near, and coming without provocation to complete our extermination.' When the soldiers came, Sitting Bull continued, 'my men destroyed the last of them in a very short time. Now they accuse me of slaying them. Yet what did I do? Nothing. The Great Spirit saved our lives because we had called him. They should then accuse the Great Spirit, for truly it was he who saved us by permitting them to die . . . We did not go out of our own country to kill them, they came to kill us and got killed themselves. The Great Spirit so ordered it.'

After the fight with Custer which 'did not last long enough to light a pipe', they left Reno's soldiers cowering on a hill, and moved off toward the Big Horn Mountains, the tribes separating along the way and taking different directions. All that Sitting Bull wanted was to be left alone. He had never sought any war with the white men; they had always brought war to him and his people, forcing them to fight or die. In that summer, he tried to keep as far away from the soldiers' forts as possible, but the country everywhere was filled with prowling columns of bluecoats, seeking Indians to kill in revenge for Custer. 'What have we done that the white people want us to stop?' he asked. 'We have been running up and down the country, but they follow us from one place to another.'

When autumn came he took his people far up the Yellowstone where buffalo were plentiful and there were no soldier forts. They had scarcely got their tipis up when they heard that soldiers were building a fort at the mouth of the Tongue and were cutting a road through the buffalo grazing grounds. The whole world seemed to be filling up with blue-coated soldiers.

In one last attempt to persuade the soldiers to leave him alone, Sitting Bull sent a message to the soldier chief, Nelson Miles, politely asking him to take his bluecoats away so that the Indians could hunt buffalo in peace. Miles asked for a council, and Sitting Bull agreed to meet with him even though he knew his life would be in danger. The meeting was a waste of time; Miles said that his soldiers would leave the country as soon as Sitting Bull surrendered his arms and took his people to live on a reservation. When Sitting Bull replied that he was not an agency Indian and did not intend to become one, Miles grew angry, and his soldiers began clicking the locks of their rifles. As Sitting Bull signaled his warriors to withdraw, some of the soldiers opened fire, and the Sioux had to start running up and down the country again.

By springtime of 1877, Sitting Bull was tired of running. There was no longer room enough in the West for white men and free Indians to live together in peace. He decided to take his people to Canada, to the land of the Grandmother, Queen Victoria. Before going he tried to find Crazy Horse, hoping to persuade the Oglalla leader to take his people to Canada also. But Crazy Horse was running up and down the country trying to escape the soldiers, and Sitting Bull could not find him.

In the Moon When the Ponies Shed (May 1877), Sitting Bull led his people into the Grandmother's country of Canada, and during the summer moons many other fleeing Indians crossed the line to join him. The Grandmother's redcoats, the Royal Northwest Mounted Police, counted 5600 Indians.

At first the redcoats were very friendly and Sitting Bull found that he could smile again. ('When he smiled, which he often did,' said one of the Canadian commissioners, 'his face brightened up wonderfully.') The redcoats invited the refugees to camp near Fort Walsh, but soon they were trying to persuade Sitting Bull to take his followers back across the border. 'Have pity on me', Sitting Bull told them. 'We are going to be raised with a new people . . . My heart was made strong, but now really it is weak, and that is why the Americans want to lick my blood. Why do the Americans want to drive me?– because they want only Americans to be there. The Great Spirit made me leader of the people, and that is why I am following the buffalo. The Great Spirit told me, if you do anything wrong your people will be destroyed, and that is why I came here. I was afraid. Look at me. See if anything wrong sticks to my body; I have nothing but my hand to fight the white men with.'

From across the border the news was all bad. The Black Hills had been stolen; the bluecoats had invaded the reservations, taking away the agency Indians' hunting rifles and horses; when Red Cloud protested they put him in the guardhouse at Fort Robinson, tied his hands, and gagged him so he could not talk. Then came the worst news of all–the soldiers had arrested Crazy Horse and stabbed him to death with a bayonet.

A few days after this, in the Moon of Falling Leaves (October 1877) Sitting Bull's camp was suddenly filled with wounded and bleeding Nez Percés. After a long hard flight from pursuing bluecoats, their war chief, Looking Glass, had been killed and Chief Joseph had surrendered. Only about a hundred Nez Percés escaped to Canada. 'They were weeping and yelling terribly', said Father Genin who was visiting in Sitting Bull's camp. 'In running away from the soldiers' reach, they had placed their small children on the backs of horses, and thus ran all night, only to find in the morning that the children were missing. The desolation of the mothers was great. To go back was to find sure death.'

The Westerners

The Catholic priest, Jean Genin, had come to Canada as an unofficial observer for both the United States and the Queen's Government. Through Commander James McLeod of the Northwest Mounted Police, Canadian officials had denied Sitting Bull's claim that his people were now British Indians entitled to the same treatment and lands as other British Indians. 'You are American Indians', McLeod told him. 'You can expect nothing whatever from the Queen's Government except protection so long as you behave yourselves.' For food, shelter and clothing, Sitting Bull's people would have to depend upon the buffalo as they had always done.

Father Genin did not find Sitting Bull receptive to the pressure from both governments for his return to the United States. 'It is very hard', the Hunkpapa said, 'to place any faith in the word of Americans. Ever since I knew them my experience with them has proved that they continually cheat the Indians, over-reaching upon their lands with big promises, never fulfilled, and at last finding some pretext to kill them . . . When you go back to my lands in Dakota, the white people will ask you what Sitting Bull says, and what he means to do. Please tell them I want none of their gold or silver, none of their goods, but that I desire to come back and live upon my lands; for there is plenty of game and grass, and we can live well if they will only let us alone.'

In hopes that his people might be allowed to return and live free in their homeland, Sitting Bull agreed to meet General Alfred Terry's commission in council at Fort Walsh during late October. Terry began the discussions by scolding Sitting Bull for being the leader of the only band of Indians in the West which had not surrendered. He promised the Hunkpapa leader

Sitting Bull remonstrating to the commission at Fort Walsh

a full pardon if he would bring his people back to the United States, surrender all arms, ammunition and horses to the soldiers, and live on the Great Sioux Reservation. 'The surrendered arms and horses would be sold,' Terry said, 'and with the money obtained from them cows will be bought and sent to you. From these cows you will be able to raise herds.'

The arrogance of Terry's proposal was almost more than Sitting Bull could bear. 'I would like to know', he retorted, 'why you came here. In the first place, I did not give you the country, but you followed me from one place to another, so I had to leave and come over to this country . . . If you think I am a fool you are a bigger fool than I am . . . The part of the country you gave me you ran me out of.' After he let Terry know that he had no intention of returning to the United States–disarmed, dismounted and helpless before the will of the Great Father's soldiers–Sitting Bull induced leaders of other tribes to speak freely. Most of them echoed his 'words, bluntly telling Terry and his commissioners, 'go back where you came from'.

As the meeting ended, General Terry realized that it was useless to make any further pleas to Sitting Bull. The Northwest Mounted Police escorted the U.S. commissioners back to the border, and Terry reported to Washington that Sitting Bull and his followers were 'a standing menace to the peace of our Indian Territories . . . they cannot fail to exercise a most injurious influence . . . giving evil counsel and advice, stimulating disaffection, and encouraging acts of hostility.'

For a time Sitting Bull's presence in Canada served as a magnet to all Plains Indians who preferred their own way of life to that of the white man's reservations. By the spring of 1878, his original refugee band of seven hundred tipis had grown to 1579–more than seven thousand freedom-seeking Indians. Had the Canadians accepted them as British Indians, most of them would have lived out their lives peacefully on the plains of Saskatchewan. The Queen's Government, however, wished to be rid of 'Sitting Bull's Indians'. No aid of any kind was offered to help them become established in the new land; their hunting range was so restricted that they could not find enough meat to eat or skins to make clothing and tipi covers. Most of them endured the misery for two years until the bad winter of 1880 brought such cold and hunger that groups of exiles began trekking across the border–traveling on foot because they were forced to eat their frozen horses. Even the loyal Gall gave up hope and crossed the border in the direction of the Great Sioux Reservation in Dakota.

Sitting Bull held out for another year, his immediate band of followers dwindling to less than two hundred. He heard that the Great Father had put a price on his head, as much as twenty thousand dollars for anyone who could deliver him across the border to Fort Buford. By the summer of 1881, all the food in his camp was gone; there was not even horse meat to eat, and the

Canadians turned their backs on his pleas for help. Yet when trader Jean Louis Legaré offered to arrange a transfer to Fort Buford, with Sitting Bull's personal safety guaranteed, the chief rebuffed him: 'You are trying to sell Indians by the pound!'

But at last Sitting Bull gave up, to save the lives of his family and loyal friends who would have starved rather than go back to the United States without him. On 19 July 1881 the Hunkpapa chief with 186 of his remaining followers arrived at Fort Buford. His clothing was tattered, and he looked old and beaten, but when he surrendered his rifle to the soldier chief, his voice was firm: 'I wish it to be remembered that I was the last man of my tribe to surrender my rifle!'

Instead of permitting Sitting Bull to accompany his people to Standing Rock, the soldiers took him to Fort Randall and kept him as a prisoner of war. He became resigned to confinement and made friends with the soldier chief who discovered that Sitting Bull was 'a very remarkable man . . . I learned to admire him for his many fine qualities . . . I marvelled at his patience and forbearance.' With time on his hands, the dispossessed leader wrote songs and poems out of his memory of the old days, and he made another pictographic record of his life. Among the numerous visitors who came to see him at Fort Randall was Rudolph Cronau, a German illustrator who helped him improve his draftsmanship and taught him to dapple the ponies in his drawings.

At last the government decided that Sitting Bull was sufficiently chastened, and in the spring of 1883 transferred him to Standing Rock reservation where he was presented with a hoe to dig in the ground along with his defeated tribesmen. It did not take him long to discover how poor his people had become. The buffalo were all gone, killed off by white hide hunters, and the Sioux were living in cheap cloth tipis which offered no protection against winter cold or summer heat. The rations doled out at the agency were scanty and of poor quality.

In August when a commission headed by Senator Henry L. Dawes came out from Washington to talk the Sioux into ceding half their reservation lands to the government, Sitting Bull went uninvited to the council. He did not have to speak against giving up land; the other leaders present were vehemently opposed to that. But he did launch a strong attack against the government for locking his people upon a reservation and expecting them to live like white men when they owned none of the things that white men had. 'It is your own doing that we are here; you sent us here and asked us to live as you do, and it is not right for us to live in poverty.' If the Great Father expected the Indians to become like white men, he added, then they must have tools and livestock, horses and wagons 'because that is the way white people make a living'. Instead of listening to what Sitting Bull had to say, the commissioners berated him for trying to assume the position of a

ABOVE The Indians' former meal tickets—bows, arrows, skill and cunning—were pitiably replaced on the reservations by ration tags.

RIGHT Some Indian possessions: a Sioux eagle feather war bonnet, like those of the 1870s and 1880s; a grizzly bear claw necklace; Sioux and Blackfoot pipe bags; Cheyenne women's leggings; Sioux, Cheyenne and Crow moccasins; knife sheaths of the Sioux and Arapaho; and a *pogamoggan* (stone-headed club) decorated with porcupine quills.

A section of painted tent sheet showing buffaloes, horses and Indians

chief. 'You have no following, no power, no control, and no right to any control', Senator John Logan shouted angrily. 'You are on an Indian reservation merely at the sufferance of the government.'

These commissioners soon departed when they saw that the Sioux were not going to sign away any more land, but other men came from Washington, prying into everything the Indians were doing, cajoling the tribal leaders, making big promises, covertly offering bribes. The Standing Rock agent, James McLaughlin, believed that it was his mission in life to destroy the culture of the Sioux and replace it with the white man's civilization. McLaughlin regarded Sitting Bull, who stood for everything Indian, as a prime enemy, and he worked hard to isolate him from the younger Sioux who were already beginning to lose any memory of tribal freedom.

In 1885 when the former Pony Express rider and stagecoach driver, Buffalo Bill Cody, invited Sitting Bull to join his traveling Wild West Show, McLaughlin readily granted official permission for the bothersome chief to leave Standing Rock. As for Sitting Bull, the offer came as a welcome release from the tedium and confinement of reservation life; it would also give him an opportunity to see the wonders of the white man's vaunted civilization in the East.

Posters and advertising for the Wild West Show featured THE RENOWNED SIOUX CHIEF, SITTING BULL, and he attracted tremendous crowds, earning for Buffalo Bill many times over the fifty dollars per week the showman paid him. Boos and catcalls sometimes sounded for the 'Killer of Custer', but after each show these same people pressed coins upon him for copies of his signed photograph. A friendly Canadian trader had taught him how to write his name in English.

During the tour of the East, Sitting Bull dictated a letter to the Commissioner of Indian Affairs, signing it in his bold script. He wanted the commissioner to know that white cattlemen were encroaching upon the grazing lands of the Great Sioux Reservation; also soldiers from Army posts were cutting reservation hay and timber, and he expressed a fear that the land would soon be entirely denuded of trees. He pointed out that only one trader was licensed to do business at Standing Rock and the trader was cheating the Indians. He concluded by suggesting that men sent out by the Indian Bureau to teach his people farming should know the Sioux language if the government expected the program to succeed. Sitting Bull never received a reply, not even an acknowledgement, to this letter.

In October when the tour ended, newspapermen asked him what he thought of the cities he had seen and whether or not he would tour with the show in its next season. 'The tipi is a better place', he told them. 'I am sick of the houses and the noises and the multitude of men.' When Buffalo Bill asked him the next year to join his show for a tour of Europe, the chief declined:

'I am needed here', he said. 'There is more talk of taking our lands.'

There was not only talk of taking more Indian land but also governmental action to take it. On 8 February 1887 Congress passed the Dawes Land Allotment Act which was designed primarily to break up the Great Sioux Reservation. Under this law, each family on the reservation would receive title to only 160 acres, the remaining land going to the government to be sold for white settlement. As the Great Sioux Reservation contained about twice the land needed for 160-acre allotments, this meant that the Sioux would lose half their land. Although the designers of this scheme in Washington surely knew that 160 acres of marginal Dakota land could not support a family either by farming or ranching, the act was hailed as the only way to 'break up the tribal mass' and force the Indians to become like white men.

The only block to this plan was the Treaty of 1868 which forbade 'cession of any portion or part of the reservation unless executed and signed by at least three-fourths of the adult male

An advertisement for Buffalo Bill's show

Denied access to insulating buffalo hide the Indians suffered terribly in winter and summer alike.

Indians'. With the treaty as a weapon, Sitting Bull struggled for two years to keep the land. 'They want us to give up another chunk of our tribal land', he told his people. 'This is not the first time or the last time. They will try to gain possession of the last piece of ground we possess . . . I do not wish to consider any proposition to cede any portion of our tribal holdings . . . If I agree to dispose of any part of our land to the white people I would feel guilty of taking food away from our children's mouths, and I do not wish to be that mean . . . let us stand as one family, as we did before the white people led us astray.'

Sitting Bull and his supporters were dealing with clever lawyers and politicians who represented powerful land-hungry interests. The land-grabbers first tried to bribe the Indians and when that failed they tried to frighten them into a belief that if they did not sign away half their land, then the government would take all of it.

In the summer of 1889 a commission headed by General George Crook toured the agencies on the Great Sioux Reservation, fully determined to obtain the required three-fourths of adult male signatures. They went first to the smaller agencies, wheedling and bullying, promising cows and bulls to those who signed, hinting retribution upon those who failed to sign.

Fearing Sitting Bull's stubborn opposition, the commissioners deliberately left Standing Rock agency to the last. As they had expected, they found the Hunkpapas adamant. With Agent James McLaughlin as a willing ally, however, the commissioners began a strong campaign to convince the Standing Rock Sioux that they would lose everything if they declined to sign. But Sitting Bull refused to yield. McLaughlin and the commissioners then concentrated their efforts upon young leaders such as John Grass who began wavering in his opposition and finally accepted the commissioners' arguments that the $1.50 per acre the Sioux would receive for their ceded lands would make them rich for the remainder of their lives.

On 3 August McLaughlin arranged a meeting to be kept secret from Sitting Bull, and at which John Grass would deliver an oration designed to stampede the Indians into signing the land cession. To prevent possible interruptions from Sitting Bull or his adherents, McLaughlin posted his Indian police in a four-column formation around the council ground.

The scheme worked. Before Sitting Bull learned of what was happening and could arrive to speak against the land cession, the commissioners obtained the signatures they needed. On that day the Great Sioux Reservation was broken apart. Within a generation the Dawes Land Allotment Act would take a hundred million acres of land away from reservations and would leave a hundred thousand Indians landless and in poverty.

'Our people were blindly deceived', Sitting Bull said. He knew now that an 'Indian giver' was a white man who gave the Indians something that already belonged to them and then took it away from them. As he was leaving the council to which he had not been invited, a newspaperman asked him how the Indians felt about giving up their land. 'Indians!', Sitting Bull shouted. 'There are no Indians left but me!'

Nor was there anything left for Sitting Bull. That winter he moved his family into a log cabin because there were not enough hides for a tipi, and the canvas issued by the Indian Bureau would not withstand even a little rain. On one pretext and another the government withheld the $1.50 per acre promised the Sioux, and then arrogantly cut their food allotments by twenty per cent. Lack of food left the very old and the very young too weak to survive winter diseases, and there was mourning in almost every family.

In their hopelessness the Indians all across the West now welcomed a new religion–the Ghost Dance with its promise of salvation. During the summer of 1890 the religion swept from reservation to reservation. The believers were sure that if they danced the Ghost Dance, the earth would soon be covered with new soil which would bury all the white men. New grass and trees would grow, streams would run clear again, and great herds of buffalo would return to the Plains.

Sitting Bull was skeptical of the Ghost Dance, but he knew that his people needed the new religion to sustain them. He did not spend much time with the dancers; he preferred to stay around his cabin listening to bird songs and remembering other summers. He wanted only to be let alone. The meadow larks spoke to him often. They told him his own people were going to kill him.

In the autumn of 1890 so many Indians were dancing the Ghost Dance that the white people became frightened at the intensity of the religious fervor. They asked the Army to send soldiers to protect them from the 'savages'. Had the Army or the Indian Bureau taken time to examine the Ghost Dance religion, they would have found that its tenets were based upon the non-violence of early Christianity; believers were forbidden to fight or to do harm to anyone. Instead the government agencies looked for an Indian leader upon whom to place the blame for the 'pernicious system of religion', as Agent McLaughlin at Standing Rock described it.

Because Sitting Bull was the best known Indian leader, the Washington bureaucrats chose him as the power behind the Ghost Dance religion. McLaughlin supported his fellow bureaucrats, the press, and the public in this view, and recommended that Sitting Bull be removed from Standing Rock and placed in a military prison. Even in his last days they would not leave the old Hunkpapa alone.

At daybreak 15 December 1890, with the backing of the Army and the Indian Bureau, McLaughlin sent forty-three Sioux dressed in agency police uniforms to arrest Sitting Bull. The Hunkpapa chief had no use for Indians who dressed in white men's uniforms to oppress their own tribesmen, but he submitted quietly. He had just stepped out of his cabin when firing broke out. A bullet tore a hole through his head. As the meadow larks had warned him, he was killed by his own people – those who had been bought by white men.

Indian agency police

17. Teddy the Rough Rider

His sixty-foot head, carved from cold granite on the face of Mount Rushmore in the Black Hills, broods over the holy land that was stolen from the Indians. Beside him are the heads of Washington, Jefferson, and Lincoln, incongruous in this setting of Western rocks and pines. It would have been more fitting for the promoters and sculptors of this 'shrine of democracy' meant for the tourist trade to have shaped the heads of Sitting Bull, Crazy Horse, Red Cloud and other native heroes here. Of the four presidents, only he belongs in this Western pantheon, and he is set back from his unsmiling companions as though uncertain of his rank, an attitude distinctly out of character. A more imaginative sculptor would have carved him Janus-fashion, one face turned to the past, the other face looking to the future.

He was the first cowboy to enter the White House, a New Yorker of the upper bourgeoisie who used the image of the Westerner– cowboy, hunter, Indian fighter, Rough Rider–to become President Theodore Roosevelt of the United States of America. Teddy was born within the same year span and only a few blocks away from the Bowery birthplace of William (Billy the Kid) Bonney. Both were puny in childhood, their constant ailments ranging from asthma to adenoids, and they spent their later years compensating for physical weaknesses and afflictions.

Billy the Kid and Teddy Roosevelt never met, but they would have recognized the similarities of their codes of honor– admiration for coolness under stress, loyalty to friends, adulation of women, and a violent belligerency toward those who held 'lesser' codes. Both loved the strenuous life of the open ranges of the West, spending long hours in the saddle, testing themselves at roundup times, accepting challenges, and fighting to win. Both believed in the power of a loaded gun and both were expert marksmen. They killed animals and men. Billy the Kid's total of twenty-one men far exceeded Teddy's one Spaniard claimed at San Juan Hill in Cuba, but Teddy's collection of animal heads would have excited the admiration of Billy Bonney. Billy became a Westerner long before Teddy;

in fact he was dead from a bullet at Fort Sumner, New Mexico Territory, two years before Teddy arrived in Dakota Territory to begin killing buffaloes, antelopes, and grizzly bears.

Teddy did not care for animals in the wild; he preferred them dead and stuffed. He did not like American Indians in their natural state, either, but he thought they looked fine dressed up in phony feather bonnets and theatrical costumes. For the Roosevelt inaugural of 1904 he released Geronimo from a military prison in Indian Territory long enough for the old Apache to ride in an open car up Pennsylvania Avenue decked out in a fancy black silk top hat.

In his first annual message to Congress, Teddy declared that it was time to dissolve the remaining reservations in the West and force the Indians to live like white men. 'The General Allotment Act', he said, 'is a mighty pulverizing engine to break up the tribal mass . . . In the schools the education should be elementary and largely industrial. The need of higher education among the Indians is very, very limited.' Some years earlier he had admitted frankly that he took 'the Western view of the Indians' as a result of his ranching experiences in Dakota Territory. 'I don't go so far as to think that the only good Indians are the dead Indians,' he told his New York friends, 'but I believe nine out of every ten are, and I shouldn't like to inquire too closely into the case of the tenth. The most vicious cowboy has more moral principle than the average Indian.' Teddy spent a considerable amount of time with cowboys, but he avoided Indians as if they were dangerous beasts, keeping them at a safe distance with rifle always ready, so that he actually knew less about Indians than about the numerous grizzly bears he shot to death.

In the early 1880s, with the Plains Indians disarmed, dismounted, and safely confined to reservations, it became the fashion for wealthy young men to visit the West and demonstrate their manliness by hunting big game with high-powered rifles. Teddy Roosevelt first saw the West on a September day in 1883 when he stepped off a Northern Pacific passenger train into a town that would have served as a set for a Hollywood Western movie. The place was called Little Missouri, and it was in the heart of what had been Sitting Bull's buffalo hunting country before the railroad came driving through in 1880, grabbing forty sections of Indian land on either side of each mile of track. Only a few weeks before Teddy arrived at Little Missouri, the Army moved Sitting Bull up to Standing Rock, less than two hundred miles away. That autumn, Sioux hunters were permitted to leave the reservations for their last buffalo hunt.

A few scraggy herds of buffalo still survived on the northern Plains, but after 1883 they were off limits to Indians. They were reserved for white hunters from the East and Europe who came in numbers greater than those of the animals they sought to

Billy the Kid

261

A tourist in the Wild West

kill. A sort of contest, stirred up by Western newspapers, developed out of this fever to find the last herd on the Plains. The nearer the species approached extermination, the more eager the hunters strove for the honor and fame of killing the last living buffalo, and in the late 1880s after the known number of surviving animals dropped to four in Dakota, ten in Montana, and twenty-six in Wyoming, the Associated Press began chronicling the kills as they did the deaths of old Western gunfighters.

At the invitation of friends who were venturing into the ranching business in Dakota Territory, Teddy Roosevelt journeyed to the West in 1883 to join the hunt for the last buffalo. From the railroad stop he traveled forty-five miles in a buckboard to a ranch cabin, talked incessantly until after midnight, slept two or three hours in blankets on an earthen floor, and then at daybreak he was up and eager to go after his buffalo. For several days through rain and across slithery gumbo mud of the northern Bad Lands, with his big teeth chattering from the cold, he astonished his guides with his tireless pursuit. He sighted three buffalo, wounded an old bull that got away, missed a shot at a cow, and finally got within fifty yards of a splendid specimen of the vanishing species. 'His glossy fall coat was in fine trim and shone in the rays of the sun,' Roosevelt said later, 'while his pride of bearing showed him to be in the lusty vigor of his prime.' He brought the buffalo down with one shot, danced a war dance of victory around the carcass, and then cut off the head to add to his trophies.

During his hunt, Teddy became entranced by the Dakota plains and so impressed with stories he heard of quick riches to be made from cattle ranching that he decided to become a rancher himself. The vast grasslands which had sustained buffalo herds and Indian tribes for centuries were now empty of both. The land could be leased cheaply from the railroad which had acquired it for nothing, and it was unnecessary to construct buildings or string fences. All that was needed was money to buy Longhorns and hire a few cowboys at low wages. The potential profits were enormous; ranchers were doubling their investments in two or three years. From his father, Teddy had inherited enough money to live in moderate comfort, but at the age of twenty-four he felt that it was time to risk some of the principal to gain even greater wealth from the West. Before he boarded the Northern Pacific to return to the East, he wrote out a check and formed a partnership with two cattlemen who were to manage his Maltese Cross Ranch.

That winter Roosevelt's wife died soon after giving birth to a daughter. To assuage his grief, he plunged deeper into New York politics which he had entered soon after graduating from Harvard in 1880. In his early twenties, Teddy had been unable to make up his mind whether he should become a lawyer or a

The Maltese Cross Ranch headquarters

writer. (In 1882 he published his first book, *The Naval War of 1812*.) After settling down with his bride in a house on West 45th Street he decided it was his duty as a man of superior breeding and education to enter politics in order to reform the government which he believed had grown corrupt under the management of unprincipled and ignorant Irishmen of the Democratic party. He joined his district's Republican club and to his astonishment was soon elected to the New York assembly. After his wife's death early in 1884, he devoted most of his energies to a campaign to prevent James G. Blaine (whom he considered to be corrupt) from being nominated as the Republican candidate for President. When he lost this fight at the Republican convention in Chicago, he turned his back on the East. He was widowed, the father of an infant daughter, and disgusted with politics. Now he would become a Westerner, start a new life, and grow rich in the cattle business.

In mid-June when he reached his Dakota destination he found that the town of Little Missouri was now called Medora, named for the wife of a French nobleman, the Marquis de Mores, who had also come to Dakota to enter the cattle business. The town and the entire Bad Lands were booming with eager seekers after quick wealth.

Hurrying to the cabin his partners had built for a Maltese Cross headquarters, Roosevelt learned that his herd had survived the winter; twenty-five Longhorns had died in snowstorms but 150 calves had been born. The prospects looked so good that he wrote more checks to buy more cattle, and made plans to found a second ranch to be called the Elkhorn farther north along the Little Missouri River.

One of his first acts as a working ranchman was to order a local seamstress to make him a buckskin shirt. 'The fringed tunic or hunting shirt made of buckskin', he said, 'was the most picturesque and distinctively national dress ever worn in America. It was the dress in which Daniel Boone was clad when he first passed through the trackless forests of the Alleghenies and penetrated into the heart of Kentucky . . . it was the dress worn by grim old Davy Crockett when he fell at the Alamo.' After donning his buckskin shirt, Teddy was convinced that he belonged at last to 'the old race of Rocky Mountain hunters and trappers, of reckless, dauntless Indian fighters . . . the forerunners of the white advance throughout all our Western land.' To celebrate, he went out and shot his first antelope. Later on he added a broad sombrero, horse-hide chaparajos, cowboy boots, and silver spurs to his costume.

When Teddy first entered into an earnest effort to learn the practical side of ranching – from roundups to branding to trail driving – the cowboys regarded him as somewhat of a joke. His pale dyspeptic face with its short reddish mustache over a mouthful of big teeth and his large round eyeglasses reminded the cowboys of an owl. They called him 'Four Eyes' and laughed

Roosevelt, in buckskin, as he liked to picture himself

openly when in his high piping voice he would cry out 'Dee-lighted!' Another of his pet phrases they imitated was 'By Godfrey, isn't that bully!' On one occasion he encouraged a cowboy to overtake an elusive Longhorn with a shrill: 'Hasten forward quickly there!' The expression spread mockingly through the Bad Lands.

His standing as a tenderfoot ended suddenly in the bar of a cattle town hotel. Hearing gunshots as he approached the hotel, Teddy entered the bar as unobtrusively as possible, intent only upon obtaining food and drying his clothes after being caught out in a storm. A drunken bully was swaggering up and down in the crowded room, occasionally firing his revolver at a clock on the wall. When he saw Teddy he roared: 'Four Eyes!' Roosevelt laughed nervously and sat down beside the stove. 'Four Eyes is going to treat!', the rowdy shouted. Roosevelt ignored him, but this only made the man more offensive.

'He stood leaning over me,' Teddy said afterwards, 'a gun in each hand, using very foul language. He was foolish to stand so near, and moreover, his heels were close together, so that his position was unstable. Accordingly in response to his reiterated command that I should set up the drinks, I said, "Well, if I've

Teddy in reality

got to, I've got to," and rose, looking past him.'

One thing Teddy had learned well at Harvard was boxing, and he prided himself upon keeping up his skill.

> As I rose, I struck quick and hard with my right just to one side of the point of his jaw, hitting with my left as I straightened out, and then again with my right. He fired the guns, but I do not know whether this was merely a convulsive action of his hands or whether he was trying to shoot at me. When he went down he struck the corner of the bar with his head. It was not a case in which one could afford to take chances, and if he had moved I was about to drop on his ribs with my knees; but he was senseless. I took away his guns, and the other people in the room, who were now loud in their denunciation of him, hustled him out and put him in a shed. I got dinner as soon as possible, sitting in a corner of the dining-room away from the windows, and then went upstairs to bed where it was dark so that there would be no chance of any one shooting at me from the outside. However, nothing happened. When my assailant came to, he went down to the station and left on a freight.

After this incident, which could be used unchanged as a script for a scene in a Hollywood western, Teddy lost his tenderfoot image. Unprepossessing though he was in appearance, Teddy even then had a certain charisma, and the sudden change in the attitude of the cowboys taught him how to develop it. From that time he was an actor-politician, sharpening his performances through the years, playing the role of hero, entertainer, statesman, romantic liberal, astute conservative, savior of national resources, warrior, hunter, cowboy, imperialist—as the occasion demanded.

He won over the cowboys, but he never tried to win the friendship of his Indian neighbors. Whenever the grass on his land allotment caught fire he blamed the Indians; whenever a steer or a horse wandered away he was sure the Indians had stolen it. One morning while riding the range alone he saw in the distance four or five mounted Sioux who had permits to leave their reservation for hunting or trading. 'I waited until the Indians were a hundred yards off,' he said, 'and then threw up my rifle and drew a bead on the foremost. The effect was like magic. The whole party scattered out as wild pigeons or teal ducks do when shot at, and doubled back on their tracks, the men bending over alongside their horses.'

The Sioux of course were alarmed; they had barely survived white men's guns pointed at them when the Army had scoured the Plains in the 1870s to drive them upon reservations. One of the Indians, evidently wanting to talk peaceably, dropped his rifle on the ground and waved his blanket over his head in a sign of friendship. Roosevelt, however, allowed him to come no closer than fifty yards, even though the Indian held up his paper permit. 'When his companions began to draw near, I covered him with the rifle and made him move off, which he did with a sudden lapse into the most canonical Anglo-Saxon profanity . . . I never saw the Indians again. They may not have intended any mischief beyond giving me a fright; but I did not dare to let them come to close quarters, for they would have probably taken my horse and rifle, and not impossibly my scalp as well.'

Late in the summer after most of the ranching chores were finished, he and two guides went to the Big Horn Mountains to kill grizzly bears. Along the way they camped on Powder River in country the Indians had fought so hard to hold while Teddy was a protected sickly child in New York City. His interest in American history, however, did not extend to this phase of the Winning of the West, and he had no desire even to meet the vanquished. One evening after a guide discovered that Cheyennes off their reservation were camped nearby, he suggested to Roosevelt that they visit the Indians.

'What do you want to go over there for?' Roosevelt asked in alarm.

'Out in this country,' the guide replied, 'you always want to know who your neighbors are.'

Somewhat reluctantly Roosevelt went along and was immensely relieved when he found the Cheyennes were not hostile. He was even more relieved the next morning after he and his companions moved on west away from them. They followed Crazy Woman's Creek, passing not far from the remains of old Fort Phil Kearny, until they reached the Big Horn country of the grizzly bears.

Last moments for Old Ephraim (one of the nicknames for grizzly bears)

Teddy respected the fierceness of the grizzlies, aiming carefully between their eyes and keeping a safe distance while the animals struggled through their death agonies. He watched without comment when one of the guides deliberately broke a grizzly's leg with his first shot 'so as to see what he'd do'. During this hunt Teddy killed three grizzly bears and six elk, piling heads and skins in a wagon which he had brought along to haul his trophies back to the railroad for shipment home to impress family and friends.

'So I have had good sport', he wrote his sister on 24 September. 'But unless I was bear hunting all the time I am afraid I should get as restless with this life as with the life at home.'

During the autumn his restlessness took him to the East where he campaigned half-heartedly for James G. Blaine who lost the election to Grover Cleveland. He spent the winter working on *Hunting Trips of a Ranchman*, an account of his experiences in Dakota, and when he was asked for publicity photos he dressed up in his cowboy suit to pose in a New York studio. One of his Western friends who received a print found the photograph hilariously amusing. 'The imitation grass not quite concealing the rug beneath, the painted background, the theatrical (slightly patched) rocks against which the cowboy leans gazing dreamily across an imaginary prairie, the pose of the hunter with rifle ready and finger on the trigger, facing dangerous game which is not there—all reveal a boyish delight in play-acting.'

The lure of the real West brought him back to Dakota for the spring roundups. He spent a busy summer developing his new Elkhorn Ranch. He built a roomy headquarters house, festooning its front porch with the horns of elk which he killed where he could find them. He attended the stockmen's convention in Miles City and was invited to deliver the Fourth of July speech at Dickinson. His widening circle of friends began suggesting that he enter Dakota politics. In his leisure moments he read from the library which he had brought out with him; he worked from time to time on a biography of Thomas Hart Benton (the man who conspired with the Magoffin brothers for the bloodless conquest of New Mexico). He also gave some thought to a major work he would like to write on the westward movement of the American frontier; he would call it *The Winning of the West*.

During the spring of 1886 Roosevelt experienced a splendid Western adventure which began with the theft of a boat he kept moored on the bank of the Little Missouri. Evidence pointed to three men, one being Mike Finnegan, a local 'bad man' who had been involved in several saloon shootouts. With two of his ranch managers, Roosevelt engaged in a fast pursuit which took him past Killdeer Mountain where twenty years earlier Sitting Bull had endured his first baptism of fire from soldiers of the United States. If Roosevelt knew of this, he made no mention of it, and would have considered the incident unworthy of a footnote in *The Winning of the West*.

The robbers were captured in Wild Western fashion, Roosevelt getting the drop on Finnegan who 'hesitated for a second, his eyes fairly wolfish . . . I walked up within a few paces, covering the centre of his chest so as to avoid overshooting, and repeating the command, he saw that he had no show, and, with an oath, let his rifle drop and held his hands up beside his head.' Eight days were spent in getting the prisoners back to the sheriff through Dakota rains and cold and mud, but during the ordeal Roosevelt managed to read Tolstoy's *Anna Karenina* which he had brought along in his saddle bag. When he finished the Russian classic he borrowed a dime novel about Jesse James that Mike Finnegan was carrying in his saddle bag and read it. Teddy was a compulsive reader.

During that summer the West was filled with excitement over a possible war with Mexico, the result of an attack by Mexican soldiers upon American forces pursuing Geronimo across the border. Captain Emmet Crawford had been killed, and the U.S. Army wanted revenge. In Roosevelt's biography of Thomas Hart Benton, he expressed the view that the United States should have conquered all of North America. 'We were the people who could use it best, and we ought to have taken it all.' He was eager therefore for any opportunity to expand the boundaries of his country, and he dashed off a letter to the Secretary of War, offering to raise a regiment of cavalry in the

The Westerners

West if war came with Mexico. In another letter to Henry Cabot Lodge, he asked his friend to telegraph him immediately if war became inevitable. Roosevelt wrote: 'I think there is some good fighting stuff among these harum-scarum rough riders out here.' This was a forecast of San Juan Hill which was to come twelve years later.

Back East that winter Teddy married a childhood sweetheart, Edith Carow, and took her off to Europe for a honeymoon. When they returned to New York in the spring of 1887, the news from Dakota was bad. Unusually severe blizzards had killed thousands of cattle on the Northern Plains. Too late the avaricious cattlemen realized they had overstocked the ranges; as bad as the blizzards were, many of the animals would have survived had there been fewer to share the winter grass. In midwinter, herds of gaunt steers had drifted up the Little Missouri to Medora, invading the town and eating tar paper from the sides of abandoned shacks until they died.

When Roosevelt arrived there in April, the Little Missouri was in flood, its waters filled with carcasses of cattle rolling in the churning current. 'We have had a perfect smashup', he wrote on 10 April. 'The losses are crippling.' Not until after several days of riding the ranges with his partners did Roosevelt realize how severe his losses were. On the Maltese Cross range they found scattered herds still surviving, but on the Elkhorn 'there wasn't a cow left'. Teddy's ranching enterprises had been virtually wiped out; his financial losses were staggering.

Although Roosevelt left the West in order to recoup his fortunes and support his growing family, he retained an interest in the Elkhorn Ranch, using it as a base for autumn hunting trips over a period of many years. Much of the time he was short of money, and he wrote voluminously to supplement his income as U.S. Civil Service Commissioner and then as Commissioner of New York City Police. In his articles on contemporary affairs, he constantly urged that the United States increase its military strength, expand its geographic limits, and become a world power. He was troubled by the civil disturbances around the 1890s – the Haymarket and Homestead riots, the Pullman strike, Coxey's Army – and regarded them as symptoms of the beginning of an upheaval comparable to the French Revolution.

'The country needs a war', he wrote in December 1895, and a year later after President McKinley appointed him Assistant Secretary of the Navy, he was in a position to help generate a war. In Cuba, insurgents were rebelling against Spanish rule and Americans sympathized with the rebels, partly out of idealism, partly because they wished to end the turmoil and regain hundreds of millions of dollars in lost trade.

At every opportunity Teddy preached 'the soldierly virtues', and declared that 'peace is a goddess only when she comes with

OPPOSITE A buffalo herd, before the white man claimed the Plains for himself

sword girt on thigh'. Although the Secretary of the Navy, John D. Long, was sometimes apprehensive over his assistant's words and actions, he did nothing to stop Roosevelt's efforts to put the Navy on a war footing and build up a powerful Asiatic squadron in the Pacific.

After the mysterious sinking of the U.S.S. *Maine* in Havana harbor on 15 February 1898, war with Spain became inevitable. 'It was our duty to intervene in Cuba,' Roosevelt said, 'and to take this opportunity of driving the Spaniard from the western world.' War was declared on 21 April, and Teddy at last had an opportunity to raise a regiment of 'harum-scarum rough riders' in the West. For lack of military experience he was unable to obtain a colonel's commission but he eagerly accepted second command under his friend Leonard Wood. Teddy took over the recruitment duties, dispatching telegrams to governors in the West, asking for volunteers who were 'young, good shots and good riders'. One of his first acts was to telegraph Brooks Brothers in New York City, ordering a 'blue cravenette regular Lieutenant-Colonel's uniform without yellow on the collar and with leggings'. He also ordered a dozen extra pairs of steel-rimmed spectacles for use in combat.

In an uncharacteristic moment of modesty during the midst of this frantic activity, Teddy commented: 'Really we are all fake heroes', and then he hurried off to Texas to whip the Rough Riders into shape. To make certain that his regiment would get to Cuba first, he seized a ship in Tampa that was awaiting arrival of another cavalry unit, and with Richard Harding Davis along to report every incident for the New York *Herald*, the Rough Riders were soon landing in front of the Spanish stronghold of Santiago. Other units joined them; Leonard Wood became a brigade commander; and Roosevelt at last was colonel of the Rough Riders.

Whether he stormed San Juan Hill or Kettle Hill is not important; Roosevelt and his Rough Riders did charge up a Cuban slope, the glory of it taking him straight to the White House. 'I waved my hat and we went up the hill with a rush', he said. 'The charge was great fun.' For Teddy it was the finest sporting event of his life. He was proud of the regiment's high casualties because he believed this proved that Westerners made the best fighters. 'The percentage of loss of our regiment', he boasted, 'was about seven times that of the other five volunteer regiments.'

Yellow fever and malaria, however, killed more Rough Riders than Spanish bullets. Conditions became so bad in late summer that the Army ordered the regiment transferred from Cuba to New York. 'I've had a bully time and a bully fight!', Teddy told reporters who met him at the landing. 'I feel as big and as strong as a bull moose!' But so few of his men were physically able to march that a planned parade down Broadway had to be cancelled. In September the Rough Riders were mustered out

OPPOSITE Cowboy gear, including a Western saddle with the typical high pommel and cantle; chaps; a rawhide *reata* or lariat; a single-action Colt ·45 (Frontier or Peacemaker) revolver with an ivory butt, c. 1873; a Stetson; and old Mexican-type spurs

after only 133 days of service, yet in that brief time they had made of Teddy Roosevelt a hero to the nation.

That autumn he was elected Governor of New York. Two years later he was nominated and elected vice-president on the Republican ticket of McKinley and Roosevelt. In September 1901 McKinley was assassinated, and Teddy the Rough Rider was suddenly President of the United States of America.

During his seven years in office Roosevelt for better or worse established the pattern that America would follow through most of the twentieth century. It was a Western pattern of good and evil, of heroic Western supermen who were ordained to subdue the vast powers of darkness. Roosevelt believed that the American way of life was so superior to all others that everyone should become like Americans even if they had to be forced to do so. If the non-believers of the world could not be chastened with words, then one should use a big stick, or a big gun.

He promised the Cubans that if 'only they will be good they will be happy' and then offered them freedom with conditions. He subjugated the Philippines in order to Americanize the inhabitants. With the U.S. Navy he supported an uprising of 'good' secessionists so that Panama would be free from Colombia, and then he built a canal across Panama. While the canal was under construction, he went to Panama and operated one of the steam shovels; he was criticized for being the first President in office to leave U.S. territory, but his critics did not understand that from Teddy's viewpoint all of America was United States territory.

On the domestic front he attacked the 'bad' trusts and left the 'good' trusts alone. He scolded the malefactors of great wealth but feared the journalistic muckrakers who were exposing them. He condemned William Jennings Bryan for having 'all the vices of Thomas Jefferson' and then adopted many of Bryan's policies. He claimed credit for conservation reforms which other men had fought for while he was busy killing so many species of wildlife that museums could not contain the endless trophies he sent them. He worked hard to preserve part of the West's forests and other resources as 'the property of the people', but he would have considered it unthinkable to restore any of the riches of this domain to the Indians. After all, the West had been 'won' from them, and victors do not surrender territory to the vanquished. He broke precedent by inviting a black man, Booker T. Washington, to dinner at the White House, but when a Negro regiment was accused of riding through Brownsville, Texas, and shooting up the town, Roosevelt without demanding evidence or a trial ordered 167 black soldiers 'discharged without honor'. That regiment had protected the Rough Riders' flank at San Juan Hill.

Near the end of his first term he journeyed to Wyoming to begin a campaign for re-election by riding sixty miles on horse-back in a single day to prove his toughness. For the photographers he wore his Rough Rider slouch hat, brown riding pants, and leggings. 'Down the mountain valley he came in a whirl of dust', the newspapers reported. 'Superbly mounted, he rode with a plainsman's ease, forward in the saddle and with shoulders loose. The West was written in every line of his frame, and clothes and bearing; he might have been a ranchman leading a roundup gang . . . He was Theodore Roosevelt, ranchman, soldier, President of the United States.'

He swept the 1904 elections with the largest number of popular and electoral votes ever before received by a Presidential candidate. Four years later, when he left office, Mark Twain commented: 'He's still only fourteen years old.' For a farewell party in the White House, Teddy surrounded himself with old comrades from the West—cattlemen, hunters, marshals—hard-muscled sun-burned followers of the strenuous life. Before the evening ended they were weeping openly because their cowboy was leaving the White House.

In 1912 he tried to get back in the White House by running for President on a third party ticket. He toured the country, shouting in his high-pitched voice that he was as strong as a bull moose, and leading audiences in singing 'Onward, Christian Soldiers'. But he succeeded only in splitting the vote of the Republican party. Woodrow Wilson and the Democrats took over the White House.

During his last years Teddy became an anachronism, a windbag charging about the world to shoot big game, lecturing kings and savants, reviewing Kaiser Wilhelm's troops and assuring the Germans that they were a 'virile and masterful people'. Not many months later when these same German troops invaded Belgium, he first supported the military strategy of the German Army, then suddenly changed his mind and rushed to Washington to beg President Wilson to let him raise another regiment of Western horse soldiers to battle the Huns. But Wilson turned him down. By this time Teddy looked older than his years; fever and other ailments acquired on African and South American hunting expeditions had sapped the strength from his body. He lived to suffer grief brought by the death of his youngest son, killed in an aerial battle in the War to Make the World Safe for Democracy, the War to End Wars, and then, on the sixth day of January 1919, Teddy the Rough Rider died.

At the time of Roosevelt's great popularity in the beginning years of the century, Americans admired him because he was the President most nearly like them—voluble, energetic, ebullient, overconfident, self-reliant, friendly toward his own kind, deeply suspicious of peoples who were different, a believer in the use of naked force to win objectives, righteous, messianic, contradictory, avaricious and generous. He represented the final distillation of the Western experience, and as President he did much to imprint these traits into the American ethos where they endure to this day.

Full Captions and Acknowledgments for Illustrations

The following abbreviations are used in the list:

BM–Courtesy of the Trustees of the British Museum, London
Calif. Hist. Soc.–The California Historical Society, San Francisco
Fort Sill–U.S. Army Artillery Center and Fort Sill Museum, Oklahoma
Freeman–Photograph by John R. Freeman & Co., London
Gilcrease–The Thomas Gilcrease Institute of American History and Art, Tulsa, Oklahoma
Heye–Courtesy Museum of the American Indian, Heye Foundation, New York
LC–Library of Congress, Washington, D.C.
Metropolitan–The Metropolitan Museum of Art, New York
Mo. Hist. Soc.–The Missouri Historical Society, St Louis
Mus. Nat. Hist.–Courtesy American Museum of Natural History, New York
Nat. Gal.–Courtesy of the National Gallery of Art, Washington, D.C.
N.Y. Pub. Lib.–The New York Public Library Picture Collection
Smithsonian–The Smithsonian Institution, Washington, D.C.
Utah St. Hist. Soc.–Courtesy Utah State Historical Society, Salt Lake City
WA–Western Americana Picture Library, Brentwood, Essex

Page numbers marked with an asterisk* indicate color illustrations

250 'The Sitting Bull Council at Fort Walsh, British Territory, October 1877', from the *Graphic*, 1 December 1877. *N.Y. Pub. Lib.*

252 Two ration tickets ($1\frac{3}{4}$ in. × $3\frac{1}{4}$ in.) from the Pine Ridge Reserve, South Dakota. *Heye*

253* Indian artifacts. *Courtesy of the owner, Mr H. Frank Humphris/photo: Robert Harding*

254* Section of a painted muslin tent sheet (unfolded width: 25 ft), Oglalla Sioux, South Dakota. *Heye*

256 Watercolor model for a poster advertising Buffalo Bill's Wild West show, artist unknown. *Bella C. Landauer Collection. Courtesy of the New-York Historical Society, New York City*

257 Sioux Indian and tipi in winter on the Devil's Lake Reservation, North Dakota, *c.* 1892. *Heye*

259 Indian reservation police, Dakota; photo: D. F. Barry, 1890. *National Archives*

261 William H. Bonney, alias Billy the Kid (1859–81). *WA*

262 'Holiday Time in the Wild West.' From *The Illustrated London News*, 19 September 1891. *London Electrotype Agency*

263 The Maltese Cross Ranch; photo: W. H. de Graff. *Theodore Roosevelt Collection, Harvard College Library*

264 Frontispiece of *Hunting Trips of a Ranchman* by Theodore Roosevelt (1885). *BM/Freeman*

266 Theodore Roosevelt with his horse; photo: Ingersoll. *Theodore Roosevelt Collection, Harvard College Library*

268 'Close Quarters with Old Ephraim', an illustration from *Hunting Trips of a Ranchman* by Theodore Roosevelt (1885). *BM/Freeman*

271* William Jacob Hays (1830–75): *Herd on the Move* (detail). Oil on canvas. 36 in. × 72 in. *Gilcrease*

272* Cowboy equipment. *Courtesy of the owner, Mr H. Frank Humphris/photo: Robert Harding*

Endpapers O. C. Seltzer: *First Furrow*. Oil on illustration board. $4\frac{1}{2}$ in. × 6 in. *Gilcrease*

*Jacket** Remington: *A Dash for the Timber. Courtesy of the Amon Carter Museum, Fort Worth, Texas*

Sources

Acknowledgment is made with thanks for permission granted by the Library of the Missouri Historical Society for use of quotations from Susan Shelby Magoffin's Down the Santa Fe Trail and Into Mexico, *and to the National Historical Society for some of the material in Chapter Two which previously appeared in* American History Illustrated.

I: Children of the Sun

Bandelier, A. F. 'Contributions to the History of the Southwestern Portion of the United States.' *Archaeological Institute of America Papers*, Vol. 5, 1890

Bolton, Herbert E. *Coronado, Knight of Pueblos and Plains.* Albuquerque, University of New Mexico Press, 1949

Cabeza de Vaca, Alvar Nunez. *Relation*, translated by Buckingham Smith. N.Y., 1871

Cushing, Frank Hamilton. *Zuni Folk Tales.* N.Y., Putnam's, 1901

Hammond, George P., and Agapito Rey. *Narratives of the Coronado Expedition, 1540–1542.* Albuquerque, University of New Mexico Press, 1940

Mooney, James. 'Quivira and the Wichitas.' *Harper's Magazine*, Vol. 99, 1899, pp. 126–35

Terrell, John Upton. *Estevanico the Black.* Los Angeles, Westernlore Press, 1968

U.S. Bureau of Ethnology. *Annual Reports*, 13th, 14th, and 23rd. 1896–1904

Winship, George P. *The Journey of Coronado, 1540–42.* N.Y., 1922

II: To the Western Sea

Audet, F. 'Les Canadiens au Nouveau-Mexico.' Soc. de Geog. de Quebec. *Bulletin*, Vol. 17, 1923, pp. 139–63

Bakeless, John. *Lewis and Clark, Partners in Discovery.* N.Y., Morrow, 1947

De Trémaudan, A. H. 'Who was the Chevalier de la Vérendrye?' *Canadian Historical Review*, Vol. 1, 1920, pp. 246–54

Folmer, Henri. 'The Mallet Expedition of 1739 through Nebraska, Kansas and Colorado.' *Colorado Magazine*, Vol. 16, 1939, pp. 161–73

Harris, Burton. *John Colter, His Years in the Rockies.* N.Y.,
Scribner's, 1952

Jackson, Donald, ed. *Letters of the Lewis and Clark Expedition, with Related Documents, 1783–1854.* Urbana, University of Illinois Press, 1962

Margry, Pierre. *Découvertes et Etablissements des Français dans l'Ouest et dans le Sud . . . 1614–1754.* Vol. 6. Paris, 1888

Thwaites, Reuben Gold, ed. *Original Journals of the Lewis and Clark Expedition, 1804–06.* 8 vols. N.Y., 1904–05

III: Knight in Buckskins

Berry, Don. *A Majority of Scoundrels, an Informal History of the Rocky Mountain Fur Company.* Harper & Bros, 1961

Camp, Charles L., ed. 'James Clyman, His Diaries and Reminiscences.' California Historical Society *Quarterly*. Vol. 4, 1925, pp. 105–41

Cleland, Robert G. *This Reckless Breed of Men, the Trappers and Fur Traders of the Southwest.* N.Y., Knopf, 1963

Dale, Harrison C. *The Ashley-Smith Explorations and the Discovery of a Central Route to the Pacific, 1822–1829.* Glendale, Calif., Arthur H. Clark, 1941

Hafen, LeRoy R., ed. *The Mountain Men and the Fur Trade of the Far West.* Vol. 3. Glendale, Calif., Arthur H. Clark, 1966

Harris, Burton. *John Colter, His Years in the Rockies.* N.Y., Scribner's, 1952

James, Thomas. *Three Years Among the Indians and Mexicans.* Chicago, Lakeside Press, 1953

Morgan, Dale L. *Jedediah Smith and the Opening of the West.* Lincoln, University of Nebraska Press, 1964

IV: Medicine Paint Catlin

Quaife, Milo M., ed. 'Journals of Captain Meriwether Lewis and Sergeant John Ordway.' Wisconsin State Historical Society *Collections*, Vol. 22, 1916

Russell, Carl P. *Firearms, Traps, and Tools of the Mountain Men.* N.Y., Knopf, 1967

Sullivan, Maurice S. *Jedediah Smith, Trader and Trail Breaker.* N.Y., Press of the Pioneers, 1936

Catlin, George. *North American Indians, Being Letters and Notes on Their Manners, Customs, and Conditions, Written during Eight Years' Travel Amongst the Wildest*

Tribes of Indians in North America, 1832–39. 2 vols. Edinburgh, John Grant, 1926

De Voto, Bernard. *Across the Wide Missouri.* Boston, Houghton Mifflin, 1947

Donaldson, Thomas. 'The George Catlin Indian Gallery in the U.S. National Museum.' Smithsonian Institution, *Annual Report,* 1890. Washington, Government Printing Office, 1892

Ewers, John C. 'George Catlin, Painter of Indians and the West.' Smithsonian Institution, *Annual Report,* 1955, pp. 483–528

Haberly, Loyd. *Pursuit of the Horizon, a Life of George Catlin, Painter and Recorder of the American Indian.* N.Y., Macmillan, 1948

McCracken, Harold. *George Catlin and the Old Frontier.* N.Y., Dial, 1959

Roehm, Marjorie Catlin. *The Letters of George Catlin and His Family; a Chronicle of the American West.* Berkeley, University of California Press, 1966

Wasserman, Emily. 'The Artist-Explorers.' *Art in America,* Vol. 60, No. 4, 1972, pp. 48–57

V: Parkman and the Year of Decision

Allen, Opal S. *Narcissa Whitman, an Historical Biography.* Portland, Ore., Binford & Morts, 1959

Cannon, Miles. *Waiilatpu, Its Rise and Fall.* Boise, Idaho, 1915

De Voto, Bernard. *The Year of Decision, 1846.* Boston, Houghton, Mifflin, 1961

Doughty, Howard. *Francis Parkman.* N.Y., Macmillan, 1962

Drury, Clifford M. *First White Women Over the Rockies.* Glendale, Calif., Arthur H. Clark, Vol. 1, 1963

Jones, Nard. *The Great Command: The Story of Marcus and Narcissa Whitman and the Oregon Country Pioneers.* Boston, Little, Brown, 1959

Parkman, Francis. *Journals . . .* edited by Mason Wade. 2 vols. N.Y., Harper & Bros, 1947

———. *Letters . . .* edited and with an introduction by Wilbur R. Jacobs. 2 vols. Norman, University of Oklahoma Press, 1960

———. *The Oregon Trail, Sketches of Prairie and Rocky Mountain Life.* Boston, Little, Brown, 1892

Wade, Mason. *Francis Parkman, Heroic Historian.* N.Y., Viking, 1942

VI: Josiah Gregg and the Wandering Princess

Connelley, William E. *Doniphan's Expedition and the Conquest of New Mexico and California.* Kansas City, Mo., 1907

Gregg, Josiah. *The Commerce of the Prairies,* edited by Milo M. Quaife. Lincoln, University of Nebraska Press, 1967

———. *Diary and Letters,* edited by Maurice Garland Fulton. 2 vols. Norman, University of Oklahoma Press, 1941–4

Keleher, William A. *Turmoil in New Mexico, 1846–1868.* Santa Fe, Rydal Press, 1952

Magoffin, Susan Shelby. *Down the Santa Fe Trail and into Mexico,* edited by Stella M. Drumm. New Haven, Yale University Press, 1926

Twitchell, Ralph E. *The History of the Military Occupation of the Territory of New Mexico from 1846 to 1851.* Chicago, Rio Grande Press, 1963

VII: The Road to El Dorado

Bruff, J. Goldsborough. *Gold Rush, the Journals, Drawings, and Other Papers . . . ,* edited by Georgia Willis Read and Ruth Gaines. N.Y., Columbia University Press, 1949.

Colton, Walter. *The Land of Gold; or, Three Years in California.* N.Y., Evans, 1860

Cooke, Philip St George. *The Conquest of New Mexico and California.* Albuquerque, New Mexico, Horn and Wallace, 1964

Frémont, J. C. *Report of the Exploring Expedition to the Rocky Mountains in the Year 1842, and to Oregon and North California in the Years 1843–44.* Washington, 1845

Gay, Theressa. *James W. Marshall, the Discoverer of California Gold.* Georgetown, California, Talisman Press, 1967

Lewis, Oscar. *Sutter's Fort, Gateway to the Gold Fields.* Englewood Cliffs, N.J., Prentice-Hall, 1966

Roberts, B. B. *The Mormon Battalion, its History and Achievements.* Salt Lake City, Deseret News, 1919

Royce, Sarah. *A Frontier Lady, Recollections of the Gold Rush and Early California,* edited by Ralph Henry Gabriel. New Haven, Yale University Press, 1932

Shaw, Reuben Cole. *Across the Plains in Forty-nine.* Chicago, Lakeside Press, 1948

Stansbury, Howard. *Exploration and Survey of the Valley of the Great Salt Lake of Utah.* Washington, 1853

Tyler, Daniel. *A Concise History of the Mormon Battalion in the Mexican War, 1846–1847.* Glorieta, New Mexico, Rio Grande Press, 1969

VIII: An Angel of Light, A Goblin Damned

Alter, J. Cecil. *James Bridger, Trapper, Frontiersman, Scout and Guide.* Columbus, Ohio, Long's College Book Company, 1951

Burton, Richard F. *The City of the Saints and Across the Rocky Mountains to California.* N.Y., Harper & Bros, 1862

Furmiss, Norman F. *The Mormon Conflict, 1850–1859.* New Haven, Yale University Press, 1960

Gates, Susa Y. and Leah D. Widtsoe. *The Life Story of Brigham Young.* N.Y., Macmillan, 1930

Greeley, Horace. *An Overland Journey from New York to San Francisco in the Summer of 1859.* N.Y., 1860

Hirshon, Stanley P. *The Lion of the Lord, a Biography of Brigham Young.* N.Y., Knopf, 1969.

Piercy, Frederick H. *Route from Liverpool to Great Salt Lake Valley,* edited by Fawn M. Brodie. Cambridge, Belknap Press of Harvard University Press, 1962

U.S. Congress. 35th, 1st Session. House of Representatives Executive Document 71 (The Utah Expedition). Washington, 1858

Werner, Morris R. *Brigham Young.* N.Y., Harcourt, Brace, 1925

West, Ray B., Jr, *Kingdom of the Saints.* N.Y., Viking Press, 1957

IX: The Swift-Wagons of of John Butterfield

Banning, William and George H. *Six Horses.* N.Y., The Century Co., 1930

Conkling, Roscoe P. and Margaret B. *The Butterfield Overland Mail, 1857–1869.* 3 vols. Glendale, Calif., Arthur H. Clark, 1947

Frank Leslie's Illustrated Newspaper. 23 October 1858

Hafen, LeRoy R. *The Overland Mail, 1849–1869.* Cleveland, Arthur H. Clark, 1926

Lang, Walter B. *The First Overland Mail, Butterfield Trail.* East Aurora, N.Y., Roycrofters, 1940

Loomis, Noel M. *Wells Fargo.* N.Y., Bramhall House, 1959

Lucia, Ellis. *The Saga of Ben Holladay.* N.Y., Hastings House, 1959

New York Herald. September–December 1858

Ormsby, Waterman L. *The Butterfield Overland Mail,* edited by Lyle H. Wright and Josephine M. Bynum. San Marino, Calif., Huntington Library, 1942

Tallack, William. 'The California Overland Express.' *Leisure Hour,* Vol. 14. London, 1865

Winther, Oscar Osburn. *Via Western Express and Stagecoach.* Stanford University Press, 1945

X: The Napoleon of the Plains

Beebe, Lucius, and Charles Clegg. *U.S. West, the Saga of Wells Fargo.* N.Y., Dutton, 1949

Frederick, J. V. *Ben Holladay, the Stagecoach King.* Glendale, Calif., Arthur H. Clark, 1940

Lucia, Ellis. *The Saga of Ben Holladay.* N.Y., Hastings House, 1959

Majors, Alexander. *Seventy Years on the Frontier.* Chicago, Rand, McNally, 1893

New York Times. 19 and 26 October, 12 December 1861

Root, Frank A., and William E. Connelley. *The Overland Stage to California.* Topeka, Kansas, 1901

Settle, Raymond W. 'The Pony Express, Heroic Effort–Tragic End.' *Utah Historical Quarterly,* Vol. 27, 1959, pp. 103–26

Settle, Raymond W., and Mary Lund Settle. 'The Early Careers of William Bradford Waddell and William Hepburn Russell: Frontier Capitalists.' *Kansas Historical Quarterly,* Vol. 26, 1960, pp. 355–82

———. *Empire on Wheels.* Stanford University Press, 1949

———. *Saddles and Spurs, the Pony Express Saga.* Lincoln, University of Nebraska Press, 1972

———. *War Drums and Wagon Wheels, the Story of Russell, Majors and Waddell.* Lincoln, University of Nebraska Press, 1966

Smith, Waddell F., ed. *The Story of the Pony Express.* San Rafael, Calif., Pony Express History and Art Gallery, 1960

Thompson, Robert Luther. *Wiring a Continent, the History of the Telegraph Industry in the United States.* Princeton University Press, 1947

U.S. Congress. 36th, 2nd Session. House of Representatives Report 78 (Abstracted Indian Trust Bonds). Washinton, D.C., 1861

———. 37th, 2nd Session. Senate Misc. Doc. 108 (Union Pacific Railroad Company). Washington, D.C., 1862

Ware, Eugene F. *The Indian War of 1864.* Topeka, Kansas, Crane and Co., 1911

XI: The Grandest Enterprise Under God

Athearn, Robert G. *Union Pacific Country.* Chicago, Rand McNally, 1971

Best, Gerald M. *Iron Horses to Promontory.* San Marino, Calif., Golden West Books, 1969

Borthwick, Alexander. Unpublished diary, in University of Oregon Library, Special Collections

Carson, John. *The Union Pacific: Hell on Wheels!* Santa Fe, New Mexico, Press of the Territorian, 1968

Howard, Robert West. *The Great Iron Trail; the Story of the First Transcontinental Railroad.* N.Y., Putnam's, 1962

Josephson, Matthew. *The Robber Barons.* N.Y., Harcourt, Brace, 1934

Lewis, Oscar. *The Big Four.* N.Y., Knopf, 1938

Moody, John. *The Railroad Builders.* New Haven, Yale University Press, 1919

North, Luther. *Man of the Plains . . . ,* edited by Donald F. Danker. Lincoln, University of Nebraska Press, 1961

Seymour, Silas. *Incidents of a Trip Through the Great Platte Valley to the Rocky Mountains . . .* N.Y., Van Nostrand, 1867

Thornton, Willis. *The Nine Lives of Citizen Train.* N.Y., Greenberg Publishers, 1948

Train, George Francis. *The Great Epigram Campaign of Kansas; Championship of Woman.* Leavenworth, Kansas, Prescott and Hume, 1867

———. *My Life in Many States and in Foreign Lands.* N.Y., D. Appleton, 1902

Trottman, Nelson. *History of the Union Pacific.* N.Y., Ronald Press, 1923

U.S. Congress. 42nd, 3rd Session. House of Representatives Report 78 (Affairs of the Union Pacific Railroad Company). Washington, 1873

———. 44th, 1st Session. House of Representatives Report 180 (Condition of the Union Pacific Railroad). Washington, 1876

U.S. War Department. *Annual Report,* 1867. Washington, 1868

Utley, Robert M., and Francis A. Ketterson, Jr. *Golden Spike.* Washington, U.S. Department of the Interior, 1969

XII: The Indian Slayers

Athearn, Robert G. *William Tecumseh Sherman and the Settlement of the West.* Norman, University of Oklahoma Press, 1956

Brown, Dee. *Fort Phil Kearny, an American Saga.* N.Y., Putnam's, 1962

Carter, R. G. *On the Border with Mackenzie.* N.Y., Antiquarian Press, 1961

Fletcher, Ellen. *By Wagon Train.* Portland, Oregon, 1967

Lewis, Lloyd. *Sherman, Fighting Prophet.* N.Y., Harcourt, Brace, 1932

Merrill, James M. *William Tecumseh Sherman.* Chicago, Rand, McNally, 1971

Nye, W. S. *Carbine and Lance.* Norman, University of Oklahoma Press, 1937

O'Connor, Richard. *Sheridan the Inevitable.* Indianapolis, Bobbs-Merrill, 1953

Sheridan, P. H. *Personal Memoirs.* 2 vols. N.Y., Webster, 1888

Sherman, William T. *Memoirs.* Bloomington, Indiana University Press, 1957

Stanley, Henry M. *My Early Travels.* Vol. 1. N.Y., Scribner's, 1895

U.S. Commissioner of Indian Affairs. *Reports,* 1868–9

U.S. Congress. 39th, 2nd Session. Senate Executive Document 15, 1867

———. 47th, 2nd Session. House of Representatives Executive Document 239 (Subsistence of Indian Tribes). Washington, 1868

U.S. War Department. *Reports,* 1866–9, 1874–5

XIII: The Father of the Cowboys

Atherton, Lewis. *The Cattle Kings.* Lincoln; University of Nebraska Press, 1972

Brown, Dee, and Martin F. Schmitt. *Trail Driving Days.* N.Y., Scribner's, 1952

Burton, Harley True. *A History of the JA Ranch.* Austin, Von Boeckmann-Jones, 1928

Cox, James. *Historical and Biographical Record of the Cattle Industry and the Cattlemen of Texas* and Adjacent Territory. St Louis, Woodward & Tiernan, 1895

Haley, J. Evetts. Charles Goodnight, Cowman & Plainsman. Norman, University of Oklahoma Press, 1949

Hamner, Laura V. Short Grass and Longhorns. Norman, University of Oklahoma Press, 1945

Osgood, Ernest S. The Day of the Cattleman. Minneapolis, University of Minnesota Press, 1929

Pioneer Days in the Southwest from 1850 to 1879 . . . Contributions by Charles Goodnight, Emanuel Dubbs, John A. Hart and others. Guthrie, Oklahoma, 1909

Sandoz, Mari. The Cattlemen. N.Y., Hastings House, 1958

Wellman, Paul I. The Trampling Herd. Philadelphia, Lippincott, 1939

XIV: The Petticoated Rebels

Brown, Dee. The Gentle Tamers, Women of the Old Wild West. N.Y., Putnam's, 1958

Chicago Tribune. 17 July 1873

New York Times. 18 July 1873; 12 and 20 May 1877

Pond, J. B. Eccentricities of Genius. London, Chatto and Windus, 1901

Stanton, Elizabeth Cady, and others. History of Woman Suffrage. 4 vols. Rochester, N.Y., 1889–1902

Stenhouse, Mrs T. B. H. An Englishwoman in Utah. London, 1882

Wallace, Irving. The Twenty-seventh Wife. N.Y., Simon and Schuster, 1961

Woodward, Helen Beal. The Bold Women. N.Y., Farrar, Straus and Young, 1953

Young, Ann Eliza. Life in Mormon Bondage. Philadelphia, 1908

———. Wife No. 19, or the Story of a Life in Bondage. Hartford, Conn., 1875

XV: Libbie and Autie

Custer, Elizabeth B. 'Boots and' Saddles' or, Life in Dakota with General Custer, with an introduction by Jane R. Stewart. Norman, University of Oklahoma Press, 1961

———. Following the Guidon. N.Y., Harper & Bros, 1890

———. Tenting on the Plains, with an introduction by Jane R. Stewart. 3 vols. Norman, University of Oklahoma Press, 1971

Fougera, Katherine Gibson. With Custer's Cavalry. Caldwell, Idaho, Caxton Printers, 1942

Frost, Lawrence A. The Court-Martial of General George

Armstrong Custer. Norman, University of Oklahoma Press, 1968

Jackson, Donald. Custer's Gold, the United States Cavalry Expedition of 1874. New Haven, Yale University Press, 1966

Merington, Marguerite, ed. The Custer Story, the Life and Intimate Letters of General George A. Custer and His Wife Elizabeth. N.Y., Devin-Adair Company, 1950

Millbrook, Minnie Dubbs. 'The West Breaks in General Custer.' Kansas Historical Quarterly, Vol. 36, pp. 113–48, 1970

Monaghan, Jay. The Life of General George Armstrong Custer. Boston, Little, Brown, 1959

Murray, Robert A. 'The Custer Court Martial.' Annals of Wyoming, Vol. 36, pp. 175–84, 1964

U.S. War Department. Reports, 1874–5

XVI: The Dispossessed

Adams, Alexander B. Sitting Bull, an Epic of the Plains. N.Y., Putnam's, 1973

De Smet, Father Pierre-Jean. Life, Letters and Travels, edited by Hiram M. Chittenden and Alfred T. Richardson. 4 vols. N.Y., Francis P. Harper, 1905

Easterwood, Thomas J. My River Life. Dundee, Oregon, 1881

Garraghan, Gilbert Joseph. 'Father De Smet's Sioux Peace Mission of 1868 and the Journal of Charles Galpin.' Mid-America, Vol. 13, 1930–1, pp. 141–63

Haydon, A. L. The Riders of the Plains. Chicago, McClurg, 1910

Olson, James C. Red Cloud and the Sioux Problem. Lincoln, University of Nebraska Press, 1965

Pfaller, Louis. '"Enemies in '76, Friends in '85"–Sitting Bull and Buffalo Bill.' Prologue, Vol. 1, No. 2, 1969, pp. 17–31

Praus, Alexis A. 'A New Pictographic Autobiography of Sitting Bull.' Smithsonian Miscellaneous Collections, Vol. 123, No. 6. Washington, 1955.

Slaughter, Linda W. 'Leaves from Northwestern History.' North Dakota State Historical Society, Collections, Col. I, 1906, pp. 200–92

Stirling, M. W. 'Three Pictographic Autobiographies of Sitting Bull.' Smithsonian Miscellaneous Collections, Vol. 97, No. 5. Washington, 1938

U.S. Commissioner of Indian Affairs. Annual Reports, 1872–7

U.S. Congress. 48th, 1st Session. Senate Report 283 (Condition of Indian Tribes). Washington, 1884

———. 49th, 1st Session. House of

Representatives Executive Document 356 (Surrender of Sitting Bull). Washington, 1886

U.S. War Department. The War of the Rebellion . . . Official Records. Series I, Vol. 48, Part 2. Washington, 1896

Utley, Robert M. The Last Days of the Sioux Nation. New Haven, Yale University Press, 1963

Vestal, Stanley. Sitting Bull, Champion of the Sioux. Norman, University of Oklahoma Press, 1957

Vogel, Virgil J. This Country Was Ours, a Documentary History of the American Indian. N.Y., Harper & Row, 1972

XVII: Teddy the Rough Rider

Deming, William Chapin. Roosevelt in the Bunk House, and Other Sketches. Laramie, Wyoming, 1927

Hagedorn, Hermann. Roosevelt in the Bad Lands. Boston, Houghton, Mifflin, 1921

———, ed. The Works of Theodore Roosevelt. 24 vols. N.Y., Scribner's, 1926

Hornaday, William T. 'The Extermination of the American Bison.' U.S. National Museum, Report, 1887, pp. 373–547

Jones, Virgil Carrington. Roosevelt's Rough Riders. N.Y., Doubleday, 1971

Lang, Lincoln A. Ranching with Roosevelt. Philadelphia, Lippincott, 1926

Lorant, Stefan. The Life and Times of Theodore Roosevelt. Garden City, Doubleday, 1959

Mattison, Ray H. 'Roosevelt's Elkhorn Ranch.' North Dakota History, Vol. 27, 1960, pp. 51–65

Morison, Elting T., ed. The Letters of Theodore Roosevelt. 8 vols. Cambridge, Harvard University Press, 1951

Pringle, Henry F. Theodore Roosevelt, a Biography. N.Y., Harcourt, Brace, 1957

Putnam, Carleton. Theodore Roosevelt, a Biography. N.Y., Scribner's, 1958

Roosevelt, Theodore. An Autobiography. N.Y., Scribner's, 1929

———. Ranch Life and the Hunting-Trail. N.Y., Century, 1920

———. The Rough Riders. N.Y., Scribner's, 1899

White, G. Edward. The Eastern Establishment and the Western Experience; the West of Frederic Remington, Theodore Roosevelt, and Owen Wister. New Haven, Yale University Press, 1968

Index

287